Alfre

The Interpretation of the Concept Hadês D

Alfredo Jr. Agustin

The Interpretation of the Concept Hadês Described in Luke 16:19-31

The Rich Man and Lazarus in the Light of the Historical-Grammatical Method

VDM Verlag Dr. Müller

Impressum/Imprint (nur für Deutschland/ only for Germany)
Bibliografische Information der Deutschen Nationalbibliothek: Die Deutsche Nationalbibliothek
verzeichnet diese Publikation in der Deutschen Nationalbibliografie; detaillierte bibliografische
Daten sind im Internet über http://dnb.d-nb.de abrufbar.
 Alle in diesem Buch genannten Marken und Produktnamen unterliegen warenzeichen-, marken-
oder patentrechtlichem Schutz bzw. sind Warenzeichen oder eingetragene Warenzeichen der
jeweiligen Inhaber. Die Wiedergabe von Marken, Produktnamen, Gebrauchsnamen,
Handelsnamen, Warenbezeichnungen u.s.w. in diesem Werk berechtigt auch ohne besondere
Kennzeichnung nicht zu der Annahme, dass solche Namen im Sinne der Warenzeichen- und
Markenschutzgesetzgebung als frei zu betrachten wären und daher von jedermann benutzt
werden dürften.

Coverbild: www.ingimage.com

Verlag: VDM Verlag Dr. Müller GmbH & Co. KG
Dudweiler Landstr. 99, 66123 Saarbrücken, Deutschland
Telefon +49 681 9100-698, Telefax +49 681 9100-988
Email: info@vdm-verlag.de
Zugl.: (Ph.D. Diss., Adventist International Institute of Studies, Silang, Cavite, Philippines, 2008)

Herstellung in Deutschland:
Schaltungsdienst Lange o.H.G., Berlin
Books on Demand GmbH, Norderstedt
Reha GmbH, Saarbrücken
Amazon Distribution GmbH, Leipzig
ISBN: 978-3-639-37548-0

Imprint (only for USA, GB)
Bibliographic information published by the Deutsche Nationalbibliothek: The Deutsche
Nationalbibliothek lists this publication in the Deutsche Nationalbibliografie; detailed
bibliographic data are available in the Internet at http://dnb.d-nb.de.
 Any brand names and product names mentioned in this book are subject to trademark, brand
or patent protection and are trademarks or registered trademarks of their respective holders. The
use of brand names, product names, common names, trade names, product descriptions etc.
even without a particular marking in this works is in no way to be construed to mean that such
names may be regarded as unrestricted in respect of trademark and brand protection legislation
and could thus be used by anyone.

Cover image: www.ingimage.com

Publisher: VDM Verlag Dr. Müller GmbH & Co. KG
Dudweiler Landstr. 99, 66123 Saarbrücken, Germany
Phone +49 681 9100-698, Fax +49 681 9100-988
Email: info@vdm-publishing.com

Printed in the U.S.A.
Printed in the U.K. by (see last page)
ISBN: 978-3-639-37548-0

ALFREDO   G.   AGUSTIN   JR.

THE INTERPRETATION OF THE CONCEPT *Hadēs* DESCRIBED IN
LUKE 16:19-31-THE RICH MAN AND LAZARUS IN THE
LIGHT OF THE HISTORICAL-GRAMMATICAL METHOD

To my ever loving, faithful, beloved
wife Arlyn and my precious children Ralph Emerson,
John Nevin, and Allyn Desiree

TABLE OF CONTENTS

LIST OF TABLES   xii

AKNOWLEDGMENTS   xiii

LIST OF ABBREVIATIONS   xv

Chapter

1. INTRODUCTION   15

    Statement of the problem and Purpose
       of the Study   18
    Significance of the Study   18
    Delimitations of the Study   19
    Methodology   19
    Plan of the Study   21
    Review of Related Literature   21
      The Description of ῾Αδης in Luke 16:19-31:
        Factual and Literal Torment or
        Blissfulness of Souls in the
        Intermediate State   22
      The Description of ῾Αδης in Luke 16:19-31:
        Factual and Literal Torment or
        Enjoyment of Souls but after the
        Judgment at the Last Day   25
      The Description of ῾Αδης in Luke 16:19-31:
        A Parable Not Factual or Literal but
        Symbolical, or Reflects Reality of the
        Torment or Blissfulness of Souls in
        the Intermediate State or the Final
        Judgment   26
      The Description of ῾Αδης in Luke 16:19-31:
        A Parable, Not Factual, Just Gives a
        Moral Lesson; No Souls in Torment or
        in Bliss in the Intermediate State   28

2. THE GENRE OF LUKE 16:19-31   33

    The OT Parable Genre   34

The NT Parable Genre   51
Luke 16:19-31: A Story Parable/Parabolic
    Story or an Example Story; Fictitious
    or True   57
    The Rich Man and Lazarus and the
      Rich Fool   57
    The Rich Man and Lazarus and Nathan's
      Parable   63
    Summary   64

3. THE HISTORICAL-RELIGIOUS BACKGROUND OF ᾅΔΗΣ   55

    The Concept of ᾅδης in the Ancient Near
      Eastern Literature   65
    ᾅδης in the Writings of Homer   67
    ᾅδης in the Writings of Plato   69
    ᾅδης in the LXX   70
      ᾅδης in the OT Apocrypha   78
    ᾅδης in the OT Pseudepigrapha   80
    ᾅδης or שְׁאוֹל in Dead Sea Scrolls   83
    שְׁאוֹל or ᾅδης in Philo   85
    ᾅδης in the NT Literature   85
    The Concept ᾅδης in James   86
    The Concept ᾅδης in Pauline
      Epistles   86
    The Concept ᾅδης in Peter and Jude   88
    ᾅδης in Revelation   93
    ᾅδης in Josephus   98
    The Concept of ᾅδης in the Babylonian
      Talmud   100
    ᾅδης in Other Greco-Roman Writers   02
    ᾅδης in the Apocryphal New Testament   107
    ᾅδης in the Early Church Fathers   109
    Summary   110
      Commonalities   110
      Differences   111

4. THE GENERAL BACKGROUND AND THE STRUCTURAL-
   THEMATIC ANALYSIS OF LUKE'S GOSPEL AND
   ACTS   115

    The General Historical Background of the
      Gospel of Luke   115
      Author and Recipients   116
      Date and Provenance   117
      Genre, Purpose, and General Theme   118
    Structural-Thematic Analysis   121
      The Structure of Luke-Acts   121

The Structure of the Travel
  Narrative   129
The Structure of Luke 16:1-31   134
Summary and Conclusion   136

5. THE EXEGETICAL ANALYSIS OF LUKE 16:19-31   139

  Lexical Analysis   139
    The Usage of ῾Άδης in Matthew   141
    The Usages of ῾Άδης in Luke-Acts   144
    The Usage of ῾Άδης in Luke 16:23   148
    The Usage of Γέεννα in the Synoptic
      Gospels   149
  Structural-Thematic Analysis of
    Luke 16:19-31   153
    Literary Structure of Luke 16:19-31   153
    The Themes of Luke 16:19-31   158
  Literary-Narrative Analysis of
    Luke 16:19-31   161
  Luke 16:19-31: In the Setting of the
    Proclamation of the Kingdom of God   177
  The Theological Implication of
    Luke 16:19-31   179
  Summary   181

6. SUMMARY AND CONCLUSION   185

  Summary   185
  Conclusion   196

APPENDIX   199

BIBLIOGRAPHY   207

This page has been intentionally left blank.

LIST OF TABLES

Table

1. Similar Characteristics between the Rich Fool and the Rich Man and Lazarus   59

2. Literary Parallelism between Luke 1-8 and Acts 1-12   122

3. Literary Parallelism between Luke 5-7 and Acts 3-11   123

4. First Feature: Divine Promise and Fulfillment   124

5. Second Feature: Parallelism between John and Jesus   124

6. Geographical Structure of Luke-Acts   126

This page has been intentionally left blank.

ACKNOWLEDGMENTS

The completion of this academic endeavor would not have been achieved without the generous, kind, and Christ-like individuals. With gratefulness, it is my pleasure to express my appreciations and deep gratitude.

First and foremost, I want to give the glory, honor and praise to my LORD and my God whose unfailing grace, love, and care have sustained me. He delivered my soul from "academic *hadēs*," and filled my mouth with singing and praise. To Him be the glory!

I would like to express my generous appreciation to my humble, kind, and very friendly adviser Dr. Richard Sabuin for his valuable insights and witty suggestions that widen the perspective of this research.

I want also to give my generous thanks to my committee members. Dr. Gerhard Klingbeil who is also our very kind Seminary dean has spent his precious hours reading my paper, and contributed valuable insights; Dr. Song Kyung Ho who also took time reading this paper and suggested good insights. I also would like to appreciate the efforts of my internal examiner Dr. Aecio E. Cairus, and my external examiner Dr. Nestor Rilloma. They, too, have given reasonable suggestions.

I am indebted to Mrs. Elsie dela Cruz who is a very efficient editor who patiently edited this paper, and provided writing insights. Thank you, Ate Elsie. Special thanks also go to Daniel Bediako for editing a portion of this dissertation. Special thanks go to Patrick Etoughé Anani for his selfless effort in converting this dissertation into a publishable book. He is really a true friend and a brother in Christ.

The General Conference and MVC-SSD bursary have provided financial xiv

support. Without their generous support, this research would have not been realized. Kindly accept my special thanks.

My wife Arlyn is my inspiration. Her love and prayers are my fortifications. She provided encouragement and hope when things weren't going our way. My children Ralph Emerson, John Nevin, and Allyn Desiree are my other source of inspiration. Their sacrifices should not go unnoticed. My time which was for them was spent for this research instead. A million thanks to you my beloved family. Of course, I also would like to thank my very self-sacrificing mother, Salvacion Gomeri Pael, who nurtured me when I was still a child.

Once again, I ascribe the glory, honor, and praise to our God for His wonderful works. To Him be the glory!

ABBREVIATIONS

AB   Anchor Bible

ABD   *Anchor Bible Dictionary*

ANET   *Ancient Near Eastern Text*

ANF   Ante-Nicene Fathers

APOT   *Apocrypha and Pseudepigrapha of the Old Testament*

BAGD   *A Greek-English Lexicon of the New Testament and Other Early
            Christian Literature*

BDB   *A Hebrew and English Lexicon of the Old Testament with an
            Appendix Containing the Biblical Aramaic*

BHS   *Biblia Hebraica Stuttgartensia*

DSS   Dead Sea Scrolls

EBC   *The Expositor's Bible Commentary*

ET   *Expository Times*

HB   Hebrew Bible

HG   Historical-Grammatical

ICC   International Critical Commentary

ITC   International Theological Commentary

JBL   *Journal of Biblical Literature*

KJV   King James Version

LCL   Loeb Classical Library

LXX	Septuagint
NAC	New American Commentary
NAGL	*New Analytical Greek Lexicon*
NASB	New American Standard Bible
NKJ	New King James
NIBC	New International Bible Commentary
NICNT	New International Commentary on the New Testament
NIDNTT	*New International Dictionary of the New Testament Theology*
NIV	New International Version
NIVAC	New International Version Application Commentary
NLT	New Living Translation
NT	New Testament
NTS	*New Testament Studies*
OT	Old Testament
OTP	*The Old Testament Pseudepigrapha*
RSV	Revised Standard Version
SDABC	*Seventh-day Adventist Bible Commentary*
TDNT	*Theological Dictionary of the New Testament*
TNTC	Tyndale New Testament Commentaries
WBC	Word Biblical Commentary

INTRODUCTION

Tʜᴇʀᴇ are several significant issues that divide biblical scholars as far as the story of the rich man and Lazarus (Luke 16:19-31) is concerned. These significant issues are the background source of the story,[1] the structure of the passage,[2] the origin of its composition,[3] and the interpretation of the parable. in the interpretation of the description of ᾅδης (hadēs)[4]

---

[1]See Richard Bauckham, "The Rich Man and Lazarus: The Parable and the Parallels," *New Testament Studies (NTS)* 37 (1991): 229; Craig L. Blomberg, *Interpreting the Parables* (Downers Grove, IL: InterVarsity, 1990), 203-04; Rudolf Bultmann, *History of Synoptic Tradition*, trans. John Marsh, rev. ed. (Oxford: Blackwell, 1972), 196-97; George Bradford Caird, *Saint Luke*, Westminster Pelican Commentaries (Philadelphia: Westminster, 1963), 191; J. M. Creed, *The Gospel According to St. Luke* (London: Macmillan, 1953), 209-10; B. S. Easton, *The Gospel According to Luke* (New York: Scribner, 1926), 254; E. Earle Ellis, *The Gospel of Luke*, New Century Bible, vol. 42 (Greenwood, SC: Attic, 1977), 205; Joseph A. Fitzmyer, *The Gospel According to Luke X-XXIV*, Anchor Bible (AB), vol. 28A (Garden City, NY: Doubleday, 1985), 1127; Norval Geldenhuys, *Commentary on the Gospel of Luke*, New International Commentary on the New Testament (NICNT) (Grand Rapids: Eerdmans, 1979), 428; Ronald F. Hock, ALazarus and Micylus: Greco-Roman Backgrounds to Luke 16:19-31," *Journal of Biblical Literature (JBL)* 106 (1987), 448-51; idem, "ALazarus and Dives," *The Anchor Bible Dictionary (ABD)*, ed. David Noel Freedman (New York: Doubleday, 1992), 4:266-67; I. Howard Marshall, *The Gospel of Luke*, New International Greek Testament Commentary (Grand Rapids: Eerdmans, 1978), 633; Ferdinand O. Regalado, "The Jewish Background of the Parable of the Rich Man and Lazarus," *Asia Journal of Theology* 16 (2002): 341-48.

[2]See Bultmann, 203; Creed, 208; John Dominic Crossan, *In Parables: The Challenge of the Historical Jesus* (San Francisco: Harper & Row, 1973), 66-67; Easton, 254; Fitzmyer, 1126-28; Hock, "ALazarus and Micylus,"449; Arland J. Hultgren, *The Parables of Jesus: A Commentary* (Grand Rapids: Eerdmans, 2000), 112; Joachim Jeremias, *The Parables of Jesus*, 2d rev. ed. (New York: Scribner, 1972), 186; George W. Knight, ALuke 16:19-31: "The Rich Man and Lazarus," *Review & Expositor* 94 (1997): 277-82; Marshall, 632; Franz Schnider und Werner Stenger, "Die Offene Tür und die Unüber-Schreitbare Kluft: Struktur-Analytische Überlegungen zum Gleichnis vom Reichen Mann und Armen Lazarus (Luke 16:19-31)," *NTS* 25 (1979): 275-83; Charles H. Talbert, *Reading Luke: A Literary and Theological Commentary on the Third Gospel* (New York: Crossroads, 1982), 156, 158.

[3]See Bultmann, 203; Aecio Cairus, "The Rich Man and Lazarus: An Apocryphal Interpolation," *Journal of Asia Adventist Seminary* 9 (2006): 35-45; Crossan, 66-67; Fitzmyer, 1127; Marshall, 634; D. L. Mealand, *Poverty and Expectations in the Gospels* (London: SPCK, 1980), 39-40.

[4]This word does not necessarily mean hell as defined and understood in our modern day. When this study mentions "hell" or "hades" this may refer to the modern definition or understanding of the New Testament (NT) word ᾅδης which may not reflect the original meaning of the word in its Old Testament (OT) and NT usages.

in Luke 16:19-31, scholars do not have a consensus.[5]

Statement of the Problem and Purpose of the Study

Some scholars and Bible commentators support the view that the description of ᾅδης in the story of the rich man and Lazarus in Luke 16:19-31 is history. This means that the description of ᾅδης is factual and literal or at least a pictorial description of it.[6] There are also several biblical scholars and theologians who disagree with the factual interpretation, arguing that the story of the rich man and Lazarus is a parable. It is a parable that does not talk about the afterlife at all.[7] In this juncture, the problem to be addressed in this research is "What is the interpretation of the concept of ᾅδης described in the story of the rich man and Lazarus in Luke 16:19-31?"

Using the Historical-Grammatical (HG) method, the purpose of this research is to extensively exegete Luke 16:19-31, to provide a more comprehensive exegetical analysis and interpretation of the concept ᾅδης described in the story of the rich man and Lazarus.

Significance of the Study

This study provides an extensive exegetical analysis of Luke 16:19-31 especially on the issue of the interpretation of the concept ᾅδης described in the

---

[5]See literature review below, pages 9-24.

[6]See Darrell L. Bock, *Luke 9:51-24:53*, Baker Exegetical Commentary of the New Testament (Grand Rapids: Baker, 1996), 1369; David Wenham, *The Parables of Jesus,* Jesus Library (Downers Grove, IL: InterVarsity, 1989), 144. See also footnotes, pp. 9-14.

[7]For example, see G. W. Knight, 281; Eugene S. Wehrli, "Luke 16:19-31," *Interpretation* 31 (1977): 277. See Review of Related Literature on pp. 9-24 for a complete citation.

story that has not been given enough attention.[81] This study presents an alternative

to the debate on method for the interpretation of Jesus' stories or parables.[92] It

also contributes to an understanding of the theology of Jesus' stories or parables.[103]

Delimitations of the Study

Since there are several issues raised in the story of the rich man and Lazarus

in Luke 16:19-31, this study is confined to the interpretation of the concept ᾅδης

as described in 16:19-31. This study does not tackle the Synoptic problem. In

dealing with the background, only the background of ᾅδης, its OT equivalent, and

its synonymous words and concepts are looked into. This is relevant especially

in shedding light to the question of whether the story is factual or true in some

sense or a fictitious story. In dealing with the structure, this study does not

engage in a deeper discussion on the historical-critical scholars' view regarding

the structure and composition of the parable. This study enters into a theological

discussion concerning the immortality of the soul only if it is necessary as part of

the exegetical analyses.

Methodology

The general methodological framework of this research is the HG method

otherwise known as the Biblical-Historical method.[111] In applying this general

---

[8]Previous studies on this passage deal more on other issues such as background, structure, and composition. With regards to the issue of this study, previous studies did not do much as far the exegesis of the passage is concerned. A very short thesis on this passage deals on the parable in general. This study deals particularly on the concept of ᾅδης.

[9]Some scholars use Historical-Critical method in interpreting the parables of Jesus. This study uses HG method in interpreting this parable. Furthermore, in using the HG, this study utilizes genre analysis, historical background, structural-thematic, and literary-narrative which are not found or lacking in previous studies on this passage.

[10]Some scholars and theologians based their theology on a parable. This study attempts to show that any element in a parable should not be used to support a theology or doctrine unless it is clearly the main point or spiritual truth emphasized in a parable.

[11]his method includes the historical backgrounds, lexical-syntactical and grammatical, literary-structural, and contextual analyses. For further details regarding this method, see Richard M. Davidson, "Biblical Interpretation," in *Handbook of Seventh-day Adventist Theology*, Commentary Reference Series, vol. 12 (Hagerstown, MD: Review & Herald, 2000), 68-87; Gerhard Maier, *Biblical Hermeneutics* (Wheaton, IL: Crossway, 1994), 375-410.

method to interpret ᾅδης as described in the story of the rich man and Lazarus, this study follows a procedure that includes some pertinent aspects of an HG exegesis:

1. It analyzes the genre of Luke 16:19-31. It begins with the analysis of OT מָשָׁל (māšāl), then the NT παραβολη (parabolē), and lastly, the genre of 16:19-31.

2. It considers the background of the parable. This includes the analysis of the specific backgrounds. It deals with backgrounds of ᾅδης its OT equivalent,[121] and its synonymous words and concepts. This background survey includes both biblical and extra-biblical literature. A study of the backgrounds of these words and concepts are vital in shedding light to the interpretation of ᾅδης in Luke 16:19-31.

3. It analyzes the structure and theme of the Luke-Acts, the immediate and wider literary context. This section analyzes the literary structure of Luke-Acts, Luke's travel narrative, and Luke 16. It analyzes special themes of the passage in relation to its immediate and wider contexts.

4. It discusses the general background of the book: the author of the entire document is identified, the recipients——who they are and where they live, the date of writing and the author's purpose, and the themes of the book.

5. It examines the lexical-syntactical issues. The usages of the word ᾅδης and γέεννα (gehenna) are analyzed in Luke-Acts and the rest of the Synoptic Gospels. Some words in the passage are also analyzed especially if they shed light on the issues. The grammatical-syntactical analysis of the passage is also considered.

6. It analyzes the structure and theme of the passage. Then the literary-narrative analysis follows.

7. It determines how Jesus originally used the parable in His own context, especially in the setting of His proclamation of the coming of the kingdom of God.

---

[12]Its OT equivalent is שְׁאוֹל. (šeʾôl). One of its translations in the LXX is ᾅδης.

8. It explores the theological implications of the parable in the light of its immediate and broader biblical-theological context.

Plan of the Study

Chapter 1 introduces the study. It includes the statement of the problem, purpose of the research, significance of the study, delimitations, methodology, plan of the study, and the review of related literature.

Chapter 2 deals with the analysis of the genre of the passage. It includes the analysis of the OT and NT parable genre, and the genre of Luke 16:19-31.

Chapter 3 constitutes the survey and analysis of the background of ᾅδης. It includes the analysis of the concept of ᾅδης in biblical and extra-biblical literature.

Chapter 4 grapples with the structural-thematic analysis. It includes the analyses of structural-thematic of Luke-Acts, Luke's travel narrative, and Luke 16.

Chapter 5 deals with the exegetical analysis of the passage in its immediate and wider contexts. It discusses the general historical background of Luke and considers the usages of ᾅδης and γέεννα in Luke-Acts and the rest of the Synoptics. The structural-thematic issues of Luke 16:19-31 are also tackled. It also analyzes the themes of Luke 16:19-31 in the light of the themes of its immediate and wider contexts. Then the literary-narrative analysis of the pericope follows. This includes the analysis of the narrative that delineates the interactions between characters, the interpretation of ᾅδης in the light of the passage and in its immediate and wider contexts; the main points of the passage; its setting in the proclamation of the kingdom of God; and the theological implications of the parable.

Chapter 6 is the summary and conclusion. First, it summarizes the study, and then proposes a conclusion with regards to the problem of this study.

Review of Related Literature

This section assorts the scholars who wrote several views concerning the description of ᾅδης in Luke 16:19-31:

1. The description of ᾅδης in Luke 16:19-31 is a factual and literal

torment or enjoyment of souls in the intermediate state between death and resurrection of the body.

2. It is a factual and literal torment or happiness of souls in the final state after the judgment at the "last Day."

3. It is a parable, but it reflects the realities that there are souls being tormented or being in bliss in the intermediate state and in the final state after the judgment.

4. It is a parable that stresses at least one or more spiritual lessons and highlights that there are no souls in torment temporarily or eternally in the intermediate state or in the final state.

The Description of Ἄδης in Luke 16:19-31:
Factual and Literal Torment or
Blissfulness of Souls in the
Intermediate State

The first view is that, as advanced by several scholars, Jesus taught the doctrine of hell in the Gospels.[13] They assert that the suffering of the soul of the rich man in the parable in Luke 16:19-31 is factual[142] and literal in hell immediately after his death and burial. However, the soul of Lazarus finds rest and enjoyment in the blissful heaven also immediately after his death, while awaiting for the resurrection and final judgment in the last day.[153] This is called by

---

[13]Simon Kistemaker, *The Parables of Jesus* (Grand Rapids: Baker, 1980), 240.

[14]Which means, what is described in the parable is the real situation of the rich man and Lazarus in Hades in the intermediate state.

[15]William Barclay, *And Jesus Said: A Handbook on the Parable of Jesus* (Philadelphia: Westminster, 1970), 94-95; Loraine Boettner, *Immortality* (Philadelphia: Presbyterian & Reformed, 1956; reprint, Cavite, Philippines: Presbyterian Theological Seminary, 1989), 96-97; Jeffrey Khoo, "The Reality and Eternality of Hell: Luke 16:19-31 as Proof," *Stulos* 5 (1997): 70; Marshall, 636-37; Robert A. Peterson, AThe Case for Traditionalism," in *Two Views of Hell: A Biblical and Theological Dialogue*, ed. Edward William Fudge and Robert Peterson (Downers Grove, IL: InterVarsity, 2000), 167; J. Renie, "Le Mauvais Riche (Luke 16:19-31)," *L' Année Théologique* (1945): 272-73; John Charles Ryle, *Expository Thoughts on the Gospels: St. Luke*, vol. 2 [book on-line] (London: W. Hunt, 1859, reproduced at google book search, accessed 23 January 2007); available from http://books.google.com/books; Internet; William M. Taylor, *The Parables of Our Saviour* (Grand Rapids: Kregel, 1975), 391; John Walvoord, "The Literal View," in *Four Views on Hell*, ed. William Crockett (Grand Rapids: Zondervan, 1996), 22, 28; Robert W. Yarbrough, "Jesus on Hell," in *Hell under Fire*, ed. Christopher W. Morgan and Robert A. Peterson (Grand Rapids: Zondervan, 2004), 67-90.

some scholars and authors as the intermediate state.[161] The early Syrian Church

Fathers, according to Edward Mathews Jr., believe that the wicked suffer in hell

in the afterlife soon after their death.[17]

J. H. D. Scourfield also observes that Jerome believes that in the parable,

souls suffer in hell immediately after death.[183] Gregory the Great, although

he allegorizes the characters in the parable, also believes the factuality of the

suffering of the unfaithful people in hell at death.[191] Martin Luther, citing the

parable of the rich man and Lazarus, likewise indicates that some souls "may feel

punishments immediately after death but others may be spared from punishment

until the day of judgment."[202] However, he also suggests that some souls "are

asleep and that they do not know where they are up to the Day of Judgment."[213]

Biblical scholars and theologians who support this view propose several

arguments to prove that, in the parable, the description of the rich man and Lazarus

in ᾅδης is factual or literal. Jeffrey Khoo in supporting this view propounds that

---

[16]See John W. Eubank, *Secrets of the Bible Unlocked* [book on-line] (n.p.: Trafford, 2005, reproduced at the google book search, accessed 24 January 2007); available from http://books.google.com/books; Internet; Sherly Isaac, *Is Jesus God* [book on-line] (n.p.: n.p., 2001, reproduced at google book search, accessed 24 January, 2007), available from http://books.google.com/books; Internet; Jeremias, 184-85; Clarence Larkin, *Rightly Dividing the Word of Truth* [book on-line] (n.p.: Cosimo Classics, 2005, reproduced at google book search, accessed 24 January 2007), available from http://books.google.com/books; Internet; Richard Lawrence, *On the Existence of the Soul after Death* [book on-line] (London: C. J. G. & F. Rivington, 1834, reproduced at google book search, accessed 24 January 2007), available from http://books.google.com/books; Internet; John Rice, *The Son of Man: A Verse-by-Verse Commentary on the Gospel According to Luke* [book on-line] (n.p., TN: Sword of the Lord, 1971, reproduced at google book search, accessed 24 January 2007), available from http://books.google.com/books; Internet; Oscar Cullman has another version of the intermediate state. In quoting Luke 16:22, he suggests that the dead in Christ are in the state of sleep. He argues against the Greek philosophy of the immortality of the soul but ended up postulating a similar version of it and uses Luke 16:19-31 as a support. Oscar Cullman, "Immortality of the Soul or Resurrection of the Dead," in *Immortality and Resurrection, Death in the Western World: Two Conflicting Currents of Thoughts* (New York: Macmillan, 1965), 36-53.

[17]Edward G. Mathews, "The Rich Man and Lazarus: Alms-Giving and Repentance in Early Syriac Tradition," *Diakonia* 22 (1988-89): 94.

[18]J. H. D. Scourfield, "A Note on Jerome's Homily on the Rich Man and Lazarus," *Journal of Theological Studies* 48 (1997): 536-39.

[19]Warren S. Kissenger, *The Parables of Jesus: A History of Interpretation and Bibliography*, ATLA Series, no. 4 (Metuchen, NJ: Scarecrow & The American Theological Library Association, 1979), 37-38.

[20]Martin Luther, *Luther's Works*, vol. 48, *Letters I*, ed. and trans. Gottfried G. Krodel (Philadelphia: Fortress, 1963), 361.

[21]Ibid., 360.

the parable is a true story[14] and that this is a "powerful passage on the reality and eternality of hell."[21] He posits several arguments:

1. The story is not fictitious, or else Jesus defeats His own purpose of presenting a warning concerning man's responsibility in this present life.

2. The account lacks the usual introduction to Jesus' parables.

3. Jesus did not use names in His parables, but here He mentioned specific names.[3]

4. Even if it is a parable, the description of what hell is, must be taken literally.[43] Furthermore, John Walvoord argues that fire is literal because the rich man is thirsty, and being thirsty is a "natural reaction to fire."[5]

Matthew Hale Smith asserts that the parable is a history and if there are embellishments, these do not destroy the thing being embellished. He further insists that if hell in the parable is not true, then heaven or bliss in the parable could not be true either. Thus, since heaven is true, then hell is also true in the parable.[6] In addition, Ivor Powell postulates that the account in this story should not be dismissed merely as an illustration or parable since the teachings expressed in this passage harmonizes with the doctrines of the Bible.[7]

Several scholars are opposed to this view arguing that if the description of the parable of the rich man and Lazarus in the afterlife is factual and literal then how can they reconcile some descriptions in the parable?

1. People who are in paradise or heaven and people who are in hell are so

---

[1]Khoo, 70. Tertullian also believes that the description of ᾅδης in the parable is a real occurrence. Tertullian *A Treatise on the Soul* (trans. Holmes, ANF, 3:187).

[2]Khoo, 75.

[3]Tertullian also urges the name as proof that the narrative is not a parable but history, and that the scene in Hades involves his doctrine that soul is corporeal. Tertullian *A Treatise on Soul* (ANF, 3:187).

[4]Khoo, 69, 70, 75.

[5]Walvoord, 28.

[6]Matthew Hale Smith, *Universalism, Examined, Renounced, Exposed* [book on-line] (Boston: Tappan & Dennet, 1844, reproduced at google book search, accessed 24 January 2007), available from http://books.google.com/books; Internet.

[7]Ivor Powell, *Luke's Thrilling Gospel* (Grand Rapids: Zondervan, 1965; reprint, Grand Rapids: Kregel, 1984), 354. Cf. Yarbrough, 74.

near to each other since they can see and can converse with each other. Does this mean that hell and heaven are just adjacent places?[8]

2. All the righteous are in the bosom of Abraham. How can he bear all the righteous in his literal bosom? Did the literal bosom exist before Abraham existed?[9]

3. The parable describes the punishments of the wicked. It seems that this is in conflict with the eschatology of the Synoptic Gospels and the rest of the NT.[10]

4. If they are souls, why do they have tongues and fingers? The rich man's body is in the grave, his soul is in hell, and him is said to suffer physical torments.[113]

5. Besides, the parable does not mention souls being taken to hell or heaven.

The Description of ʾΑδης in Luke 16:19-31: Factual and
Literal Torment or Enjoyment of Souls but
after the Judgment at the Last Day

Proponents of the second view insist that the description of ἄδης in Luke 16:19-31 has a setting after the judgment in the last day. Souls will suffer or rejoice for eternity. This is called by some scholars as the final state.[12] John Calvin suggests that Christ is telling the story in the level of our understanding Adescribing spiritual things under figures."[13] He further declares that Jesus paints a picture that represents the condition of the future life and sees the suffering of

---

[8]Alfred Plummer notes that "the Jews believed that Gehenna and paradise are close to one another. . . . We need not suppose that the parable teaches us to believe this. The details of the picture cannot be insisted upon." Alfred Plummer, *The Gospel According to Luke: A Critical and Exegetical Commentary*, International Critical Commentary (ICC) (Edinburgh: T. & T. Clark, 1977), 394.

[9]Robert Leo Odom, *Is Your Soul Immortal?* (Wilwood, GA: Discovery Reading, 1989), 88.

[10]Cairus, 44.

[11]William F. Arndt, *Luke*, Concordia Classic Commentary Series (St. Louis, MO: Concordia, 1956; reprint, St. Louis, MO: Concordia, 1986), 363.

[12]Hultgren, 113. Cf. C[hristopher] F. Evans, *Saint Luke*, TPI New Testament Commentaries (Philadelphia: Trinity Press International, 1990), 614.

[13]John Calvin, *Calvin's Commentaries: A Harmony of the Gospels of Matthew, Mark, and Luke*, vol. 2, trans. A. W. Morrison, ed. David W. Torrance and Thomas F. Torrance (Edinburgh: St. Andrews, 1972), 118-19.

the rich man in hell as eternal after the judgment in the last day.[14]

This view is not so popular in biblical scholarship because many scholars see the event in the afterlife in this parable as happening before the last-day judgment as indicated in vv. 27-31.[15] Since the rich man asked Abraham to send Lazarus to warn his brothers on earth, it indicates that the setting is not after the final judgment.

The Description of ᾍδης in Luke 16:19-31: A Parable Not Factual or Literal but Symbolical, or Reflects Reality of the Torment or Blissfulness of Souls in the Intermediate State or the Final Judgment

The third view is that, as intimated by Darrel Bock, "this detail pictures the conscious awareness of where one resides after death. . . . It is graphic and pictorial and reflects a reality rather than describing it literally."[16] Furthermore, he maintains that the "fire" in Hades is metaphorical of conscious suffering.[17] I. Howard Marshall denotes that what is meant here is the intermediate state after death, but the details are not to be taken literally.[18] In addition, Michael Gilmour points out that although the "glimpse into Hades was observable,"[19] yet the parable may not be a specific event in actuality.[20] Norval Geldenhuys contends that this is just a parable, and we should not assume that this story really happened in real life.[21] Jesus, he continues, just "presents in intuitive forms

---

[14]Ibid., 117, 119.

[15]Marshall, 636. Cf. Joachim Jeremias, "ᾅδης," *Theological Dictionary of the New Testament (TDNT)*, ed. Gerhard Kittel and Gerhard Friedrich, trans. Geoffrey W. Bromiley (Grand Rapids: Eerdmans, 1964-76), 1:146-49.

[16]Bock, 1369. Cf. Darrell L. Bock, *Luke*, The NIV Application Commentary (NIVAC) (Grand Rapids: Zondervan, 1996), 433-34; D. Wenham, 144; Leon Morris, *Luke*, Tyndale New Testament Commentaries (TNTC), vol. 3 (Grand Rapids: Eerdmans, 1984), 254; Robert H. Stein, *Difficult Passages in the New Testament: Interpreting Puzzling Texts in the Gospels and Epistles* (Grand Rapids: Baker, 1990), 100.

[17]Bock, *Luke*, 435. Cf. I. Powell, 356.

[18]Marshall, 636.

[19]Michael J. Gilmour, "Hints of Homer in Luke 16:19-31," *Didaskalia* 10 (1999): 32 [journal on-line]; available from Academic Search Premier database; Internet; accessed 24 January 2007.

[20]The source of the parable is the world of human observation and experience. Ibid.

[21]Ibid., 428. Cf. Arndt, 363; Blomberg, 206; Caird, 191; Walter L. Liefeld, "Luke," *The Expositor's Bible Commentary (EBC)*, ed. Frank E. Gaebelein (Grand Rapids: Zondervan, 1984), 991; Daniel

which were familiar to his hearers an imaginary narrative in order to make them

see and realise vividly what awaits them."[223] Furthermore, W. Powell argues that

"we need not accept the story as having occurred. However, we may take it that

basic conditions of a parable are to be understood as true to fact."[234] Thomas

Huntingford and Jean Calvin acknowledge that Luke 16:19-31 is a parable, but,

also maintain that if the comfortable state of good souls in Abraham's bosom

immediately after death is true and real then the state of the wicked souls in hell

is also true and real.[241] Franz Mussner notes that "the parable shows that Jesus

shared about the coming life . . . and it would also appear that this other life

begins immediately after death."[252]

Walter L. Liefeld avouch that 'the story can be understood as a parable that

realistically portrays the fate of those who have rejected the Lord.'[263] He adds

that "it is no mere story chosen for its usefulness as an illustration but a rather

sober portrayal of yet unseen realities."[274]

W. Graf also contests that the passage is a parable that is a story just

invented by Jesus for the purpose of driving home a moral lesson. Therefore, it

is wrong, as far as the parable is concerned, to "exploit it as a *locus theologicus*

for a description of the state of the dead."[285] He adds that "the parable is not

Parker Livermore, *Proof-Texts of Endless Punishment Examined and Explained* [book on-line] (Chicago, IL: Livermore, 1862, reproduced at google book search, accessed 25 January 2007); available from http:// books.google.com/books; Internet; Charles H. Pinnock, "The Conditional View," in *Four Views on Hell*, ed. William Crockett (Grand Rapids: Zondervan, 1996), 156-57.

[22]Geldenhuys, 429.

[23]W. Powell, "The Parable of Dives and Lazarus (Luke 16:19-31)," *Expository Times (ET)* 66 (1954-55): 351.

[24]Thomas Huntingford and Jean Calvin, *Testimonies in Proof of the Separate Existence of the Soul in the State of Self-Consciousness between Death and Resurrection* [book on-line] (London: C. J. G. & F. Rivington, 1829, reproduced at google book search, accessed 25 January 2007); available from http://books.google.com/books; Internet.

[25]Franz Mussner, AThe Synoptic Account of Jesus' Teaching on the Future Life,@ in *Immortality and Resurrection* (n.p.: Herder & Herder, 1970), 47-48.

[26]Liefeld, 993.

[27]Ibid.

[28]W. Graf, "Dives and Lazarus (Luke 16:19-31)," *Homiletic & Pastoral Review* 38 (1937-38): 1184. Cf. David L. Tiede, *Luke*, Augsburg Commentary on the New Testament (Minneapolis: Augsburg, 1988), 289.

meant to be a complete description of the state of the reprobate, although there is an obvious hint of its finality."[291]

Another scholar, Peter Rhea Jones, reasons that the "language of the parable is apocalyptic"[302] like the book of Revelation. Hence, it should be viewed as symbolic, and "it is wooden to literalize."[313] Furthermore, he insists that the primary purpose of the parable is not to describe the afterlife but to impact on the present world, and the "impact depends on its force on the view of the life to come."[324] On the other hand, he suggests that it can be surmised that the parable favors an intermediate state immediately at death.[335]

The Description of ἍΑδης in Luke 16:19-31: A
Parable, Not Factual, Just Gives a Moral
Lesson; No Souls in Torment or in
Bliss in the Intermediate State

George W. Knight upholds that it is a parable rather than a true story. It "is not to satisfy curiosity concerning Hades, or Heaven, not the 'intermediate state,' nor any other fascinating esoteric topic related to life beyond death."[34] He adds, "It is set in a collection of parables that calls for careful stewardship . . . and emphasizes that there is a point in time when it is too late."[35] Eduard Schweizer points out that it is not a "guidebook to the next world."[36] Furthermore, Richard Bauckham clearly notes that the story in effect deprives itself of any claim to

---

[29]Tiede, 289.

[30]Peter Rhea Jones, *Studying the Parables of Jesus* (Macon, GA: Smyth & Helwys, 1999), 186; Bock, *Luke 9:51-24:53*, 1369.

[31]Jones, 186.

[32]Ibid., 188.

[33]Ibid., 188-89.

[34] G. W. Knight, 281. Eugene Wehrli points out that "the narrative is not an attempt to give information about the unseen world." Wehrli, 277. Cf. Larry Kreitzer, "Luke 16:19-31 and 1 Enoch 22," *ET* 103 (1992): 139; Christopher F. Evans, "Uncomfortable Words–V: Neither Will They Be Convinced," *ET* 81 (1969-70): 230; Thorwald Lorenzen, "A Biblical Meditation on Luke 16:19-31," *ET* 87 (1975-76): 42.

[35]G. W. Knight, 281.

[36]Eduard Schweizer, *The Good News According to Luke*, trans. David E. Green (Atlanta: John Knox, 1984), 261.

offer an apocalyptic glimpse of the secrets of the world beyond the grave. It cannot claim eyewitness authority as a literal description of the fate of the dead. It has a status of a parable. It is a part of a story to make a point.[37] Proponents of this view just understand the passage as a parable. It does not give a true picture of the afterlife, whether of the intermediate state or the final state. What they underscore is that Jesus told the parable to stress a moral lesson or a spiritual truth about stewardship. They do not state their own view of the suffering of souls in the afterlife in their interpretation or comments on the parable. Some scholars, aside from asserting that the parable should not be understood as a real description of the souls in the intermediate state, insist that the parable was "designed to teach that future destiny is determined by the use men make of the opportunities of this present life."[38] They also believe that there is no such thing as souls in torment or in joyful bliss in the intermediate state.[39]   On this line of thought Edward William Fudge, in his dialogue with Robert A. Peterson, points out,

> Few serious interpreters attempt to take the details of the story literally. To do so would require us to imagine the saved and the lost conversing with each other after death, in full view of each other and at close range. We also would have to think of literal tongues that burn with literal fire and literal water that does not cool them, not to mention physical bodies that can be tortured by fire but somehow do not burn up.[40]

He also notes that Jesus had told the story not to answer the question concerning the afterlife but to further illustrate His discourse on covetousness and stewardship in the preceding section of Luke 16 (vv. 1-13).[41] Fudge concludes that both OT and NT teach the resurrection of the wicked for the purpose of judgment

---

[37]Bauckham, 245. Cf. Bruce Reichenbach, *In Man the Phoenix?: A Study of Immortality* (Washington, DC: Christian University Press, 1978), 184.

[38] "A Certain Rich Man" (Luke 16:19), *Seventh-day Adventist Bible Commentary (SDABC)*, rev. ed., ed. Francis D. Nichol (Washington, DC: Review & Herald, 1976-80), 5:830. Cf. M. L. Andreasen, *Man: Here and Hereafter* (Mountain View, CA: Pacific Press, 1937), 65.

[39] "A Certain Rich Man," *SDABC*, 5:833; Andreasen, 64-65; Angel Manuel Rodriguez, "Using a Parable to Make a Point," *Adventist World*, January 2007, 26; Odom, 88-91.

[40] Edward William Fudge, "The Case for Conditional-ism," in *Two Views of Hell: A Biblical and Theological Dialogue* (Downers Grove, IL: InterVarsity, 2000), 41.

[41]Ibid.

in the lake of fire. They will be finally annihilated in everlasting extinction.[42] Seventh-day Adventist also holds this view, arguing that Scripture teaches the concept tormenting of the wicked does not precede the second advent of Jesus (2 Thess 1:7). Thus the parable of the rich man and Lazarus "in no way proves the consciousness of the dead, and the present and eternal torment of the wicked."[43] The Seventh-day Adventist also concludes that this "parable is spoken for the purpose of influencing the living, and is adapted to the time."[44] However, Kim Papaioannou, in his dissertation, argues that although Jesus deliberately modeled His story with the popular folktale of His time, He nevertheless de-constructs the themes of those stories in His story. He then concludes that the credibility of those stories are destroyed. He consequently proposed that "any contribution of the Parable to a Synoptic understanding of the afterlife is, in essence, negative."[45]

Some scholars do not submit to this view because they contend that if it is not true why did Jesus use this story which is not true? It would weaken His purpose of warning people to be responsible in the present life. Furthermore, if it is a parable, why are there no customary words for introducing a parable? In addition, this view is thought to be in conflict with some biblical data (see for example, Luke 23:43; Acts 2:27; 1 Pet 3:18-19; Rev 6:9-10). It is also in conflict with the popular belief held by the Jews during the time of Jesus and with the majority of the Church Fathers.

In summary, scholars are divided into four major views as regards the interpretation of the description of ᾅδης in Luke 16:19-31. The first view is that ᾅδης in the story describes the factual and literal torment of souls, the intermediate state of souls in Hades and a blissful life of the righteous souls in heaven who

---

[42]Edward William Fudge, *The Fire That Consumes* (Carlisle, UK: Paternoster, 1994), 4.

[43]George R. Knight, ed., *Questions on Doctrine*, Adventist Classic Library, annotated Edition (Berrien Springs, MI: Andrews University Press, 2003), 430. Cf.   LeRoy Edwin Froom, *The Conditionalist Faith of Our Fathers* (Washington, DC: Review & Herald, 1966), 2:234-44; Marvin Moore, *Where Is Bobby?* (Nashville, TN: Southern Pub. Assn., 1976), 21-22.

[44]G. R. Knight, 431.

[45]Kim G. Papaioannou, "Places of Punishments in the Synoptic Gospels" (Ph.D. diss., Durham University, Durham, England, 2005), 153.

await the final day of judgment. This description is factual and literal and was taught by Jesus. The second view, similar to the first, considers ᾅδης in the story as having a setting after the final judgment in the last day. The wicked souls will suffer for eternity but the righteous souls will live in blissful heaven for eternity.

The third view regards that the description of ᾅδης in Luke 16:19-31 as not factual. It does not show the literal situation of the afterlife. However, it reflects the reality of the suffering or the enjoyment of souls in the intermediate state or in the final state.

The fourth view asserts that it is just a parable used by Jesus to emphasize faithful stewardship, the importance of the Law and the Prophets, and the uselessness of someone raised from the dead to generate faith. Furthermore, there is no such thing as souls being in torment in the intermediate state or in the final state. The wicked will be resurrected at the last day judgment and will be annihilated by fire. This review of literature has shown that scholars are divided over the issue being tackled in this study. There is no unanimity that several views above show various interpretations of the description of ᾅδης in Luke 16:19-31. However, it is evident that scholarship tends to focus on some other issues such as the background, structure, and origin of composition. No thorough study has yet been done on the interpretation of ᾅδης in the story of the rich man and Lazarus.[46] Thus, there is a need to fill in these gaps.

---

[46]There was a thesis written that dealt with the parable of the Rich Man and Lazarus. However, it is a general analysis of the parable. Besides, the thesis is very old and is so short (sixty-eight pages). See Walter Dingfield, "A Study of the Rich Man and Lazarus," (Th.M. thesis, Dallas Theological Seminary, Dallas, Texas, 1954). Articles written by scholars regarding the topic are also short and incomplete as far as exegesis is concerned. A dissertation by Papaioannou deals so much on the issue of the places of punishments in the Synoptic Gospels. It touched Luke 16:19-31, but he deals so much with the extra-biblical background and the literary analysis of the passage. Hence, this research provides an extensive exegetical analysis of the concept ᾅδης in Luke 16:19-31 which is lacking in previous studies

THE GENRE OF LUKE 16:19-31

THE NATURE of the genre of NT parables[22] is a controversial issue in NT studies.[23] The genre of Luke 16:19-31 is also an issue among scholars. There are at least two important issues that should be settled as far as genre of Luke 16:19-31 is concerned.

First, is the story a factual event or fiction? Several scholars say that it is a folktale[24] which may be considered to be factual or a fictitious event.[25]

As a fictitious story, it is more on a "pictorial and representative than a real story."[26] It was just used by Jesus as a parable to stress a truth on faithful stewardship.[27] Others assert that Luke 16:19-31 is a true story,[28] or at least it may

---

[22]Although the word *parabolē*, does not occur in Luke 16:19-31, this study presupposes, like other NT scholars (see the discussion on third and fourth views in the review of related literature), that this narrative is a parable. Based on this presupposition, this chapter begins with the discussion on OT מָשָׁל the equivalent of NT parabolē.

[23]David Parris points out that the focus on the issue of genre in NT parables today is on whether or not there are allegorical elements in NT parables. David P. Parris, "Imitating the Parables: Allegory, Narrative, and the Role of Mimesis," *Journal for the Study of the New Testament* 25 (2002): 35 [journal on-line]; available from Academic Search Premier database; Internet; accessed 23 January 2007.

[24]Scholars suggest divergent background sources of Luke 16:19-31. The widely accepted background source of this story was an Egyptian folktale of Si-Osiris. See F. L. Griffith, *Stories of the High Priests of Memphis* (Oxford: Clarendon, 1900), 42-43, quoted in John Nolland, *Luke 9:21-18:34*, Word Biblical Commentary (WBC), vol. 35B (Dallas, TX: Word, 1989), 826. Bauckham suggests a wide spectrum of background. Bauckham, 229. Rudolf Bultmann argues that the narrative was influenced by a Jewish story of Bar Mayan. Bultmann, 196-97. Ronald Hock on the other hand asserts that the background source for this story was Lucian's story of Micyllus the cobbler. Hock, "Lazarus and Micyllus," 448-51. Larry Kreitzer argues for 1 Enoch 22 as the background source. Kreitzer, 139-43.

[25]For example, see Papaioannou, 137.

[26]See Bock, *Luke*, 432.

[27]G. W. Knight, 281.

[28]See Khoo, 70; Louis Richard Batzler, "The Parable of Jesus Concerning the Afterlife: Spiritual and Psychical Insights," *The Journal of Religion and Psychical Research* 23 (2000): 87 [journal on-line]; available

just reflect a reality.[29] Second, is this story categorized as a narrative parable[30] or an example story?[31] To decide whether Luke 16:19-31 is a true or a fictitious story,[32] and whether it is a parabolic narrative or an example story,[33] it seems appropriate to survey first the OT parables and to examine their characteristics, especially their subgenres. This section also surveys several parables in Luke to find some parallels and bases for the analysis of the genre of Luke 16:19-31. Then, the genre of the passage itself is determined

The OT Parable Genre

In genre identification, Gerald Klingbeil notes that, customarily, biblical scholars tend to follow the predominant presuppositions and axioms of the "turn-of-the-century biblical scholarship."[34] It considers the "form and content" as the basis for genre identification.[35] However, OT biblical scholars are still not in agreement in identifying the genre of some OT books.

Jens Bruun Kofoed observes the animated debate on the issue of whether the books of Kings are under "historiography" or "antiquarianism" genre.[36] Some scholars, as noted by Kofoed, use the Greek historiography as the standard in

from Academic Search Premier database; Internet; accessed 19 January 2007.

[29]See Morris, 254.

[30]Joel B. Green, *The Theology of the Gospel of Luke*, (Cambridge: Cambridge University Press, 1995), 604.

[31]A Ph.D. dissertation examines four parables which were labeled by Adolf Jülicher as example narratives. Some of these parables are the Good Samaritan, the Foolish Rich Man, and the Rich Man and Poor Lazarus. See Jeffrey Thomas Tucker, "Four Parables in the Gospel of Luke: Perspectives on the Example Narratives" (Ph.D. Diss., Vanderbilt University, 1994), abstract available from http// www .aiias.edu/database/proquest/dissertation and thesis; internet; accessed 22 January 2007.

[32]If it is a factual event, then it is a true story. If it is not a factual event, then it is a fictitious story or a fiction.

[33]It is a narrative parable if one of the characters in the story corresponds to one of the audience in the literary context. If the characters in the narrative do not correspond to individuals in the audience, then it may be called an example story.

[34]Jens Bruun Kofoed, *Text and History: Historiography and the Study of the Biblical Text* (Winona Lake, IN: Eisenbrauns, 2005), 227-34.

[35]Ibid.

[36]Jens Bruun Kofoed, *Text and History: Historiography and the Study of the Biblical Text* (Winona Lake, IN: Eisenbrauns, 2005), 227-34.

measuring whether the historical books of the Hebrew Bible (HB) are historical production or a product of an imaginative literary and poetic traditions of epic and mythology.[37] Kofoed does not agree with this view. As a result, he presents a new approach using the procedure of John Marincola.[38] In this approach, Kofoed rejects the "too rigid definitions and applications of the historiographical subgenres." In another research, Kofoed proves that ancient Israel history writing, although may be deployed with religious purposes, belongs to "historiographical genre." He does this by making a comparison between the books of Kings and several Ancient Near East inscriptions: (1) Assyrian Royal Inscriptions, (2) Babylonian Chronicles, and (3) North West Semitic Royal Inscriptions. He concludes that the Books of Kings can safely be continued to be included as historical information in the pool of evidence for a historiographical reconstruction of ancient Israel.[39]

Klingbeil, in his semantic analysis of the Aramaic ostraca of Syria-Palestine during the Persian period, also proposes an alternative approach in identifying genres. This approach is "based upon the semantics and their content."[40] In view of divergent approaches in genre identification among biblical scholars, this study, like Klingbeil, will not just uncritically accept the presupposed axioms being laid out by previous biblical scholars on the identification of genre. This study seeks to analyze and establish the genre of Luke 16:19-31. It starts from the OT where some narrative parables seemed similar to the supposed parable in Luke 16:19-31.

This study starts with the analysis of the OT parable genre. The Hebrew word for parable is מָשָׁל. It has a variety of meanings. It means "proverbial saying" (1 Sam 10:12), "by-word" (Deut 28:37; 1 Kgs 9:7), "prophetic figurative

---

[37]Ibid., 227.

[38]Ibid., 235. For John Marincola's procedure, see John Marincola, "Genre, Convention, and Innovation in Greco-Roman Historiography," in *The Limits of Historiography: Genre and Narrative in Ancient Historical Texts*, ed. Christina Shuttleworth Kraus (Leiden: Brill, 1999).

[39]Ibid., 14. For a close scrutiny of Kofoed's research, see ibid., 1-14.

[40]Ibid. For a detailed demonstration of this approach, see Klingbeil, 36-46. This methodology was adapted from J. P. Louw and E. A. Nida. See ibid., 33. See also J. P. Louw and E. A. Nida, *Greek-English Lexicon of the New Testament Based on Semantic Domains*, 2 vols. (Cape Town: Bible Society of South Africa, 1988).

discourses" (Num 23:7,18; 24:3,15; 20,21,25), "similitude and (allegorizing) parable" (Ezek 17:3-10), "poem" (Job 29; Ps 49, 78), and "sentences of ethical wisdom" (Prov 1:6).[41] D. Brent Sandy and Ronald L. Giese Jr. note that מָשָׁל, "the Hebrew term for allegory and parable is used to describe a wide range of wisdom forms in the OT narrative and poetic literature. The essence of מָשָׁל is comparison."[42] David Gowler also notes that מָשָׁל "is difficult to describe and almost impossible to define, but its 'root meaning' can be seen as 'to represent' or 'to be like'."[43] Analyzing the context and content of some of the occurrences of the OT מָשָׁל in relation to their proposed semantics can be helpful in identifying the genres of the said texts. The root word מָשָׁל occurs in the HB 141 times in 126 verses. It comprises several ranges of meanings: (1) verb——represent, be like; (2) noun——proverb, parable which includes proverbial saying, by-word, prophetic figurative discourse, similitude, parable, and sentences of ethical wisdom; (3) verb——denominationally used as a proverb, speak in parable or sentences of poetry; (4) noun—— likeness, one like; (5) verb——rule, have dominion, reign.[44] This section classifies the OT מָשָׁל being analyzed into subgenres. The first is the "Ancient Saying" or "Proverb." The example of this מָשָׁל is in 1 Sam 24:13[14]. In this passage, king David used a מָשָׁל[45] which says, "out of the wicked comes forth wickedness." The preposition כְּ (kᵉ) "like" indicates that there is an element of

---

[41]Francis Brown, with S. R. Driver and Charles A. Briggs, *A Hebrew and English Lexicon of the Old Testament with an Appendix Containing the Biblical Aramaic* (BDB), based on the lexicon of William Gesenius (1952), s.v. "מָשָׁל."

[42]D. Brent Sandy and Ronald L. Giese Jr., *Cracking the Old Testament Codes: A Guide to Interpreting the Literary Genres of the Old Testament* (Nashville, TN: Broadman & Holman, 1995), 259.

[43]David B. Gowler, *What Are They Saying about the Parables?* (New York: Paulist, 2000), 42.

[44]Brown, BDB, s.v. "מָשָׁל." Cf. Benjamin Davidson, *Analytical Hebrew and Chaldee Lexicon* (1997), s.v. "מָשָׁל"; Gerald Wilson, "מָשָׁל," *New International Dictionary of Old Testament Theology and Exegesis*, ed. Willem A. VanGemeren (Grand Rapids: Zondervan, 1997), 2:1134-36. Gesenius elaborates further in saying that it consists of an ingenious comparison of two things or opinionsBsententious saying, sentence, opinion (cf. Prov 26:1,2,3,6,7,8,9,11,14, 17). It also means a *song, poem* (Num 23:7,18; Job 27:1; 29:1; Ps 49:5), aside from similitude, parable, and proverb. Freidrich Heinrich Wilhelm Gesenius, *Gesenius' Hebrew and Chaldee Lexicon*, trans. Samuel Prideaux Tregelles (1978), s.v. "מָשָׁל."

[45]It is translated as "proverb" (KJV; NASB; NLT).

comparison. David used this מָשָׁל to compare the situation between him (David) and king Saul to an ancient saying or proverb. The point of the מָשָׁל is that, usually, wickedness produces wickedness, which implies that he (David) is not wicked. He does not want to show wickedness to Saul, as what the king did to him. The מָשָׁל here is used by David as a basis of his action, although his action runs contrary to the מָשָׁל he quoted. It seems that this מָשָׁל has a comparative usage, but it is different from an allegorical/narrative parable מָשָׁל. This מָשָׁל in 1 Sam 24:14 may be called a "proverbial saying," or specifically, "proverb of the ancients" subgenre.

The second is the "Song" or "Taunt Song," or "a Poem." The example is in Num 21:27-30. This seems to be a poem which is constructed in parallelism. An example is v. 28, (כִּי־אֵשׁ יָצְאָה מֵחֶשְׁבּוֹן לֶהָבָה מִקִּרְיַת סִיחֹן)[46] "For a fire went forth from Heshbon" [first line], "A flame from the town of Sihon" [second line], NASB. The second line is parallel with the first. They emphasize the same idea, a typical and common Hebrew poetry.

Philip J. Budd labels this מָשָׁל as a "song" and it has some form of a ballad, perhaps a taunt song.[47] The basic idea of a מָשָׁל is evident in the passage. It is in a noun form which means, "to be like." The idea of comparison is seen in the parallel structure of Hebrew poetry.[48]

The third is the "Prophetic Oracle" or "Prophetic Figurative Discourse." Other passages which have the same idea with the מָשָׁל of Num 21:27-30 are Num 23:7,18; 24:3,15, 20,21,23. The word מָשָׁל is used here to describe the discourse of Balaam (23:7-10; 18-24; 24:3-9; 15-24). These passages are structured again with a common Hebrew poetry parallelism. An example is Num 23:8, ( )[49] "How shall I curse, whom God has not cursed? And how can I denounce, whom the

---

[46]The Hebrew texts in this study are taken from a software Bible Works. See Bible Works, version 7 (Norfolk, VA: LLC, 2007). For a hard copy, see K. Elliger and W. Rudolph, *Biblia Hebraica Stuttgartensia* (*BHS*) (Stuttgart: Deutche Bibelgesellschaft, 1977), 252.

[47]Philip J. Budd, *Numbers*, WBC, vol. 5, 246.

[48]Ibid.

[49]See Elliger and Rudolph, *BHS*, 256.

LORD has not denounced? (NASB)" This מָשָׁל, although, has poetic structure,

(מָה אֶקֹּב לֹא קַבֹּה אֵל וּמָה אֶזְעֹם לֹא זָעַם יְהוָה) but could be different from a poem מָשָׁל. Since the content indicates their prophetic nature, this מָשָׁל could be labeled as "prophetic oracle" or "prophetic figurative discourse."[50]

The fourth is called "By-Word." This מָשָׁל is also used in Deut 28:37 (cf. 1 Kgs 9:7; 2 Chr 7:20; Job 17:6). In these passages, מָשָׁל is closely connected with שְׁנִינָה. (sheˁnînāh), "Sharp word, taunt."[51] In the contexts of these passages, except in Job, the people of Israel were cut off from the land promised by the covenant. Their disobedience cut them off from the covenant land. Consequently, they became a מָשָׁל, "by-word" which means, in the contexts, an object of ridicule and taunt.

The fifth is called "Ethical Wisdom," or "Proverb." The usage of this מָשָׁל is in the book of Proverbs. In 1:1, king Solomon is declared as the author of these מִשְׁלֵי (mishˁlê). In the context of Prov 1:6, מָשָׁל may mean "wisdom saying" or "the words of the wise (NASB)." Since the main objective of these wisdom sayings is for moral behavior (1:3), this מָשָׁל may be called "ethical wisdom" מָשָׁל. This ethical wisdom is accepted as an authoritative rule as indicated through the meaning of the verb form "to rule." Tremper Longman suggests that מָשָׁל "simply refers to the fact that this literary vehicle is a part of the wisdom teacher's pedagogical repertoire."[52] Furthermore, he points out that מָשָׁל denotes "what we recognize as many different types of writing."[53]

The sixth is "Narrative מָשָׁל." One example of this מָשָׁל is found in Ezek 17:3-10. Michael Goulder admits that there are only five HB texts that could qualify for a "narrative מָשָׁל": (1) Jotam's מָשָׁל of the trees (Judg 9:7-15), (2) Nathan's the

---

[50]The word נְאֻם (neˁ'um) means "utterance." Brown, BDB, s.v. "נְאֻם." It is translated "oracle" in NASB. It occurs six times (24:3,4,15,16) in Balaam=s discourses and it refers to his whole discourses. Cf. R. Dennis Cole, *Numbers,* New American Commentary (NAC), vol. 3B (Nashville, TN: Broadman & Holman, 2000), 409; Brown, BDB, s.v. "מָשָׁל."

[51]Brown, BDB, s.v. "שְׁנִינָה."

[52]Tremper Longman, *Proverbs* (Grand Rapids: Baker, 2006), 30.

[53]Ibid. He adds, "One would expect comparison to be a constituent part of the proverb, and indeed, many of the proverbs use simile and metaphor to communicate important ideas." Ibid.

Poor Man's only Lamb (2 Sam 12:1-4), (3) Jehoash's מָשָׁל of the Thistle (2 Kgs 14:9), (4) Isaiah's מָשָׁל of the Vineyard (Isa 5:1-6), and (5) Ezekiel's מָשָׁל of the Vine and the Eagles (Ezek 17:3-10).[54]

Gowler points out that of the five, only Nathan's מָשָׁל is found similar to the parables in the Synoptic Gospels. The rest are fables and allegorizing parables.[55] In this juncture, it is fitting to analyze these five OT narrative מָשָׁל in order to determine the nature of these narratives which Goulder labeled as narrative מָשָׁל. These narrative מָשָׁל could be classified into different subgenres.

The first one is called a "Fable." An example is Jotham's fable (Judg 9:7-15). The historical narrative of Judg 9 describes the evil deeds and rule of Abimelech the son of Gideon who was also called Jerubbaal (8:35; 9:2). This chapter can be divided into three sections: (1) Judg 9:1-6——Abimelech and the men of Shechem's corroboration to kill the seventy sons of Gideon, and Abimelech's ascendancy to kingship; (2) Judg 9:7-21——Jotham's narrative parable of trees and its interpretations,[56] and (3) Judg 9:22-57——The fulfillment of Jotham's curse against Abimelech and the people of Shechem.

Abimelech's historical narrative in Judg 9 begins with his quest to become the king over Israel. He went to the people of Shechem, his mother's relatives, and convinced them to set him as king over them. With the support of the Shechemites, he succeeded in destroying his father's household by killing all his brothers except Jotham. Abimelech was then made king by them (vv. 1-6). This is the preceding context of the narrative fable.

In v. 7, upon hearing what had happened to his brothers, Jotham, the surviving son of Jerubbaal, then went to mount Gerizim and at the top of his voice uttered this narrative מָשָׁל, while Abimelech and the people of Shechem were listening to him. Analyzing this narrative (vv. 8-15), it seems apparent that

---

[54]Michael Goulder, *Midrash and Lection in Matthew* (London: SPCK, 1974), 47.

[55]Gowler, 45.

[56]Daniel I. Block notes that this "is carefully constructed in standard Hebrew narrative style." Daniel I. Block, *Judges, Ruth: An Exegetical and Theological Exposition of Holy Scripture*, NAC, vol. 6, 315.

this is a fable. It is also plausible to suggest that this fable is used as a parable[57] in the technical sense of the word rather than an allegory. Here are the evidences:

1. The literary context indicates it. This narrative serves as Jotham's rallying point in the pronouncement of a curse on Abimelech and the people of Shechem. This is evident in vv. 15-20. Verses 15 and 20 are the highlights of the parable. This is Jotham's main thrust: the bramble who was made king by the trees, invites them (the trees) to take refuge in his shades provided "in truth" they made him king. But if not "in truth" then the curse will fall on them, "may fire come out of the bramble and consume the cedars of Lebanon" (v. 15). Now the literal meaning of this figure of speech is clearly set forth in vv. 16-20. If "in truth and integrity" the people of Shechem made Abimelech king over them, then they could rejoice with him and he could rejoice with them. But if not "in truth and

---

[57]It is necessary at this point to define what is a parable and an allegory. According to John Dominic Crossan, the Hebrew literary tradition gave the OT מָשָׁל (parabolē,, LXX) a much wider understanding. It has a wide range of application. John Dominic Crossan, "Parable," *ABD*, 5:146. He adds, "Contemporary literary criticism agrees with the Greco-Roman tradition emphasizing the narrative element in parable but with the Hebrew tradition in allowing both impossible and possible stories into the genre." Ibid. Our definition of parable in this study is the contemporary definition. According to Crossan, "There are three elements stressed in modern parabolic theory. Parables combine qualities of narrative, metaphor, and brevity. A parable must tell, in as short a space as possible, a story with a double meaning. One meaning will usually be quite clear on the surface of the narration. Another, and presumably deeper meaning, or other, and possibly multiple meanings lie hidden within the complexities of the narrative." Ibid., 146-47.

According to Craig Blomberg, parable Arevolves around one main point of comparison between the activity in the story and Jesus' understanding of the kingdom of God, and thus they teach one primary lesson. Subordinate details are significant only to the extent that they fit in with and reinforce the central emphasis." Blomberg, 30. He defines allegories as "more complex stories which require numerous details in them to be Adecoded." Blomberg notes that AChristian Bugge argued that OT and rabbinic literature rather than Aristotle provide the background for interpreting Jesus' use of parables. In Hebrew the word מָשָׁל (often translated as parabolē, in the Greek Bible (Parable in English translations) is used for all types of figure of speech—proverbs, riddles, taunts, simple comparisons, and complex allegories." Ibid., 36. Based on this discussion, it is apparent that allegory is one of the subgenres of OT lv;m; and NT parabolē,.

Carl Heinz Peisker defines allegory as Aa freely invented story, which says something other than it appears to say on the surface by heaping metaphor on metaphor. It is a continuous metaphor (Matt 22:2-10; John 10:15; Rom 11:17-24; 1 Cor 3:10-13; Ezek 16; 17; 19; 23; 31; 34; Ps 80:8-19). "Carl Heinz Peisker, Aparabolē," *New International Dictionary of New Testament Theology (NIDNTT)*, ed. Colin Brown (Grand Rapids: Zondervan, 1975-78), 2:747. Allegory in the NT are designated as parabolē, rather than *allēgoria* (Matt 22:1). Ibid., 2:748.

Crossan adds, AAn allegory has many separate but connected points of reference and each detail is important in itself, but the parable has only one major point and all the details serve only to build up this single reference. "Crossan, *In Parables*, 9. However, he notes that Athe possibility that allegory, with its many points, and parable, with its single point, were but ends of a sliding scale within which one had to talk of parabolic allegories and allegorical parables." Ibid. Jeremy Schipper also insists that in an allegory, each element would represent a corresponding reality. Jeremy Schipper, "Did David Overinterpret Nathan's Parable in 2 Samuel 12:1-6?"*JBL* 126 (2007): 385.

integrity," then Abimelech would destroy the people of Shechem, and the people of Shechem would also destroy Abimelech (vv. 16-20).

2. The story of Jotham is nonsense if it has no literal meaning. It has only one possible primary meaning as the context indicates. The bramble is apparently referring to Abimelech whose fire would consume the men of Shechem and Beth-Millo who are represented by the trees in the parable if they have not set him king over them in truth and integrity (v. 20).

3. The fulfillment of the curse is also one of the evidences. Since the people of Shechem did not set Abimelech king over them in truth and integrity, so Abimelech destroyed them (vv. 34-49). However, Abimelech was also killed by a woman's millstone (vv. 50-57).

4. Not all items in the parable have literal correspondence. The olive tree, fig tree, and the vine do not have literal representations.

5. Jotham, in this narrative parable, explicitly drives only one point. It is the curse of destruction against Abimelech and the people of Shechem if they did not deal "in truth and integrity" in making him king and in killing Jerubbaal's household.

There are few observations regarding this narrative parable:

1. The story is not true to life; it is sometimes called a fable.[58]

2. Not all items in the parable have literal correspondence.

3. The literal meaning goes beyond what was described in the parable. Daniel Block calls it "the tensions between the fable and the surrounding text."[59]

---

[58]Block notes that "in terms of genre, vv. 8-15 contain the finest example in Scripture of a fable which by definition typically involves a short narrative in poetry or prose that teaches a moral lesson and involves creature like plant, and/or inanimate objects speaking or behaving like human characters." Block, 316.

[59]Ibid.

In the parable, the trees were looking for a king; in the context, it was Abimelech who approached the people of Shechem to set him as their king. Furthermore, only the bramble caused fire and burned the trees. That means, supposedly, only Abimelech would destroy the people of Shechem. However, Abimelech was also destroyed in the fulfillment of the curse.

4. This narrative parable explicitly drives only one point that is the curse of destruction against Abimelech and the people of Shechem. In the contrary, George F. Moore, aside from the main point above, suggests another lesson from this fable; those men whose character and ability fit them to rule are hesitant to take the position. On the contrary, men who are useless and obnoxious are the ones ready to be king.[60]

Arthur E. Cundall and Leon Morris also note that the refusal of the olive, fig, and vine may represent the men of dignity and influence to be king in Israel.[61] Although this interpretation is possible in the context, but, explicitly, Jotham did not hint on this in his application of the parable. Besides, in the preceding narrative, only Gideon was asked by the Israelites to rule over them (8:22). If Gideon represents one of the trees (for example, the vine),[62] then who would represent the olive and the fig? There was no explicit event before the time of Gideon that the Israelites asked either Othniel, Ehud, or Deborah to rule over them. Thus, the narrative is not an allegory per se. There are at least three items in the narrative which are clearly represented in real life. The trees represent the Israelites,[63] and the bramble represents Abimelech.[64] The

---

[60]George F. Moore, *A Critical and Exegetical Commentary on Judges*, ICC, 248-52.

[61]Arthur E. Cundall and Leon Morris, *Judges and Ruth*, Tyndale Old Testament Commentaries, vol. 7 (Downers Grove, IL: InterVarsity, 1968), 129. They also point out that the later Rabbis suggested that Othniel, Deborah, and Gideon were represented by the olive, fig, and vine in the fable. Ibid.

[62]See Judg 8:22.

[63]David Jackman, *Judges, Ruth*, Communicator's Commentary, vol. 7 (Dallas, TX: Word, 1991), 158.

[64]E. John Hamlin, *Judges: At Risk in the Promised Land*, International Theological Commentatry (ITC) (Grand Rapids: Eerdmans, 102.

"fire" may represent the instruments used to destroy both Abimelech and the Shechemites.

This narrative may be considered a parable. In this case, this is different from other parables in the OT and NT because it is not a real-life story. Some scholars may be right in calling this a fable. It may be labeled then as "Fable Parable." In the context, Jotham's purpose in using this parable is to pronounce a prophetic curse against Abimelech and the people of Shechem.

The second narrative מָשָׁל is the one told by prophet Nathan to king David (2 Sam 12:1-4)[65] immediately after the later's heinous crime of adultery and murder (2 Sam 11). There are two issues that should be tackled with this narrative:

1. What is the subgenre of this narrative מָשָׁל?

2. Is this narrative a true story, or a fictitious one?

Apparently, based on the context and content of the narrative, this is a parable. But unlike Jotham's parable, this one is not a fable but a real-life story. There are several evidences to show that this is a parable:

1. Based on the context, there is no one-to-one correspondence between the items in the narrative and Nathan's application.[66]

2. There are only at least four items in the narrative which have correspondences in Nathan's application. The most explicit one is the rich man who represents David (v. 7).[67] The poor man may represent Uriah (v. 9).[68] The flocks and herds of the rich man may represent David's many wives and Harem (v. 8).[69] The ewe lamb may represent Bathsheba (v. 9).

3. The traveler is not represented.

---

[65]The narrative is about two men, one was rich and one was poor. The rich man had many flocks and herd, while the poor man had only one ewe lamb. When a visitor came, the rich man, instead of slaughtering a sheep out of his flocks, took the ewe lamb of the poor man and butchered it for his visitor.

[66]See also J. P. Fokkelman, *Narrative Art and Poetry in the Books of Samuel*, vol. 1, *King David* (Assen, The Netherlands: Van Gorcum, 1981), 78.

[67]Joyce G. Baldwin, *1 & 2 Samuel*, Tyndale Old Testament Commentaries, vol. 8, 237.

[68]Henry Preserved Smith, *The Book of Samuel: A Critical and Exegetical Commentary*, ICC, 323.

[69]Ibid.

4. Uriah was killed; whereas in the parable, the poor man was not. It was the ewe lamb that was killed; whereas in Nathan's application, Bathsheba was not. Arnold A. Anderson may be right in saying that the "lack of correspondence between the parable and David's crimes need not create a problem because what was stressed is not identity but comparison. David is like the rich man in the parable."[70] The parable may be defined as "juridical parable."[71] Uriel Simon defines juridical parable as a realistic story. It is about a legal violation told to someone who also had a similar offense with one of the characters in the parable, in order that the offender may pass judgment to himself. The offender will be caught in a trap, only if he does not prematurely detect the parable.[72] However, just recently, Schipper argues that David did understand Nathan's parable as a parable rather than a legal case.[73] On the other hand, in the context, it seems clear that Nathan unsuspectingly tells the parable as a really legal case. J. P. Fokkelman also suggests that in David's reaction, "it is evident that Nathan's story contains none of the linguistic or stylistic devices which would indicate the story's being fictitious."[74]

Clearly, Nathan's purpose in using this parable is to trap David in pronouncing condemnation against himself. There are other passages similar to Nathan's juridical parable. Anderson notes, "There are similar judgment-eliciting parables in 2 Sam 14:1-20; 1 Kgs 20:35-43; Isa 5:1-7), and they all share a similar basic structure well illustrated by Nathan's parable."[75]

In the application of the parable, Nathan did not intend to show a one-to-one correspondence between the parable and real situation, but to pronounce

---

[70] Arnold A. Anderson, *2 Samuel*, WBC, vol. 11, 161.

[71] Ibid., 160.

[72] Uriel Simon, "The Poor Man's Ewe-Lamb: An Example of a Juridical Parable," *Biblica* 48 (1967): 221.

[73] Schipper, 383.

[74] Fokkelman, 72.

[75] Anderson, 160. To show the structure, "there is the introduction (11:27b-12:1a) which is followed by supposed legal case (vv. 1b-4) and the judgment elicited (vv. 5-6), finally the judgment is reapplied to the actual culprit himself (v. 7a)." Ibid.

God's judgment against the sins of David. This is emphasized in the statement,
"you are the man!" (v. 7a), and the ensuing declaration of punishment (vv. 7b-12).
Apparently, Nathan's narrative parable is not an allegory but a parable per se.

The next question, is this narrative parable a true legal story which happened
or not? At first, the story seems to be a true story that prophet Nathan brought
out as a legal problem of a really poor man who was oppressed by a rich man
and needs the king's judgment. However, the subsequent application that follows
betrays the historicity of the story. Anderson notes,

> It has been assumed that the judgment eliciting parable in 2 Samuel depict
> authentic legal cases which were actually brought to David but, on the
> other hand, it is more likely that they were literary device (as in Isa 5:1-7)
> or constructions to provide an interpretation of events in retrospect.[76]

In short, this story is fictitious. Although, it might happen in real life, the
context shows that it is not a true story. It was just probably crafted by Nathan
to primarily conceal God's pronouncement of judgment against king David.
Nathan's statement, "you are the man!" instead of "you are like this rich man" is
an evidence against the historicity of the story. The third narrative מָשָׁל is 2 Kgs
14:9. This is a very short narrative. This narrative parable is similar to that of
Jotham's parable. Hence, this is also a fable. This fable like that of Jotham's is
again a parable instead of an allegory.

Jehoash in using this parable,[77] to convey his message to Amaziah in
response to the hostile proposal[78] of the later, is just to tell Amaziah not to dare to
fight him in a battle (v. 10). For the reason that, as implied in the application of
Jehoash' parable, Amaziah, like a thorn bush, has no match with him who is like a
cedar.[79] The application of this parable of Jehoash king of Israel, in relation to the

---

[76]Ibid., 160-61.

[77]Mordechai Cogan and Hayim Tadmor notes that "the use of fables and proverbs in political
contexts is well attested" in ancient near east. Mordechai Cogan and Hayim Tadmor, *II Kings*, AB, vol. 11,
156.

[78]In v. 8, Amaziah challenges Jehoash to meet him face to face. Cogan and Tadmor note that the
meaning of the Hebrew phrase has a hostile sense of confrontation. They also note that the Akkadian
equivalent is not only used for peaceful meetings, but occasionally for confrontations with an enemy as well.
Ibid. Cf. John Gray, *1 & 2 Kings*, Old Testament Library (London: SCM, 1977), 607.

[79]See Paul H. House, *1 & 2 Kings*, NAC, vol. 8, 324.

challenge issued by Amaziah king Judah, is a little bit far from the content of the
parable. The parable is about the proposal of the thorn bush to cedar concerning
the marriage of their children, but a wild beast trampled on the thorn bush. The
application is not about the marriage proposal of Amaziah to Jehoash concerning
the marriage of their children. The point of Jehoash is just to warn Amaziah not
to engage in a battle with him (v. 10). Again, like that of Jotham's and Nathan's
parables, Jehoash's use of the parable is prompted by a preceding situation. The
parable was used to convey a certain message to the receiver on the other end. In
short, Jotham, Nathan, and Jehoash used parables as vehicles (as an illustration)
to convey their messages to their intended recipients.

The fourth narrative מָשָׁל is Isa 5:1-7. Although the word מָשָׁל does not
occur in the passage or in its context, the content of the passage evidently
shows that this is a poetical or hymnic (v. 1) and a figurative passage (v. 7). The
comparative nature of the passage indicates that this is a parable (v. 7ab), but this
one may be labeled as "allegorical parable." There are several correspondences
between the parable and the application which were pointed out by Isaiah: (1)
the vineyard owner——Yahweh (v. 7a), (2) the vineyard——men of Jerusalem and
Judah (v. 7b), (3) the bad fruits——bloodshed, and injustice (v. 7cd); and (4) the
destruction of the vineyard——destruction of Jerusalem, and the captivity of her
people (vv. 8-13). Joseph Blenkinsopp notes that medieval exegetes interpret
this passage allegorically (for example, removing stones means extirpating the
Canaanites, the watchtower——the temple),[80] but the application of the parable
does not indicate that this is an allegory. To a certain extent, there was one-to-
one correspondence given by the prophet himself, yet not all details were given a
one-to-one correspondence by the prophet. Hence, this one could not be labeled
as an "Allegory" but, to some extent, an "Allegorical Parable."

John D. W. Watts asserts that "the original genre is a complaint or, better,
an accusation. The setting is that of the court of justice."[81] As mentioned earlier,
this is a judgment-eliciting parable or juridical parable. The structure is similar

---

[80]Joseph Blenkinsopp, *Isaiah 1-39*, AB, vol. 19, 207.

[81]John D. W. Watts, *Isaiah 1-33*, WBC, vol. 24, 54.

to that of Nathan's juridical parable. There is an introduction (v. 1ab). There is a supposed legal case (vv. 1c-2f). Then judgment is elicited (vv. 3-6),[82] but, unlike in Nathan's parable, the one who pronounced judgment were not the culprits (Jerusalemites and Judaeans), but the complainant—the owner of the vineyard, Yahweh. Finally, judgment was reapplied to the offenders in real life (v. 7).

It is unarguable that this parable may happen in real life. However, like Nathan's juridical parable, it is apparent in the context that this is not a true story. The application of the parable shows that the song-parable is just an illustration (v. 7);[83] the purpose is to trap the people of God to pronounce judgment against themselves. However, unlike in Nathan's parable (David pronounced judgment against himself), it is not the Jerusalemites and Judaeans who pronounced judgment on themselves, but Yahweh (vv. 5-6).

In the application of the parable, like Nathan, it is prophet Isaiah who pronounced the judgment of Yahweh for His people. Another significant feature in the application is the unraveling of Isaiah as regards the correspondences of several items in the parable. Isaiah explicitly reveals that the vineyard represents the house of Israel or the men of Judah (v. 7ab), and of course the LORD of hosts is the owner of the vineyard. Yahweh's desire for good fruits represents His desire for justice and righteousness; bad fruits represent a bloodshed and a cry for distress (vv. 4b,7cd).

There is an implicit element in the application. The statement in v. 7, "Thus he looked for justice, but behold, bloodshed; for righteousness, but behold, a cry of distress" implies that God had already done His part of nurturing and caring for His people. This element is not stated in the application but understandably implied.

In relation to its subsequent context, the parable, according to John

---

[82]S. H. Widyapranawa asserts that this call of judgment by the owner "is merely rhetorical. The owner knows exactly what he will have to do with his own vineyard." S. H. Widyapranawa, *Isaiah 1-39*, ITC, 21-22.

[83]Otto Kaiser suggests that "v. 7 discloses the parabolic, metaphorical character of the song." Otto Kaiser, *Isaiah 1-12*, Old Testament Library (London: SCM, 1983), 92.

Oswalt, "sets the stage for the rest of the chapter, which includes a discussion of six conditions (wild grapes) that exist in the people and are contrary to God's expectation."[84]

The last narrative מָשָׁל is Ezek 17:1-10. The word מָשָׁל occurs twice in v. 2. The first one is a verb, and second is a noun. The structure shows a popular Hebrew parallelism where the first clause is parallel with the second clause: (1) Son of man, propound a riddle [first clause]; and (2) speak a parable to the house of Israel [second]. The word "chîdāh" of the first clause is parallel with the word מָשָׁל of the second clause. Moshe Greenberg notes, "While the two terms appear in parallelism (Ps 49:5; 78:2; Prov 1:6) they are not interchangeable as Judg 14:2ff., and 1 Kgs 10:1 show."[85]

The word חִידָה means "riddle, enigmatic, perplexing saying or questions."[86] As a riddle, this is an "obscure utterance of something put indirectly and needing interpretation—an allegory."[87] Moshe may be right in saying that the parallelism of מָשָׁל with חִידָה does not mean that a riddle is also a מָשָׁל, at least in this context, but rather it may "point to the two levels on which the fables move."[88] The sentence structure, semantic, content, and context, indicate that this מָשָׁל is an allegory. Leslie C. Allen also suggests that this is an allegory about two eagles, a cedar, and a grapevine. It is a fable type of allegory—a story in which animals and plants are invested with human characteristics and behavior.[89] Analyzing the application of this riddle מָשָׁל may further support the semantic aspect. Unlike

---

[84]John Oswalt, *The Book of Isaiah Chapters 1-39*, New International Commentary on the Old Testament (Grand Rapids: Eerdmans, 1986), 151.

[85]Moshe Greenberg, *Ezekiel 1-20*, AB, vol. 22, 309.

[86] Brown, BDB, s.v. "חִידָה."

[87]Ibid.

[88]Greenberg, 309. See ibid., 320 for the two-level structure where the fable moves.

[89]Leslie Allen, *Ezekiel 1-39*, WBC, vol. 28, 254. Cf. Bruce Vawter and Leslie J. Hoppe, *Ezekiel: A New Heart*, ITC, 97; Walther Zimmerli, *Ezekiel 1*, Hermeneia, trans. Ronald E. Clements (Philadelphia: Fortress, 1979. Peter Craigie calls this a "parable." Peter Craigie, *Ezekiel*, Daily Study Bible, ed. John C. L. Gidson (Philadelphia: Westminster, 1983), 123-24. If Craigie meant the same as that of the biblical meaning, then this fable is a parable.

the preceding parables already considered, there are detailed correspondences[90] between the riddle or allegory and the application:

1. The great eagle of v. 3 who took away the top of the cedar is the king of Babylon——Nebuchadnezzar (v. 12b).

2. The topmost of the cedar's young twigs that were brought to the land of merchants and traders (v. 3b-4) represent the king and princes who were brought to Babylon (v. 12b).

3. Some seeds of the land which were taken by the eagle and planted in fertile soil whose branches turned toward the first eagle (vv. 5,6) may represent one of the royal families and the mighty of the land (v. 13).

4. Another eagle in v. 7 may represent Egypt in v. 15 to whom the vine turned its roots.

5. The turning of the roots of the vine to the second eagle in v. 7 may represent the change of loyalty of the vassal king of Judah from the king of Babylon to the king of Egypt when he sent envoys to Egypt for the military support of the latter (v. 15).

6. The questions, "Will it thrive? Will he not pull up its roots and cut off its fruits, so that it withers——so that all its sprouting leaves wither?" in v. 9 correspond to the questions, "Will he succeed? Will he who does such things escape? Can he indeed break the covenant and escape?" in the revelation of the meaning in v. 15.

7. The clause, "And neither by great strength nor many people can it be raised from its roots again" may mean that he will die in Babylon (v. 16), he will not escape (v. 18).[91]

Looking at the immediate context of this allegory, interestingly, it is obvious that this is placed among a series of Yahweh's parabolic messages for His rebellious people of Judah——that started in Ezek 12 up to chap. 24. Chapter 12:1-16 is about

---

[90]Leslie Allen also sees correspondences between the fable and its interpretation. See Allen, 254-55.

[91]For a very detailed presentation of correspondences between the fable (vv. 1-10) and the interpretation (vv. 11-21), see Daniel I. Block, *The Book of Ezekiel 1-24*, New International Commentary on the Old Testament, 536-37.

a parable of the prophet's baggage going to exile. Chapter 12:17-28 is a parable of trembling. Chapter 13:1-23 is a message against false prophets and prophetesses. Chapter 14:1-23 is a message against the idolatrous elders. Chapter 15:1-8 is a parable of the fruitless vine. Chapter 16:1-63 is a parable of the adulterous woman. Chapter 18:1-32 is a proverb of the sour grapes repudiated. Chapter 19 is the lamentation given in a figurative language for the princes of Israel. Chapter 20:1-44 is the message concerning Israel's unfaithfulness. Chapter 20:45-59 is a parable of the forest fire. Chapter 21 is a parable of the sword. Chapter 22 is a parable of the smelting furnace of judgment. Chapter 23 is a parable of the two sisters. Chapter 24:1-14 is a parable of the boiling pot. Chapter 24:15-27 is a parable of the death of Ezekiel's wife.

It is apparent that the מָשָׁל is a "Fable Allegory." Like some of the previous parables being analyzed, this fable allegory was used by the prophet with a series of parabolic messages because of the spiritual and moral situations among God's people that need to be addressed. Hence, this מָשָׁל may be labeled as "parabolic allegory" as opposite of Isa 5:1-7 which is an "allegorical parable." It is obvious that this allegory has a meaning or application, but unlike the previous ones, this one has one-to-one correspondences between the fable allegory and its application.

In summary, OT מָשָׁל has a wide range of meanings; and as a genre, it has several subgenres. Its subgenres and also meanings are (1) proverbial saying, (2) by-word, (3) prophetic figurative discourse, (4) similitude and parable, (5) poem, and (6) sentences of ethical wisdom. Its essence is comparison.

The literary contexts of the occurrences of the word מָשָׁל was analyzed in order to find basis or pattern in identifying the genre of Luke 16:19-31. Several points were drawn out in the analysis of several OT מָשָׁל:

1. A proverbial saying has also a comparative usage.

2. A poem מָשָׁל is constructed in parallelism with the idea of comparison.

3. The idea of a by-word מָשָׁל is "object lesson." The object (people) of taunt gives lessons to the beholder.

4. The proverb מָשָׁל have ethical values. They are called "ethical wisdom." It serves as behavioral rules.

5. Narrative parables are classified into several subgenres: *(a)* Fable Parable, *(b)* Juridical Parable,*(c)* Allegorical Parable, and *(d)* Fable Allegory or Parabolic Allegory. There are five narratives being examined in this chapter. Several significant points came out in the analysis:

1. Some of these parables are fables——they are not real-life stories. They may be called "Fable Parables."

2. Not all items in the parables have correspondences in the application or interpretation of these parables.

3. At least one of these five narrative parables is an allegory——it has one-to-one correspondences explicitly indicated in the passage.[92]

4. Sometimes the application given by the prophet goes beyond what was stated in the parable.

5. OT narrative parables are just fictitious stories used only as vehicles to convey rebuke, divine   judgments, and to convict the one to whom the parable was intended.

6. Some of these narrative parables are called   "juridical parable" created to convey divine judgments.

7. The narrative parables were told because of the preceding events that need to be dealt with. This means that these narrative parables are illustrations or vehicles to convey messages to their intended audience.

NT Parable Genre

The NT word for parable is parabolē. It occurs fifty times in forty-eight verses.[93] The word parabolē is used "as a rhetorical figure of speech, setting one

---

[92]In parable, the prophet or the user does not give a one-to-one correspondence in the figurative portion and the application: for example, Jotham' s Fable Parable; Nathan's Juridical Parable. Whereas in parabolic allegory, the prophet gives a one-to-one correspondence between the figurative portion of the passage and the application portion of the passage.

[93]In Matthew, it occurs seventeen times, twelve are found in Matt 13 (vv. 3,10,18,24, 31,34[twice],35,36,53); 15:15; 21:33,45; 22:1; 24:32. In Mark, it occurs thirteen times (3:24; 4:2,10,11,13 [twice],30,33,34; 7:17; 12:1; 12:12; 13:28). In Luke, it occurs eighteen times (4:23; 5:36; 6:39; 8:4,9,10,11;

thing beside another to form a comparison or illustration."[94]   It means "type,"
"figure," and "parable."[95]   The meaning of parabolē in classical literature might
have been derived from Plato that probably was taken from the verb "paraballē"
which means "to place alongside, hold beside, throw to, compare," and may come
from "para" "alongside" and *ballô* "throw, bring, place."[96] Peisker notes,

> According to Aristotle, the similitude and the pure parable serve as an
> introductory means of proof (Rhet. 2,20). Through the comparison of the
> known with the unknown, in which the listener himself has to find the
> similarity (the *tertium comparationis* is not in general named, in order to
> set in motion the listener's thought processes of grasping, comparing and
> considering) the point of analogy is reached.[97]

In the NT, it has the following meaning:[98] (1) type or symbol (Heb 9:9;
11:19), (2) saying (Matt 15:15; Mark 7:17), (3) proverb (Luke 4:23), and (4)
parable. The "Parable" has various senses:

1. Figurative sayings (Matt 5:14), in this case the image and reality, are put
together without a comparative adverb.

2. Metaphor (Matt 7:13f.; 9:37f.; 15:13), in which the image is placed
instead of reality.

3. Simile (Matt 10:16; Luke 11:44), in which reality and image are placed
beside one another by means of a comparative adverb.

4. The pure parable (Matt 13:33; Luke 13:20; Matt 13:31f.; Luke 14:28-
33; 15:4-10), in which two things (image and reality) are compared so that the
known will elucidate the unknown.

12:16,41; 13:6; 14:7; 15:3; 18:1,9; 19:11; 20:9,19; 21:29). It occurs only twice outside the Synoptic Gospels
(Heb 9:9; 11:19).

[94]Walter Bauer, *A Greek-English Lexicon of the New Testament and Other Early Christian Literature*
(BAGD), trans. and adapted by William F. Arndt and F. Wilbur Gingrich, 3d ed., rev. and augmented by F.
Wilbur Gingrich and Frederick W. Danker (2000), s.v. "parabolē."

[95]Peisker, 2:743.

[96]Ibid., 2:743.

[97]Ibid., 2:743-44.

[98]The NT concept of parabolē may be drawn from its OT equivalent which is lv;m rather than the
Greek's concept of parabolē. This is probable since OT lv;m of the HB is translated into parabolē in the LXX
(Num 23:7; 24:15,20, 21,23; Deut 28:37; 1 Sam 10:12; 23:14; 1 Kgs 5:12; 2 Chr 7:20; Ps 43:15; 48:5; 68:12;
77:2; Prov 1:6; Ecc 1:17; 12:9; Ezek 12:22,23; 16:44; 17:2; 18:2,3; 19:14; 21:5; 24:3; Mic 2:4; Hab 2:6).

5. The parabolic story (Luke 18:2ff.; 11:5-8; 14:16-24) differs from a pure parable only in that its fictional story is recounted as if it had once happened.

6. An illustrative story (Luke 18:10-14; Luke 10:30-37; Luke 12:16-21), in which a story gives an example, a model case. This story is usually invented.

7. Allegory (Matt 22:2-10; John 10:15), in which the story is freely invented saying something other than it

appears to say on the surface by heaping metaphor on metaphor.[99]

In the Gospels, it is often used to convey truths that pertains to the kingdom of God in a comparative way as indicated by the Greek word "homoios" "as, like" introducing similarity (Matt 13:24,31,33,).[100] Crossan asserts that the term Parable "covers both the aphoristic and narrative metaphors of Jesus."[101]

It would be appropriate to briefly look into the literary contexts of some parables where the word parabolē occurs. It considers a few where the word did not occur and analyzes these parables. It also compares several of these uncontested parables with Luke 16:19-31 and decides whether Luke 16:19-31 is a fictitious or true story, a parabolic story, or an example story.

In Luke, parabolē occurred eighteen times (Luke 4:23; 5:36; 6:39; 8:4,9,10,11; 12:16,41; 13:6; 14:7; 15:3; 18:1,9; 19:11; 20:9,19; 21:29). In Luke 4:23, parabolē is translated unanimously as "proverb" (KJV, NIV, NLT, NASB). It carries one of the OT meanings of the word מָשָׁל. In its occurrence here, Jesus reacts on the unbelief of His town's people in Nazareth, prompting Him to say a parabolic proverb "Ἰατρέ, θεράπευσον σεαυτόν (physician heal yourself).[102] The passage indicates that this proverb was well-known in the time of Jesus. It was quoted by Jesus for His townsfolk.[103] Jesus states this proverb anticipating that this would be quoted by His own townfolks to Him. Here, Jesus is compared

---

[99]Peisker, 2:746-47. Cf. Friedrich Hauck, "parabolē." *TDNT*, 5:752-60.

[100]Bauer, BAGD, s.v. "ὅμοιος."

[101]Crossan, "Parable," 5:148.

[102]This is similar to an "ancient saying or proverb" in OT classification of lv;m; (2 Sam 24:13 [14]).

[103]No doubt that Jesus did use an existing piece of saying to stress His point. Robert Stein notes that this proverb has several extra-biblical parallels, namely in Greek and Hebrew literature. Robert Stein, *Luke: An Exegetical and Theological Exposition of Holy Scripture*, NAC, vol. 24, 187.

to a physician in this parabolic proverb, who should perform in Nazareth His miraculous deeds in Capernaum. In the context, the proverb was spoken in view of Jesus' confrontation with his own townsfolk.

In Luke 5:36, parabolē is translated as "parable" (KJV, NIV, NASB). Here it may function, using an everyday life scenario,[104] as an illustration in order to convey a spiritual truth.[105] Here, παραβολή mean "metaphorical or figurative saying."[106] The material things in the parable correspond to things in the spiritual realms in a form of analogy. Stein may be right when he argues that the emphasis of Luke, in the context, is in "newness" of the kingdom brought by Jesus, which is not compatible with an old Pharisaic Judaism.[107] This metaphor or figurative saying[108] is stated in the context of the Pharisees' question on Jesus' disciples' lack of fasting.

In Luke 8:4-15, a parable refers again to an everyday life scenario (the sower or farmer), which Jesus used to teach a spiritual truth about the mysteries of the kingdom of God (v. 10). However, Jesus explains the meaning of the parable (v. 11). The parable, in this context, reveals a spiritual truth about how men received the word of God. It is clear here that the literal things in the parable correspond to spiritual things taught by Jesus in its interpretation. There are several items in the parable that correspond with that of its interpretation:

1. The seed is the word of God (vv. 5,11).

2. The seeds beside the road are those who have heard the message of the kingdom but the devil takes it away from their hearts (vv. 5,12).

---

[104]Putting a new cloth on an old garment; or putting an old wine into a new wine skin.

[105]E. Earle Ellis suggests that the "two parables illustrate the dichotomy between Christianity and traditional Judaism." Ellis, 107. However, the context of the passage does not explicitly or implicitly say so. The context tells about the conflict about fasting. The Pharisees and scribes question the lack of fasting and prayer of the disciples of Jesus compared with the disciples of John.

[106]Stein, *Luke*, 185.

[107]Ibid., 186.

[108]This kind of parabolē is similar to the classification, "Proverbial saying" of the OT מָשָׁל. There is an idea of comparison between two things in the figurative saying in the lv;m; or parabolē and its spiritual counterpart.

3. The seeds on the rocky soil are those who heard the word and received it with joy. They believed for a while but fell away when temptations came because they did not have firm roots (vv. 6,13).

4. The seed on thorns are the ones who have heard the word and believed but have been choked with worries, riches and pleasures of life (vv. 7,14).

5. The seeds in good soil are the ones, which have heard the word in honest and good heart, have held fast on it, and have borne fruits (vv. 8,15).

This parabolē could not be taken as an allegory if the OT classification is considered. There are items in the parable which do not have spiritual correspondences: the farmer or sower and the fruits. This parabolē may be classified, based on the OT, as "Allegorical Parable" like Isa 5:1-7. Interestingly, Isa 5:1-7 and Luke 8:4-15 have agricultural setting.

As far as the classification given above by an NT scholar, this is a "pure parable." There is a comparison between the image and the reality, between the known and the unknown. This parable is also in the context of Jesus' proclamation of the good news of the kingdom of God (v. 1). Although the seed has been given a spiritual meaning here, the focus of this parable is the different kinds of soil.[109] This parable may usually happen in real life but Jesus may not be pointing to a specific farmer.

The parable of the good Samaritan (Luke 10:25-37) seems to be classified as an "example story" or "illustrative story" NT parabolē. This parable serves as a model to the expert of the Law (v. 1) to show him who his neighbor is (v. 27). There are evidences showing that this is an example story:

1. The parable is intended primarily to an expert of the Law. The parable has several characters which do not have correspondences in the audience. If the expert of the Law is the Samaritan, who then represents the Priest, the Levite, and the innkeeper?

2. Jesus' statement, "go and do likewise" (v. 37) indicates that this is

---

[109]Liefeld, 906.

apparently an example story. There is also one spiritual truth being stressed in this parable. The parable does not have a one-to-one correspondence with the real situation in Jesus' audience. The parable is prompted by a problem or question being posed by Jesus' audience. Hence, it has a literary setting like other OT and NT narrative parables.

The word parabolē occurs also in Luke 12:16. Here, Jesus tells a parable of a rich fool (vv. 16-21).[110]

This parabolē is, most likely, a story parable or parabolic story because of several reasons:

1. In the literary context (vv. 15,21), the spiritual truth is clearly stated by Jesus before and after the parable intended for His audience.

2. The rich fool in the parable represents primarily someone who asked Jesus to mediate between him and his brother concerning their inheritance (v. 13) and to everyone in Jesus' audience who was greedy and stored riches only for himself (vv. 15,21).

In summary, NT parabolē have similarities with OT מָשָׁל. They have a wide range of meanings and subgenres. One subgenre is what we technically term as "parable." This subgenre has also different types: (1) figurative saying, (2) metaphor, (3) simile, (4) a pure parable, (5) a parabolic story or story parable, (6) illustrative or an example story, and (7) allegory.

Luke's parables discussed above have similar characteristics with some OT narrative מָשָׁל. For example, Nathan's juridical parable is similar to the parable of the rich fool. Both parables are intended to give a rebuke to the audience. Isa 5:1-7 is similar to the parable of the sower (Luke 8:4-15). Both have several one-to-one correspondences pointed out by both Isaiah and Jesus. However, not everything in both parables has correspondences.

Furthermore, some similar characteristics between OT narrative מָשָׁל and Luke's parables are the following:

1. The basic idea of comparison is present in both.

2. Both are told to convey a specific message to their audience.

---

[110]In OT classification, this parabolē is similar to Nathan's "juridical parable."

3. Both are given because of a certain problem or situation preceding them.

4. Some parables in both have allegorical elements.

5. Some items in both have correspondences in real life, application, and interpretation.

6. Both have an ethical or a behavioral focus.

There are also differences between OT מָשָׁל and NT parabolē. Some OT מָשָׁל differ from NT parabolē in literary structure. Many OT מָשָׁל are poems and proverbs using Hebrew literary structural parallelism while NT parabolē are prose. OT מָשָׁל which have ethical instructions are the proverbs while almost all NT parabolē have ethical or moral instructions. Some OT narrative parables subgenres are used to convey divine judgments against the apostasies of its intended audiences,[111] whereas NT parables convey spiritual truths and principles pertaining to the kingdom of God that Jesus proclaimed and taught to His audience.

Luke 16:19-31: A Story Parable/Parabolic Story or an Example Story; Fictitious or True

At this juncture, the conclusions being drawn above are the basis in analyzing Luke 16:19-31. If Luke 16:19-31 belongs to parabolē genre, what is its subgenre? Is this a fictitious or a true story? One way to answer these questions is to compare the parable of the rich man and Lazarus with the parable of the rich fool (NT), and with the parable of Nathan (OT).[112]

The Rich Man and Lazarus and the Rich Fool

There are few issues to settle in comparing these two narratives:

1. Does the absence of the word parabolē in 16:19-31 negate the view that this is a parable?

2. Does Luke 16:19-31 have correspondence in spiritual realms, especially

---

[111]The parable of the rich fool (Luke 12:16-21) has a theme of judgment. God pronounced judgment against the rich fool. The judgment is in the story, but not in the application. The intended audience was not judged like the rich fool in the story.

[112]If Nathan's parable and the parable of the rich fool are fictitious, then it is also possible that the parable of the rich man and Lazarus is a fictitious story.

for Jesus' audience described in Luke 12:16-21?

  3. Do they have similar features?

  4. Do they have specific messages to convey to their intended audience?

  5. Are these parables true story or fictitious? The answer to the first question is negative. The absence of the word parabolē does not mean that this is not a parable. There are actually many parables of Jesus in which the word parabolē is

his Guests." But unlike in the parabolē of old/new cloth and old wine/new wineskins, Jesus did not say it is a parabolē. However, it is obvious that it is a parable since the imagery in the saying conveys spiritual correspondence.

  The word parable, does not occur in some parables. These parables are the following: (1) the parable of the house builders (Luke 6:46-49); (2) the parable of children in a marketplace (Luke 6:31-35); (3) the parable of two debtors (Luke 7:40-50); (4) the parable of the good Samaritans (Luke 10:30-37; (5) the parables of watchful servants, a wise and faithful manager, and an unfaithful servant (Luke 12:35-48); and (6) the parable of a shrewd manager (Luke 16:1-8). Furthermore, the expression "There was certain rich man" (:Aνθρωπος δέ τις ἦν πλούσιος) in Luke 16:19 is a similar expression used in Luke 12:16 (᾽Ανθρώπου τινὸς πλουσίου) "a certain rich man." This is the evidence that Luke 16:19-31 is a parable.

  The answer to the second question is positive, which means that the parable of the rich man and Lazarus have spiritual correspondence especially for Jesus' audience. To support this idea, Luke 16:19-31 may be compared with Luke 12:16-21. In 12:16-21, Jesus speaks the parable to the crowd after being asked by a man that he acts as an arbitrator between him and his brother to divide the family inheritance equally (12:13-15). The spiritual correspondence is clear in this parable.

  In Luke 16: 19-31, the primary spiritual correspondences of the parable of the rich man and Lazarus are the Pharisees whom Jesus labeled as φιλάργυροι (philargyroi) "lovers of money" or "covetous" (16:14). It is clear in the context that Jesus directs this parable to them. In Luke 16:1-8, Jesus directs the parable of the shrewd manager to His disciples exhorting them to be as wise as the children of this world by taking advantage of the unrighteous wealth to make sure of heaven (v. 9).

The Pharisees reacted to the teachings of Jesus about the proper handling of wealth (vv. 10-13) because they were greedy (v. 14); in a way, it is a form of idolatry in relation to v. 13. Jesus then confronted the Pharisees. In v. 15, He tells them that even though they are highly esteemed among men, they are βδέλυγμα (bdelygma) which means "detestable" or "abominable" in the sight of God. Green asserts that this term is the key in Jesus' criticism of the Pharisees. He notes that this word may mean (1) idolatrous activity (Isa 1:13; 66:3), (2) immoral financial dealings (Deut 25:16), and (3) the act of remarrying a woman who has been divorced (Deut 24:4).[113] In Jesus' indictment, these three abominations are present in the Pharisees (vv. 14-18).[114] Then Jesus directs the parable of the rich man and Lazarus (19:16-31) to the Pharisees who scorned His teaching on how to deal with wealth.

For the third question, the characteristics of both narratives indicate that they are similar. These are shown in table 1.

TABLE 1

SIMILAR CHARACTERISTICS BETWEEN THE RICH FOOL
AND THE RICH MAN AND LAZARUS

Similar Characteristics	References
1. Both passages are narratives told by Jesus	Luke 12:16; 16:19
2. Both have similar introductions	12:16; 16:19
3. Both passages speak about two rich men who care only for themselves—they both enjoy their wealth	12:18-19; 16:19 4.

---

[113]Green, 604.

[114]The literary context will be further discussed in chapter 5 of this study.

Table 1-*Continued*

4. Both were not good stewards	12:19; 16:19-21
5. Both stories have spiritual truths being taught by Jesus to His audience	12:15,21; 16:29,31
6. Both rich men's brothers were involved. In the rich fool, someone asks Jesus to tell his brothers; in the rich man and Lazarus, the rich man asks Abraham to tell his brothers.	12:13; 16:27
7. Both were intended for specific individuals in their literary contexts	12:13-14; 16:14-15
8. Both rich men have tragic endings	12:20-21; 16:23-24

As for the fourth question, the answer is still positive. In the parable of the rich fool, Jesus stresses a spiritual truth. Jesus tells this parable to liken the rich fool to anyone in His audience who is greedy (v. 21). In Luke 16:19-31, the message would be for the Pharisees who, in neglecting the poor by being lovers of money, disregarded the Law and the prophets who clearly set out the rules on how to deal with the poor and wealth.[115] The comparison of 12:16-21 and 16:19-31 show overwhelming similarity. Hence, this evidence shows that Luke 16:19-31 is a narrative parable.[116] Based on the criteria set up above, it is a "story parable" or "parabolic story."

Lastly, are these two parables fictitious or true stories? In deciding on this question, the suggestion of Kofoed may be very helpful. He accepts Paul Ricoeur's proposal on how to judge the fictionality and factuality of certain literature. He notes that Ricoeur "pointed out three distinct phases in the process of history-writing: the documentary phase, the explanatory or comprehensive

---

[115]Green, 610.

[116]Many biblical scholars suggest that Luke 16:19-31 is a parable but do not give evidences of doing so. Probably they think it is not an issue anymore. For example, see Craig A. Evans, *Luke*, New International Biblical Commentary (NIBC), vol. 3 (Peabody, MA: Hendrickson, 1990), 248; Bock, *Luke*, 432; Green, 604-05; Morris, 252.

phase, and the literary phase."[117] Basing on one's judgment on this theory, one
could decide on the fictionality or factuality of this narrative on literary level—
that is the literary form of the narrative. It may be decided in the explanatory
level because the documentary level is not possible today. Luke accepts the
historicity of Jesus on the explanatory level (1:1) and on the documentary level
(1:2). However, although Jesus is a factual person and someone who once lived
on earth, in His teachings He may have used folktale stories which some may be
fictitious.

How do we go from here as far as His parables are concerned? In my idea,
it is better to classify these parables through analyzing Jesus' intent in telling
stories, as far as the account of Luke is concerned. In Luke's perspective, Jesus'
primary intent in telling the parable is to drive spiritual truth of the kingdom of
God. Jesus did not intend to tell a historical event. This is evident in the literary
level:

1. Jesus did not even mention the name of the foolish rich man.

2. He did not mention the place where he lives, his family, and relatives.

3. Jesus did not also dare to mention any datum in relation to time. On the
contrary, in Luke' literary style in writing the story of Jesus as a historical event,
he usually indicates the dates, the historical prominent persons, historical places,
and historical events (1:5; 2:1,2,3; 3:1,2). Judging from this evidence, it may be
proposed that Jesus' story parables may not be historical events that happened
to certain historical persons, that is, when we based on the way Luke wrote a
historical event, although these stories may happen in real life.

Furthermore, the images in the parable of the Rich Man and Lazarus (Luke

---

[117]Kofoed, *Text and History*, 201-02. He explains, "The initial stage is dubbed 'documentary'
because it is from written documents or 'testimonies' that the historiographer takes his departure. Ricoeur
defines 'testimonies' as 'a declaration of a witness who says three things': (1) I was there, (2) believe me or
not, and (3) if you don't believe my word ask somebody else' and stresses that 'the whole structure of the
linguistic community to which I belong relies on whether the truth-claim of a given testimony is trusted or
not.' It is such a trusted testimonies that, according to Ricoeur, constitute the basic scientific component
of truth-claims raised by historical knowledge. The next step is explanatory/comprehensive phase, in
which causes and reasons are asked- or, to use the terminology of the *Annales* School, the phase in which
explanations are sought for the relationship between structures, conjectures, and events. In the final literary
phase, the trusted, 'raw' material of the first phase is given order, based on the explanation of the second
phase, in a literary representation, the narrative or historical discourse." Ibid., 202.

16:19-31) may show that it is not factual. Verses 19-21 may be real and factual, but the question arises in vv. 22-31. The imagery in vv. 22-31 goes beyond what is earthly that could be historically verifiable. Therefore, the basis of historicity and factuality is the rest of the unambiguous parts of the Scripture. Here are the possible unreal and not factual images in the parable:

1. The dead Lazarus was carried by an angel to the bosom of Abraham—this is not supported by the rest of the Scripture (v. 22). The Scripture says that all the dead, righteous and wicked alike, will go to the grave (Ecc 9:10; John 5:28-29; 1 Thess 4:16).

2. The rich man is consciously tormented in ᾅδης. This is the crux of this passage. Chapter 3 of this study further deals with this issue. Some scholars say this is factual. Other passages of the Scripture speak about the dying persons' expectation of descending to ᾅδης, but it does not say that they are conscious or at least their so called "disembodied souls" are conscious in there.

3. The dead are conscious in ᾅδης, they are having a conversation; the rich man conversed with Abraham (vv. 24-31).

4. If what some scholars are suggesting is true that the bosom of Abraham is paradise or heaven, then ᾅδης as the place of the wicked and heaven as the place of the righteous are just in close proximity. This is not supported by the rest of the literal description of the Scripture about heaven (1 Cor 12:1-4; John 14:1-3; Rev 21).

However, chapter 3 of this study further sheds light to this problem.

5. After their death, the wicked are immediately punished, and the righteous are immediately rewarded. The rest of the Scripture does not agree to the eschatology of this parable (John 5:28-29; John 14:1-3; 1 Thess 4: 16-17; 2 Pet 3:7,10). Based on these evidences, the parable of the rich man and Lazarus may not be based on a historical event, but rather a fiction story (see chapter 3) used by Jesus to teach spiritual truths which pertain to the kingdom of God.

The Rich Man and Lazarus and
Nathan's Parable

In all OT narrative parables, only Nathan's parable is similar to Jesus'
parable of the rich man and Lazarus. There are similarities between these two
parables:

1. Both are fictitious.

2. Interestingly, both parables speak about two contrasting characters——a
rich man and a poor man (2 Sam 12:1; Luke 16:19-20).

3. In both narratives, their contrasting socio-economic situations were
described (2 Sam 12:2-3; Luke 16:19-21).

4. Both rich men in both stories did something wrong to their poor
neighbors. In Nathan's story the rich man actively offended the poor by taking
his ewe lamb (2 Sam 12:4). In Jesus' parable, the rich man passively neglected
Lazarus (Luke 16:19-21).

5. Both stories were told in order to correct or rebuke someone or some
people in the audience. In Nathan's parable, the object is David (2 Sam 12:7-
12), whereas in Jesus' parable the objects are the Pharisees.[118]

6. Both stories have a special purpose or message. In Nathan's parable,
the purpose of Nathan is to rebuke and correct king David's immoral acts (2
Sam 12:7-10); whereas in Jesus' parable, He wants to rebuke the Pharisees who
were lovers of money (16:14).

7. Both parables do not have one-to-one correspondence. In Nathan's
parable, only the rich man was clearly identified representing David (2
Sam 12:7). In Jesus' parable, He did not say who represents the Pharisees.
However, the context indicates that the five brothers of the rich man represent
the Pharisees (vv. 27-31). There are also several differences between the two
parables:

1. The parable of Nathan is in the setting of God's pronouncement of
judgment and reconciliation against David. Jesus' parable is in the setting of
His teaching and proclamation of the principles of the kingdom of God.

---

[118]It is apparent in the literary context——Luke 16:15).

2. Nathan's parable is intended to rebuke an erring member of the Old Covenant community. Jesus' parable is intended to rebuke arrogant outsiders who prevented people from entering the kingdom of God.

Summary

In summary, the narrative of the rich man and Lazarus in Luke 16:19-31, like the parable of the rich fool in Luke 12:16-21 and Nathan's parable in 2 Sam 12:1-7, is a parable. The subgenre is a story parable or parabolic story. There are several reasons for this conclusion:

1. One of them (the rich fool) has an explicit label— parabolē. If it is true to one, it may be true to the other two.

2. They have similar characteristics.

3. They have identical introductions, usually a common introduction of parables.

4. They are prompted with moral issues among their audience.

5. They are specifically intended to an individual or group of individuals.

6. There is at least one character in the story who corresponds to one of the audience.

7. They are used to convey a special message(s) or purpose.

On the issue on factuality or fictionality, it is also suggested that Luke 16:16-31 is a fictitious story like the rich fool and Nathan's parable. The parable's imagery itself betrays some of the scholars' claim to its factuality.

THE HISTORICAL-RELIGIOUS BACKGROUND OF ʿAᵢDHS

I N THIS chapter, the backgrounds of ᾅδης will be tackled in order to shed light on the problem of the interpretation on the rich man and Lazarus in Luke 16:19-31. The historical-religious background of ᾅδης will be examined in Ancient Near Eastern literature, Homer, Plato, Septuagint (LXX), OT Pseudepigrapha, Qumran writings, NT biblical literature, Lucian of Samosata, other Greco-Roman writers, Talmud, and NT Apocrypha.

The Concept of ʿΑδης in the Ancient Near Eastern Literature

In the Sumerian myths and epic tales, the equivalent of ᾅδης is the netherworld. It is poetically described in a mythical story of the death of Gilgamesh.[119] According to the story, Enlil, the father of the Sumerian gods, had not granted eternal life to Gilgamesh. However, he granted Gilgamesh the kingship of the netherworld. When Gilgamesh died, he descended to the netherworld and became king there.[120] It is clear that the Sumerians believed in men and women still existing in the netherworld after their death.

In another Sumerian myth, Inanna, queen of heaven, descended to the netherworld[121] to meet her sister, Ereshkigal, the queen of the netherworld.

---

[119]The date of the text of the "Death of Gilgamesh" is reconstructed from the three tablets excavated from Nippur dating from the first half of the second millennium B.C.

S. N. Kramer, "Sumerian Myths and Epic Tales," in *Ancient Near Eastern Texts Related to the Old Testament (ANET)*, 3d ed., ed. James Benneth Pritchard (Princeton, NJ: Princeton University Press, 1969), 50.

[120]Ibid., 50-51.

[121]This myth was inscribed in the first half of the second millennium B.C. However, the date of its first composition is unknown. Ibid., 52-53.

Unfortunately, Ereshkigal put her to death. Her messenger returned to heaven and sought the help of Enlil and Nanna to rescue Inanna. When they refused to help, the messenger appealed to god Enki, a god of wisdom. The messenger of Inanna finally got help from him. Eventually, Inanna was brought back to life. When she was leaving the netherworld, she was accompanied by the dead who dwelled in the netherworld. Again, in this myth, it is obvious that the Sumerians believed that the dead inhabit the netherworld. There is also a god who is in charge of the netherworld.[122]

In Egyptian myths, tales, and mortuary texts it is also apparent that the Egyptians believed in a "life after death." They believed that death is a continuation of this present life. In a mortuary text,[123] the dead are described as happy and peaceful in the land of the dead which is called the "West" or necropolis. For them, dead men do not cease to exist after their death.

In Akkadian myths and epics, like the Sumerians, there is also a version of a goddess who descended to the netherworld. In this Akkadian version,[124] Isthar,[125] the goddess of fertility, was also detained in the netherworld or land of the dead but eventually returned to the land of the living.[126] In this Akkadian myth, the netherworld was called the "land of no return."[127] In this myth, the netherworld is dark. It has gates like the OT שְׁאוֹל, but, unlike OT שְׁאוֹל, it has gatekeepers. Another Egyptian story which speaks about the concept of ᾅδης is the story of Setme and his son Si-Osiris. Although, according to Bauckham, it was written in the second half of the first century C.E., it was most likely based on an older tale because Setme Khamuas was the high priest of Memphis ca. 1250 B.C.E.[128] In

---

[122]Ibid., 52-57.

[123]John A. Wilson, "Egyptians Myths, Tales, and Mortuary Texts," in *ANET*, 32-34. These mortuary texts were carved inside the pyramids of Unis (twenty-fifth and twenty-fourth centuries B.C.). Ibid., 32.

[124]This version dates from the end of the second millennium. E. A. Speiser, "Akkadian Myths and Epics," in *ANET*, 107.

[125]She is Inanna in the Sumerian myth.

[126]Speiser, 106-09.

[127]Ibid.

[128]Richard Bauckham, *The Fate of the Dead: Studies on the Jewish and Christian Apocalypses* (Leiden:

this story, a soul from Amente, the Egyptian equivalent of ᾅδης, was reincarnated into a child, Si-Osiris. He had to deal with an Ethiopian magician who was powerful than the Egyptian magicians. One time, Si-Osiris observed the funerals of a rich man and a poor man. The rich man was buried in a very extravagant fashion, whereas the poor man's burial was so pitiful. The father of Si-Osiris, Setme, desired the fate of the rich man but his son told him that, in Amente, he would rather desire the fate of the pauper. Si-Osiris brought his father to Amente. There, Setme witnessed the suffering of the dead being punished in the fourth and fifth halls. The rich man's eye was fixed in the door's pivot, while the pauper was elevated to sit near Osiris,[129] the god of Amente and judge of the dead.[130] There are three classes of the dead in Amente: (1) those whose good works outnumbered their evil works, (2) those whose evil works outnumbered their good works, and (3) those whose good equaled their evil works.[131]

῾Ἄδης in the Writings of Homer

In "The Odyssey,"[132] written by Homer, an often-repeated phrase "had been stricken by fate and had gone to the house of Hades"[133] is often referred to those who died and went down to the underworld, the realm of the god Ἀιδης (Aidēs).[134] It is apparent that in the context of this passage when the word Ἀιδης occurs, it does not refer directly to the underworld but rather to a god who rules the underworld. In this context, the underworld damei.j (dameis) is just attached to the name of the god Ἀιδης. This is evident in a similar expression, "go down

---

Brill, 1998), 97.

[129]Lazarus in Abraham's bosom in Luke 16:19-31 seems parallel to this imagery.

[130]This concept is absent in Luke 16:19-31.

[131]Bauckham, *Fate of the Dead*, 98.

[132]There is no exact date for this writing. But as early as 660 B.C., Homer's poems were already mentioned by Callinus of Ephesus. See Homer *The Odyssey* "Introduction" (trans. Murray, LCL, 1:vii).

[133]The earliest Greek form of the NT word ᾅδης was "'αιδόσδε" (aidosde). It was first found in Homer's writing. See Homer *The Odyssey* 3.410 (LCL, 1:99).

[134]Ibid. See also ibid., 6.10-15 (LCL, 1:207); ibid., 4.830-35 (LCL, 1:167). The forms that occur in these passages are Ἀιδόσδε (aidosde) and Ἀίδαο (Aidao) respectively.

to the house of Hades."[135] In Homer's myth, 'Αιδης is believed to be the god of the underworld.[136] Another significant goddess present in the underworld is Περσεφονείης (Persephone).[137] She is always associated with 'Αιδης. She has power over the dead in 'Αιδης, granting reason to the dead.[138] The rest of the dead are just flitting as shadows.[139]

Homer also tells of a godlike Θειοιο (Theioio) Odysseus who by the help of a goddess undertook a journey to 'Αιδης. In this context, 'Αιδης directly refers to the underworld.[140] It is now apparent that Homer uses the word 'Αιδης to refer to the god of the underworld as well as the underworld itself. 'Αιδης is described as having a wide gate.[141] In the house of 'Αιδης, the dead are described as ψυχαὶ (psychai).[142] Odysseus, after a ritual, was able to talk with the ψυχαὶ of the dead,[143] especially with the soul of an old seer, to seek soothsaying from him.[144] He also saw a god, Minos, judging the dead.[145]   It should be pointed out that there is a conceptual imagery in Homer that is parallel with the imagery in the story of the rich man and Lazarus. Homer reports that in the house of 'Αιδης, Odysseus saw the soul of Tantalus in violent torment. Tantalus was standing in a pool of water, yet, while thirsty, he was not able to drink.[146] In Luke 16:19-31, the rich man

---

[135]Ibid., 10.175 (LCL, 1:357); ibid., 12.380-84 (LCL, 1:459).

[136]Ibid., 11.45-50 (LCL, 1:347-49). The form that occurs here is 'Αιδη (Aidē). This is probably the dative form of the nominative form 'Αιδης. The form has a hard breathing mark. In Homer, it often refers to a god of the underworld. The underworld in this context is called the "house" of this god.

[137]Ibid.

[138]Ibid., 10.495 (LCL, 1:381).

[139]Ibid.

[140]Ibid., 10.500-20 (LCL, 1:381-83).

[141]Ibid., 11.570 (LCL, 1:427). One passage indicates that 'Αιδης has several gates. In this context, 'Αιδης refers to a place. Ibid., 14.155 (LCL, 2:45).

[142]It is translated as "ghost." Ibid., 10.525-30 (LCL, 1:383). However, the word could also mean "souls."

[143]Ibid., 11.50-90 (LCL, 1:389-93).

[144]Ibid., 11.160-65 (LCL, 1:397-99).

[145]Ibid., 11.565-70 (LCL, 1:427).

[146]Ibid.

was also in torment. He was asking Abraham to send Lazarus to cool his tongue with Lazarus' finger dipped in water. However, Abraham refused because of the chasm that divided the rich man and Lazarus (v. 26). It should be noted, however, that while in Homer the dead are already judged in ᾄδης, this concept is absent in Luke 16:19-31.

Ἄδης in the Writings of Plato

The dichotomy between soul and body of man is very much emphasized in the writings of Plato. The body is just considered as a tomb or a jar.[147] Consequently, it is told that the souls of the wicked are conscious in 'Αιδης. And after a man dies, his soul goes to ῞Αιδης (Haidēs).[148] In that place, a stone is balanced above his head.[149]

According to Plato, ῞Αιδης is the name of the Invisible, that is, ἀειδής (aeidēs). He is also called Pluto, the god of the underworld. The Greeks were afraid of him because, according to their belief, the souls of men would enter into his realm without the covering of the body.[150] These souls would be restrained in ῞Αιδης by a strong desire of virtue,[151] enabling them to desist from all the evils and desires of the body.[152]

Plato also describes 'Αιδαο (Aidao)[153] as having gates within which the souls of men are hidden. It is sometimes used in a figure of speech especially with someone "who hides one thing in his heart and says another."[154]

---

[147]Plato *Georgias* (trans. Lamb, LCL, 3:419). The form that occurs here is ῞Αιδου (Haidou). In this context, it refers to the place.

[148]The form that occurs is also ῞Αιδου (Haidou). Unlike in Homer, the form has a smooth breathing mark and an accent. In this context, it is the name of the underworld, which is probably the short cut of the phrase "house of Hades."

[149]Plato *Cratylus* (trans. Fowler, LCL, 4:47).

[150]Ibid., (LCL, 4:71).

[151]Ibid., (LCL, 4:78).

[152]Ibid.

[153]This is the form that occurs in this passage.

[154]Plato *Lesser Hippias* (LCL, 4:435). Cf. ibid., (LCL, 4:451).

Plato, in his book of Laws, says, "Vengeance . . . is exacted in Hades,"[155] especially for those who murder their fellow Greeks who divulged their secrets.[156] In addition to this, when the murderers return to earth from Ἅιδης, they would still pay the penalty for their crimes.[157] Furthermore, those who lay hands on their fathers or mothers or their progenitors would receive punishments in Ἅιδης more severe than death.[158] So, for Plato, Ἅιδης is a place of judgment and punishment.

Another idea is that the souls of most wicked people would "move toward the deep and the so-called lower regions—under the name Ἅιδης and the like. Men are haunted by most fearful imaginings, both when alive and when disparted from their bodies."[159] However, when souls get a share with the divine virtue, they would move to an eminent region, being transported by a holy road to another and a better region.[160]

Ἅιδης in the LXX

The word ᾅδης occurs seventy-two times in the OT (LXX version), sixty-two instances of which translate the Hebrew word שְׁאוֹל.[161] ᾅδης also translates בּוֹר (bôr) in four instances,[162] דּוּמָה (dûmāh),[163] in two instances, and once רְפָאִים (rᵉphā ʾîm), —מָוֶת (māweth),[164] מוּת (moth), and צַלְמָוֶת (tsālᵉmāweth). In the

---

[155]Plato *The Laws* 2.9.870 (trans. Bury, LCL, 11:256-7).

[156]Ibid.

[157]Ibid.

[158]Ibid., 2.9.881 (LCL, 11:291).

[159]Ibid., 2.10.904 (LCL, 11:367).

[160]This is most likely the equivalent of the bosom of Abraham in the story of the rich man and Lazarus or the paradise in Jewish belief.

[161]Bauckham also notes, "In the LXX . . . Sheol is usually translated as Hades, and the Greek term was naturally and commonly used by Jews writing in Greek." Richard Bauckham, "Hades," *ABD*, 3:14. Cf. L. Wächter, "שְׁאוֹל," *Theological Dictionary of the Old Testament*, ed.   G. Johannes Botterweck, et al., trans. Douglas W. Stott (Grand Rapids: Eerdmans, 2004), 14:241-42.

[162]It means "pit." Ibid., s.v. "בּוֹר."

[163]דּוּמָה means "silence." Brown, BDB, s.v. "דּוּמָה."

[164]It means "death." Ibid., s.v. "מָוֶת."

occurrences of ᾅδης as a translation of שְׁאוֹל in majority of OT passages,[165] it may mean "place beneath the earth"[166] or simply "the grave" or "death."

שְׁאוֹל means "underworld," "place of inquiry (reference to necromancy)," and "hollow place."[167] It is the place where men descend at death (Gen 37:35; 42:38; 44:29-31). In some instances, it means "pit," and it is sometimes personified (Isa 28:15; 5:14; Hab 2:5). Sometimes it is used in figurative language as extreme degradation in sin (Isa 57:9; Hos 13:14; Isa 26:19).[168] Furthermore, the feminine noun שְׁאֵלָה (šᵉ'lāh) means "thing asked" (Judg 8:24; 1 Sam 1:27).[169] The masculine noun שָׁאוּל (ša'ûl) is a proper name which means "asked."[170] The verb שָׁאַל (ša'al) means "to ask" or "to demand," and "to inquire."[171]

Benjamin Davidson points out that the verb שָׁאַל (ša'al) means "to ask," "to inquire," "to demand" or "to require," "to request" or "to petition," and "to ask as a loan" or "to borrow."[172] He also notes that the Chaldee word שְׁאֵל (ši'ēl) means "to ask or interrogate," and "to demand" (Ezra 5:9,10).[173] B. Davidson also notes that the masculine noun שְׁאוּל means "grave," and "the abode of the departed souls," while the root שָׁאַל (ša'al) means "to be hollow."[174]

G. Gerleman points out that the common Semitic root שׁאל (š'l) appears primarily in Hebrew as a verb which means "to ask," "to request," "to ask permission" (1 Sam 1:17; Isa 7:11). The semantic range of meanings includes "to

---

[165]E.g., 1 Sam 2:6; 1 Kgs 2:6; Job 21:13; Ps 17:5; 30:18; 48:14,15; 54:16; 85:13; 88:49; Prov 7:27; 9:18; 15:24 Isa 38:10; 57:9 (LXX).

[166]KJV and NIV translate it "grave," while the NASB just uses the transliteration "sheol."

[167]Brown, BDB, s.v. "שְׁאוֹל"

[168]Ibid.

[169]Ibid., s.v. "שְׁאֵלָה"

[170]Ibid., s.v. "שָׁאוּל."

[171]Ibid., s.v. "שָׁאַל"

[172]B. Davidson, s.v. "שָׁאַל"

[173]Ibid., s.v. "שְׁאֵל" Cf. Ludwig Koehler and Walter Baumgartner, *The Hebrew and Aramaic Lexicon of the Old Testament*, trans. and ed. M. E. J. Richardson (2000), s.v. "שָׁאַל"

[174]B. Davidson, s.v. "שָׁאַל"

beg," "to borrow," and "to ask for a loan" (Exod 22:13; 2 Kgs 4:3; 6:5).[175] Gerleman also observes that in the theological context it means "the question of one seeking an oracle (Hag 2:11; 1 Sam 10:22; 14:37; Hos 4:12)."[176] Furthermore, Gerleman suggests that the feminine substantive—שְׁאוֹל (šᵉʾûl), meaning "realm of the dead," is peculiar to Hebrew. It appears as a loan word to Syriac and Ethiopic.[177] He notes, like many other scholars, that שְׁאוֹל is derived from the basic root שאל which means "to ask," "to require," "place of inquiry," "the cravings," or from the second root שאל which means "to hollow out."[178]

In view of the discussion above, it seems that scholars unanimously agree that שְׁאוֹל may be derived from the Semitic root שאל which has a wide range of meanings. It means "to ask," "to request," "to demand," "to inquire," "to require," "to be hollow," "to ask for a loan," and "to borrow." They also agree that the noun שְׁאוֹל means "the underworld," "the place or the abode of the dead," and "a hollow place." However, one scholar says that it is the place of the departed souls, an idea that it is not shared by other scholars.

It is significant to note that the meaning of the verb is not explicitly reflected in the meaning of the noun. However, we may say that שְׁאוֹל implicitly carries the meaning of the verb in the sense that it is described as craving, or devouring the lives of men (Prov 15:11). In the Scripture, it is also portrayed as just a temporary resting place of the dead because Yahweh will not abandon the righteous in it (Ps 16:10; 49:16; 73:23). In this sense, the meaning "to borrow" is being reflected.

In analyzing the contexts, שְׁאוֹל is the place where Jacob would go down because of his sorrow for the death of his son Joseph (Gen 37:35), and for the possible loss of his son Benjamin (42:38; 44:29,31). However, in commenting on Gen 37:35, Gordon Wenham says, "Sheol is the place of the dead in the OT,

[175]G. Gerleman, "שאל," *Theological Lexicon of the Old Testament*, ed. Ernst Jenni and Claus Westermann, trans. Mark Biddle (Peabody, MA: Hendrickson, 1997), 3:1282.

[176]Ibid., 3:1283.

[177]Ibid.

[178]Brown, BDB, s.v. "שְׁאוֹל"

where the spirits of the departed continue in a shadowy and rather unhappy

existence."[179] He cites Isa 14:14-20 as evidence. He probably refers to vv. 15-

16 where Lucifer was cast down to שְׁאוֹל (v. 15). Then v. 16 tells about those

who see him. Nonetheless, v. 16 does not say whether the meeting is in שְׁאוֹל.

This description of Lucifer being cast down to שְׁאוֹל should not be taken literally

because in other biblical data, he was just thrown down to earth (Ezek 28:17,

18; Rev 12:9). Furthermore, looking at the context of Isa 14, it is evident that

it is a very poetic and metaphorical chapter telling even the rejoicing of cypress

and cedars over the demise of Babylon (14:8).

In Deut 32:22-24, in a poetic context, Moses describes the destruction

of Israel to שְׁאוֹל if they turn away from Yahweh. God would kindle fire which

will burn as far as ᾍδης (LXX)[180] below and would devour (καταφάγεται) the

earth and its harvest (v. 24). Although ᾍδης or שְׁאוֹל burns, the description is in

poetic language, and may not be taken literally. S. R. Driver also notes, "The

verse contains a graphic but hyperbolic description (for the context requires the

judgment to be limited to Israel) of the far-reaching and destructive operation

of the Divine Anger."[181] The next verses contain the literal description of the

destruction of these rebellious people mentioned here (vv. 23,24). They are not

to be burned literally in the fire of ᾍδης.[182] They are to be destroyed by famine,

pestilence, and deadly plague instead. So, ᾍδης here may still literally mean

"grave," or "a place beneath the earth" (v. 22b and d). In this case, the Israelites

who would be destroyed by calamities would make ᾍδης their graves (vv.

23,24).

Furthermore, in Num 16:30,33 שְׁאוֹל or ᾍδης refers to the place below the

ground or a pit which opened and swallowed the rebellious leaders of Israel

[179] Gordon J. Wenham, *Genesis 16-50*, WBC, vol. 2, 357. Cf. John Skinner, *Genesis*, ICC, 449.

[180] KJV and LXX (English translation) translate it "Hell," NIV translates it "realms of death," and NLT translates it "grave."

[181] S. R. Driver, *Deuteronomy*, ICC, 366.

[182] Fire is a "symbol of great calamities (see Ezek 30:8) or a flaring up of anger (Jer 15:14; 17:4). 'Hell' is a figure of destruction (see Prov 15:11; Ps 86:13)." "Fire" (Deut 32:22), *SDABC*, 1:1070.

the wilderness on their way to Canaan.[183] In addition, in a common Hebrew

parallelism, ᾅδης of the first line of Ps 29:4 (LXX) is parallel with the λάκκος

"pit."[184] However, in some instances, ᾅδης in LXX is a translation of the Hebrew

word בּוֹר which means "pit" (Isa 14:19; 38:18). This may mean that בּוֹר is a

synonym of שְׁאוֹל. This is also clear in Isa 14:15 where the word שְׁאוֹל of the

first phrase is explained further by בּוֹר in the second phrase: תּוּרָד אֶל־יַרְכְּתֵי־בוֹר

אֶל־שְׁאוֹל אַךְ[185] (But you are brought down to the grave [first phrase], to the

depths of the pit [second phrase], NIV).

In several passages, ᾅδης or שְׁאוֹל is parallel with θάνατος (thanatos, LXX)

or מָוֶת—(which means "death" (Ps 54:16).[186] However, in few passages, ᾅδης is

also a translation of the Hebrew word מָוֶת(Prov 14:12, KJV, NIV, NLT, and

NASB; see also 16:25). Interestingly, in few instances, ᾅδης is a translation of

the Hebrew word דּוּמָה "silence" (Ps 115:17; Ps 93:17). This is indicated in the

phrase "the dead do not praise the LORD" (Ps. 115:17; 113:25 [LXX]). The

word ᾅδης is also a translation of the Hebrew word רְפָאִים "dead"[187] (Prov 2:18).

This word form occurs twenty times. In LXX, it is translated as (1) Ραφαὶν

(raphain) which means "giants"; (2) τιτάνων (titanôn) which is translated into

English as "Rephaim" and often in the phrase "valley of Rephaim"; and (3)

νεκρός (nekros) which is translated "dead." In the contexts of its occurrences,

the word רְפָאִים does not mean "ghosts" or "conscious dead spirits." This word

may just be translated as "dead" in the context of Prov 2:18. Furthermore, the

---

[183]R. Dennis Cole suggests that the word שְׁאוֹל here means "grave." He says, "Sheol at this point in Israel's history seems to have been the grave, or perhaps a shadowy, unknown realm where one was gathered to his fathers at death." Cole, 269. Katharine Doob Sakenfeld, in commenting on Num 16:30,33, says, "Sheol is the most common Hebrew term for the dwelling place of the dead. It is thought of as very low, below the earth, and a place of watery silence and darkness. . . . By contrast to the later Christian idea of hell, Sheol is not a special place of punishment reserved for the wicked." Katharine Doob Sakenfeld, *Numbers*, ITC, vol. 4, 101.

[184]KJV, , NASB, NKJV, and LXX English translation. See also Isa 14:15,19; 38:18; Ezek 31:16

[185]See Elliger and Rudolph, *BHS*, 696.

[186]For example, see Ps 17:6; 114:3; Prov 7:27; Isa 28:15,18; 38:18; Hos 13:14 (LXX).

[187]NASB, KJV, NKJV. NIV translates it "spirits of the dead"; TEV translates it "world of the dead"; while RSV translates it "shades." BDB takes this to mean "ghosts," or "dead spirits." Brown, BDB, s.v. "רְפָאִים."

LXX translation, "ἔθετο γὰρ παρὰ τῷ θανάτῳ τὸν οἶκον αὐτῆς καὶ παρὰ τῷ ᾅδῃ μετὰ τῶν γηγενῶν τοὺς ἄξονας αὐτῆς"[188] indicates that ᾅδης is parallel with θανάτος. This may further indicate that רְפָאִים may just mean "dead" people who are not conscious.

῾Αδης is also a translation of מוּת[189] "death——natural or violent"[190] (Job 33:22). Lastly, it translates the word צַלְמָוֶת which means "shadow of death" (KJV, NKJV, NIV) or "deep darkness" (NASB, RSV).[191]

There is also an OT concept of ᾅδης or שְׁאוֹל as a place in the deep part of the earth. Zophar tells Job in a form of a question that the "mysteries of God" are higher than the heavens and "deeper than" שְׁאוֹל or ᾅδης (Job 11:8).[192] It is also implied in some passages like Prov 15:24; Job 38:17;[193] Ps 86:13; Isa 14:15. However, Jonah poetically describes his experience in the belly of the whale as in the "belly of sheol" or "depths of the grave" (Jonah 2:2, NIV).

Another point that needs to be considered is that OT writers believe that people who rest in ᾅδης or שְׁאוֹל do not remember God nor praise Him (Ps 6:6; 113:25; Isa 38:18). Job also believes that those who go down to שְׁאוֹל vanish away and never return (Job 7:9). He just hopes a resurrection from the dead (19:25-27). The author of Ecclesiastes also believes that people who go down to שְׁאוֹל neither work nor think. They do not have any knowledge or wisdom anymore. Their memory, hatred, and love are also forgotten (vv. 5,6). Hence, he advises his listeners to do their best in every endeavor they undertake (9:10) while they are

---

[188]The NIV translates it as, "For her house leads down to death and her paths to the spirits of the dead (NIV)," and the KJV, "For her house inclineth to death, her paths unto the dead (KJV)." For the Greek text, see Charles Lee Brenton, *The Septuagint Version of the Old Testament and Apocrypha* (London: Samuel Bagster, 1851; reprint, Grand Rapids: Zondervan, 1970), 789.

[189]It is translated "death" (NIV, NASB, and RSV).

[190]Brown, BDB, s.v. "מות."

[191]It means "death-like shadow, deep shadow or darkness." Ibid., s.v. "צַלְמָוֶת"

[192]KJV translates "deeper than hell"; NIV "deeper than the depths of grave"; NLT "deeper than the underworld."

[193]Here, the word ᾅδης is a translation of the Hebrew word צַלְמָוֶת (death-like shadow or deep shadow or darkness).

still alive. שְׁאוֹל or ᾅδης is also described in the OT in a metaphorical language. It is pictured as having a mouth (Ps 140:7; Isa 5:14). It is compared to men who are not satisfied (Prov 27:20) and a barren womb (30:16). It is also pictured as having חֶבֶל (ḥeḇel) "cord," which in the LXX is translated ὠδῖνες (odines) "birth pains" or "pangs" (Ps 17:6). שְׁאוֹל or ᾅδης is also portrayed as surrounding the Psalmist (Ps 114:3), and God describes it as having gates (Job 38:17; cf. Isa 38:10) and having power to imprison His own people (Ps 88:49, LXX). However, God declares that He has the power to ransom them from it (Hos 13:14).

In another instance, it is described as τὰ ταμίεια τοῦ θανάτου (the chambers of death, Prov 7:27) which is situated down the earth. In another passage, ᾅδης or שְׁאוֹל is featured as excited by the casting down of Babylon to its domain (Isa 14:9a). The second line is parallel with the first: ὁ ᾅδης κάτωθεν ἐπικράνθη συναντήσας σοι ("*Hades* below is excited to meet you") συνηγέρθησάν σοι πάντες οἱ γίγαντες[194] ("it rouses all the dead for you"). It pictures the dead being alive and ready to welcome Babylon (14:9b).[195] Although it is tempting to conclude here that the dead have some kind of existence in ᾅδης,[196] the evidence is not overwhelming since the language of the passage is highly poetic and metaphorical. For example, in vv. 7-8, the lands, the cypress trees, and the cedars of Lebanon are portrayed as rejoicing over the overthrow and destruction of Babylon.

The OT concept of ᾅδης or שְׁאוֹל and death seem to go beyond the literal

---

[194]Brenton, 849.

[195]Eugene Merrill asserts that here in this passage the dead "have an existence of some kind, though their description as shades (repaim) (Isa 14:9) makes it clear that theirs is a weak and unrewarding style of life (14:10)." Eugene Merrill, " שְׁאוֹל," *New International Dictionary of Old Testament Theology and Exegesis*, ed. Willem A. VanGemeren (Grand Rapids: Zondervan, 1997), 4:7.

[196]L. Wächter asserts that the OT Israelites, the Greeks, and the Babylonians "conceived the world of the dead as a great space in the depths, as an underworld. The spirits of the dead (Job 26:5; Prov 9:18; Isa 14:9) enter into this realm of darkness (Job 10:21; Ps 88:7,13[6,12]: etc.) and silence (Ps 22:3[2]; 94:17) that is closed off with locks and gates (Job 38:17; Ps 9:14[13]; Isa 38:10)." Wächter, 14:241-42. See also Harry Buis, "ᾅδης," *The Zondervan Pictorial Encyclopedia of the Bible* (1976), 3:7. In addition, Adela Yarbro Collins points out that the "dead are referred to as 'shades,' pale reflections of the men and women they had once been (Isa 14:10; Ecc 9:10). Existence in lAav. is characterized by forgetfulness and inactivity (Ps 88:12; Ecc 9:10)." Adela Yarbro Collins, "Hades," *The HarperCollins Bible Dictionary*, ed. Paul J. Achtemeier (New York: HarperCollins, 1985), 395.

grave and lifeless, physical body. It means that ᾅδης or שְׁאוֹל.[197] "cannot be squared exactly with that of the grave of the ancestors, the family burial place, where the dead are to be found."[198] This is supported by the fact that in some instances, the OT writers use קֶבֶר—(qeber)[199] "burying place," "sepulcher," or "grave," to refer to the physical grave or tomb (Gen 50:5, 2 Sam 19:37; 1 Kgs 13:30; 2 Chr 34:28; Job 5:26; Ps 88:11; Isa 53:9). The difference is also apparent in Ps 88:1-5. This Psalm portrays a picture of the Psalmist, who is in trouble, crying and praying day and night before God (vv. 1-2). His life is in the edge of ᾅδης or שְׁאוֹל (v. 3a); he is counted as dead (v. 4) and forsaken among the dead (v. 5a). He also considers himself as a slain man lying in the קֶבֶר (v. 5b) who is forgotten by God (v. 5c) and is cut off from Him (v. 5d). The difference here is that when the Psalmist mentions ᾅδης or שְׁאוֹל in v. 3, he associates it with his soul ψυχή (psychē, LXX) or life ζωή (zoē, LXX). But when he mentions μνημεῖον or קֶבֶר, he associates it with a slain body (v. 5b). This may indicate that ᾅδης goes beyond μνημεῖον or קֶבֶר in meaning. It seems that the Psalmist likens his separation from his God to his experiencing of ᾅδης or שְׁאוֹל. The Psalmist describes this condition as being put in the lowest pit (v. 6a) or being in dark places or in the depths (v. 6b). It is also a condition of being rejected by God (v. 14). It is furthermore attested by the fact that the Psalmist expresses thanks to the Lord for delivering him from ᾅδης or שְׁאוֹל (Ps 30:3[4]).[200] The Psalmist is literally alive but he considers his troubled life as if he were in ᾅδης.[201]

---

[197]Merrill says, "It is place, one beneath the earth's surface to which people descend at death or even while still alive (Num 16:33; Ps 55:15[16]." Merrill, 3:7.

[198]Hans Bietenhard, " ᾅδης," *NIDNTT*, 2:206.

[199]μνημεῖον (mnēmeion) in LXX.

[200]See also Ps 29:4; 49:16[15]; 86:13.

[201]Hans Bietenhard notes that שְׁאוֹל does not only lie "on the border of life in the beyond. It also penetrates the circle of the living on every side, through illness, weakness, imprisonment, oppression by enemies and by death." Bietenhard, 2:206.

῞Αδης in the OT Apocrypha

n the book of Tobit, ᾅδης, as in the LXX, is described as being below the earth (13:2).[202] Tobit, in his prayer of joy, blesses God and expresses his view about God in relation to ᾅδης. He views God as the one who chastises and shows mercy (13:2a) by leading men down to ᾅδης (13:2b) but "brings them up again" (13:2c).[203] Since the third line is in contrast with the second line in Hebrew poetry, ᾅδης could be viewed in a negative way. Here is the contrast᾿ κατάγει εἰς ᾅδην ("He leads down to *Hades* [first line], καὶ ἀνάγει and He brings up [again]" [second line]).[204] In this context, ᾅδης is considered as a scourge or a severe punishment. It is a figurative description of the troubles and sufferings that Tobit experienced. The point here is that the author of Tobit views ᾅδης in a very negative manner like OT writers. It is something that the Jews dreaded.

In the apocryphal book of the Wisdom of Solomon,[205] ᾅδης is considered as having royal dominion, though he could not have his dominion upon the earth (1:14).[206] Furthermore, the author exposes the philosophy of some wicked men who believed that at death, man ceases to exist. According to these men, the reason of a dead man is extinguished, his body turns to dust, and the spirit is dispersed. Besides, none was ever known that returned from ᾅδης (2:1-6). However, the author believes that when the righteous die, their souls "are in the hand of God, and no torment will touch them" (3:1). Furthermore, the author believes that the

---

[202]This Apocryphal book was most likely written in the Pre-Maccabean Period. See D. C. Simpson, "The Book of Tobit," in *The Apocrypha and Pseudepigrapha of the Old Testament in English (APOT)*, ed. R. H. Charles (Oxford: Clarendon, 1978), 1:183. For the texts, see ibid., 1:202-41.

[203]See also Wisdom of Solomon 16:13.

[204]All LXX Greek texts in this study come from Bible Works Software. For a hard copy, see Charles Lee Brenton, "Tobit," *The Septuagint Version of the Old Testament and Apocrypha with an English Translation; and with Various Readings and Critical Notes* (London: Samuel Bagster, 1851; reprint, Grand Rapids: Zondervan, 1978), 1-35; see also Simpson, 1:235; J. A. F. Gregg, "Addition to Esther," in *APOT*, 1:675.

[205]There is no consensus on the date of this book but after considering all the proposed dates with their arguments, Samuel Holmes proposes 50 B.C. to A.D. 10. Samuel Holmes, "The Wisdom of Solomon," in *APOT*, 1:521.

[206]Ibid., 1:535-68.

souls of the dead are held back in ἅδης and only God can release them (16:13-14). There is already a clear indication that, in the inter-testamental period, the Jews believed that a person's soul continued to exist in ἅδης after his/her death.

In the book of Sirach,[207] ἅδης is synonymous with θάνατος as seen in a parallel poetic pattern (14:12).[208] In the context, the author admonishes his son to be prudent in dealing with his short life on earth. He exhorts him to do good to his friends (v. 13) in view of the nearness of death. At this point, ἅδης may refer to death or grave as evident in the context.

῾Αδης is also a place, as in the OT, where the dead cannot praise the Lord (17:27-28). The idea in vv. 27-28 seems parallel to Ps 115:17. There is also a hint of a fiery ἅδης (21:9). Like in the OT, ἅδης is also believed to be a deep pit (21:10). In Sirach 51, the author seems to echo the Psalmist (Ps 88). He praises God for redeeming his soul from death (51:2a), for keeping his flesh back from the pit (51:2b), and for delivering his foot from the power of ἅδης (51:2c; v. 4). This may be a metaphorical description of the author's deliverance from the certainty of death (v. 6) especially from a slanderous tongue (v. 2d,e; v. 5), or from those who rise up against him (v. 2f). Hence, death is the metaphorical meaning of ἅδης or שׁאול.

In the book of Baruch,[209] ἅδης, as in the OT, is also regarded as the grave (Cf. 2 Macc 6:23) where the dead, those whose breaths are taken from their bodies, go down when they die. The dead give neither glory nor righteousness to the Lord (2:11; 3:11,19). The Israelites who were taken captives were already counted among those who go down to the grave. This indicates that some hopeless people, though alive, were considered as dead in the grave (2:11). In the Prayer

---

[207]The date of the composition is later than 300-275 B.C. based on internal evidence and the character of the Hebrew diction. G. H. Box and W. O. E. Oesterley, "The Book of Sirach," in *APOT*, 1:296. For the texts, see ibid., 1:316-517.

[208]Ὅτι θάνατος οὐ χρονιεῖ καὶ διαθήκη ᾅδου οὐχ ὑπεδείχθη σοι "that **death** will not delay [first line], and the decree of *hadēs* has not been shown for you [second line] (RSV)."

[209]A.D. 78 is the most probable date of composition according to O. C. Whitehouse. O. C. Whitehouse, "The Book of Baruch," in *APOT*, 1:576. For the texts, see ibid., 1:583-95.

of Azariah and the Song of the Three Children,[210] the deliverance of the three Hebrew captives from the fiery furnace was also considered as a deliverance from ᾅδης. In this context, deliverance from ᾅδης may mean deliverance from death (1:66).

ᾅδης in the OT Pseudepigrapha

One of the extra-biblical Jewish stories similar to the story of the rich man and Lazarus in Luke 16:19-31 is 1 En 22:1-14.[211] In Enoch's vision, angel Rafael tells Enoch that inside a high mountain (v. 2) there is a place where the spirits of the souls of the dead are assembled (vv. 3,4). The souls of the people are kept here until the great judgment (v. 4). This is called the intermediate state of the dead.

Furthermore, Enoch states that the voices of the spirits of the dead reach unto heaven (v. 5). In this temporary place, the souls of the righteous are separated by a spring of water (v. 9), and the souls of the sinners are also set apart (v. 10). The souls of the sinners are in great pain in that place (v. 11). The author adds, "Their spirits too—with anguish" (v. 11). After the judgment, they will stay there in pain forever (v. 13).

There are conceptual or thematic similarities between the story of the rich man and Lazarus and the supposed vision of Enoch in 1 En 22:1-14. Kreitzer notes this resemblance by presenting several thematic and verbal parallels between the two.[212] This close affinity may indicate that the conceptual belief

---

[210]According to W. H. Bennett, the most probable date of composition is about 170-168 B.C. W. H. Bennett, "The Prayer of Azariah and the Song of the Three Children," in *APOT*, 1:629. For the texts, see ibid., 1:632-37.

[211]E. Isaac, "1 Ethiopic Apocalypse of Enoch," In *The Old Testament Pseudepigrapha (OTP)*, ed. James H. Charlesworth (Garden City, NY: Doubleday, 1983), 1:1-89. According to George W. E. Nickelsburg, 1 En 1-36 was already known before the death of Judas Maccabeus in 160 B.C.E., "Hence we are justified in treating these chapters as a product of the period before 175 B.C.E." George W. E. Nickelsburg, *Jewish Literature between the Bible and the Mishnah* (Philadelphia: Fortress, 1981), 48.

[212]These are the parallel thematic concepts:
1. There is a separation between the righteous and the wicked in ᾅδης (1 En 22:9; Luke 16:22).
2. There is reference to a deep and dark void which may parallel the great chasm in Luke (1 En 22:1-2; Luke 16:26).
3. There is a mention of water in the place of the righteous (1 En 22:9; Luke 16:24).
4. The wicked are tormented in both accounts (1 En 22:9-10; Luke 16:23). Kreitzer, 139-42.

concerning ᾍδης was already popular in Jesus' time. Hence, one can argue that the story in Enoch may have influenced the conceptual framework of the people in Jesus' time including the story of the rich man and Lazarus. In 1 En 102:5,11[213] (see also 103:7), שאול is a place where the dead descend. The author adds, "Their spirits too—with anguish" (v. 11), the wicked, will experience evil and great tribulation—in darkness, nets, and burning fire (103:7,8).

In Pseudo-Philo,[214] ᾍδης is called "the chambers of souls" (32:13). In 15:5, it is called "chambers of darkness" where the souls of the children of Israel who died in the wilderness were shut up. In 21:9, it is called "the secret dwelling places of souls."

In Sibylline Oracles, the author exposes the evil deeds of some of God's children who had forsaken the true and eternal God. Instead of offering sacrifices to Him, they made "sacrifices to the deities in Hades."[215] The author is aware of the influence of Greek paganism and rebukes them of their evil ways. He also urges them to return to the God of light (Frag. i.23-35).[216] It seems that conservative Jews did not condone Greek pagan practices and beliefs.

In another fragment of Sibylline Oracles, an author portrays God's judgment in the last day. God will raise men from the ashes and judge them. The wicked will be covered by "murky Tartarus and black recesses of hell." However, the righteous will live again on earth (iv:79-92).[217] In book V of Sibylline Oracles, the author mentions ᾍδης as the nether region of the earth (v:78).[218] He speaks also of Tartarus, which may refer to the place of punishment for the wicked after God's last judgment, while ᾍδης is the place of the dead awaiting judgment.

---

[213]Nickelsburg dates 1 En 92-105 in the reign of Alexander Jannaeus or perhaps John Hyrcanus. Nickelsburg, 149.

[214]According to D. J. Harrington, the earliest possible date of this book would be 135 B.C. But a date around the time of Jesus is most likely. D. J. Harrington, "Pseudo-Philo," in *OTP*, 2:299. For the texts, see ibid., 2:304-77.

[215]H. C. O. Lanchester, "The Sibylline Oracles," in *APOT*, 2:377-406.

[216]Ibid., 2:377. This fragment may be dated during the reign of Ptolemy VI Philometor around the middle of the second century B.C.E. See Nickelsburg, 164.

[217]Lanchester, 2:396.

[218]Ibid., 400.

In 4 Ezra,[219] ᾅδης is described as having portals (4:7) and is situated in the deepest part of the earth (4:8). In the great resurrection and final judgment, the pit of torment will appear (7:36a), but over against it shall be the place of refreshment (7:36b). This pit of torment is also called the "furnace of Gehenna" (7:36c). The descriptions in 4 Ezra and Luke 16:19-31 bear a striking similarity in that both accounts refer to a place of torment and a place of refreshment, which stand adjacent to each other. Nonetheless, 4 Ezra account is in the context of the last-day judgment, whereas the context in Luke is a time before the last-day judgment.

Another interesting statement is that ᾅδης will flee at the time when death will vanish (8:53). But before the disappearance of ᾅδης at the last-day judgment, it remains "the underworld and the chambers of souls" (4:41-42; 7:32) where the souls are kept till the judgment. This ᾅδης is likened to a womb which is a temporary place for the souls entrusted to it. These souls are waiting to be delivered out of ᾅδης (4:36-43). They even ask how long they will remain in those chambers (4:35).

In 4 Ezra 7:75-101,[220] the condition of souls immediately after their death is described. The spirits of the wicked would wander in torments, ever grieving and sad in seven ways (v. 80). In contrast, the spirits of the godly will be separated from the body and will immediately see the glory of God. They will have rest in seven orders (vv. 89-92). They will stay there until the last days when their reward of immortality will be given to them and when they will be glorified (vv. 95-99). Based on these data, ᾅδης is a temporary place below the earth where souls are kept. The wicked are already being tormented, while the righteous are at rest. At the last-day judgment, the righteous will be released through the resurrection. They will be glorified and will receive immortality; by that time death and ᾅδης will be no more.

---

[219]The date of the composition of this book is probably A.D. 100 based on internal evidence. G. H. Box, "IV Ezra," in *APOT*, 2:552. For the texts, see ibid., 2:561-624.

[220]B. M. Metzger, "The Fourth Book of Ezra," in *OTP*, 2:525-59.

ˈΑδης or שְׁאוֹל in Dead Sea Scrolls (DSS)

In 1QH XI:8-18, the Psalmist describes a woman giving birth in a שְׁאוֹל-like experience.[221] The womb of the woman where the child came from is likened to שְׁאוֹל. The womb is called "the breakers of death" (v. 8) or "pangs of sheol" (v. 9). It seems apparent in this passage that death is synonymous to שְׁאוֹל (Cf. 4Q548 [4QVision of Amram], Frag. 1:2).[222] In this passage also, שְׁאוֹל is synonymous to "pit" in the phrase "breakers of the pit" (v. 12). שְׁאוֹל is also synonymous to אבדוף "Abaddon" (v. 16).

שְׁאוֹל is described as "abyss" or "deep" (1QH XI:17; 1QH XI:31; 11Q11 [Apocryphal Psalms], col. IV:7-9) which is synonymous to "pit." It is also described as having gates[223] which open to receive all the dead (1QH XI:17).[224] The gates are then closed and fastened with an everlasting bolt (1QH XI:18). Furthermore, the souls of the dead are believed to descend into the "depth" (4Q418b, Frag. 1:3).

In one instance, the hymnist, like the often repeated phrase of the Psalmist of the OT, expresses his thanks to the Lord because he is saved from the pit, and from שְׁאוֹל of *abaddon* (1QH xi:19). In this context, שְׁאוֹל or pit may refer to a near-to-death situation of the author (see 1QH XI:28).

Similar to this idea, another Qumran[225] author blesses the Lord for lifting up his soul from lAav. or reviving his spirit (4Q437, Frag. 2, col. I:11-13). This is most likely a metaphorical language of a very desperate situation or even of a physical ailment. The idea that שְׁאוֹל is the prison house of the spirits of the dead in the Pseudepigrapha is also present in Qumran. This belief was adapted from

---

[221]Florentino Garcia-Martinez and Eibert J. C. Tigchelaar, *The Dead Sea Scrolls: Study Edition* (Leiden: Brill, 1997), 1:165-67.

[222]Ibid., 2:1093.

[223]In another passage it is called "gates of death" (4Q418 [Instructions], Frag. 127:2). Ibid., 2:877. Cf. 4Q429, Frag. 2, col. II:4.

[224]Cf. 4Q432 (4QH), Frag. 4, col. I:4-6.

[225]Qumran is the place where the DSS were found. The DSS are dated between 134 B.C.E. and 68 C.E. See James Vanderkam and Peter Flint, *The Meaning of the Dead Sea Scrolls* (London: T. & T. Clark, 2002), 22; Menahem Mansoor, *The Dead Sea Scrolls: A College Textbook and Study Guide* (Grand Rapids: Eerdmans, 1964), 23-25.

the book of Enoch. As quoted from Enoch, the spirits who are confined in the so-called "everlasting prison" are tortured. They are shackled in that prison house until the day of their destruction, that is, in the day of judgment (4Q204 [4QEn ar] v:1-2).[226] On the day of judgment, all the wicked spirits will be exterminated (4QEn v:2).

Again, in another passage, it is mentioned that the souls of men are in a prison called "pits" (4Q206 [4QEn ar] Frag. 2 ii:1). They will be in this prison until the great judgment, the day of the end, when they will be judged (II:2,3). However, the reference is made to a complaint of a dead man's spirit, which rose up to heaven (II:3,4).

The expression "everlasting pit" (4QBer [4Q286] Frag. 7, col. II:4; Frag. 5, 4Q418 69 II:3)[227] occurs only in Qumran writings. This idea is similar to the expression "everlasting prison" in the book of Enoch which was also found in one of the Qumran caves. This eternal pit is also called "dark places" (Frag. 5, 4Q418; Frag. 69 II:3; 4Q418; 4Q544 [Visions of Amram], Frag. II:4-6; 11Q11 [Apocryphal Psalms], col. ii:7-9). The wicked are told to "return to eternal pit" (Frag. 69 II, 4Q418; Frag. 5, 4Q418). This pit has a powerful angel placed in charge of it, and is specifically referred to as the "angel of the pit."[228] In this pit, the wicked dead groan probably because of the pain caused by the fire that burns them (Frag. 5, 4Q418 69 II:2; Frag, 69 II, 4Q418).

There is also a belief in Qumran that there is a fire burning in שְׁאוֹל. For example, in a war scroll [4QM], the author pleads to God to scatter the sons of darkness, who will be burned and consumed in the dark places of Abaddon, or in the places of destruction of שְׁאוֹל(4Q491 [4QM], Frag. 8-10, col. I:14-16).[229]

Another idea in Qumran regarding שְׁאוֹל which is identical with an OT idea is that of שְׁאוֹל as a spiritual catastrophe. Through transgressions and iniquities

---

[226]Garcia-Martinez and Tigchelaar, 1:423-25.

[227]Ibid., 2:647. Cf. Frag. 5, 4Q418 69 II:3.

[228]Cf. 11Q11 (Apocryphal Psalms), col. IV:5.

[229]Cf. 4Q525 [4QBeat] Frag. 15:5-8; 4Q542 (4QTQahat ar) Frag. 1, col. II:7-8.

a person may have sold himself or herself to שְׁאוֹל or death (11Q5 [Psalms], col. XIX:9-10). Since this is hardly a physical death, we may say that in this context it is a spiritual death. It is a broken relation with Yahweh which is regarded as שְׁאוֹל-like experience.

שְׁאוֹל or ʽἍδης in Philo

In one of Philo's writings, he indicates that שְׁאוֹל. is situated in the lower region of the earth. He indicates further that souls travel from ἅδης to heaven in a road laid down by God.[230] Philo, in describing the wanderings of the Israelites in the wilderness after their exodus from Egypt, also tells us that Moses led the Israelites from an inhabited to an uninhabited world, and then led them to ἅδης. In the context, ἅδης may mean grave, or a place beneath the earth.[231] Philo, probably influenced by the LXX, also uses the word ἅδης for the Hebrew word שְׁאוֹל in describing the earth which opened and swallowed the rebellious Israelites in the wilderness of Sinai. He describes them "descending into ἅδης."[232] In another passage, Philo seems to have a shared belief with his fellow Jews of the Apocrypha, Pseudipigrapha, and Qumran that to ἅδης is the place where the souls would go when a person dies.[233]

Ἅδης in the NT Literature

In this section, ἅδης and its synonyms in the NT writings, aside from the Synoptic Gospels and Acts, will be scrutinized. It will include the writings of James, Paul, Peter, Jude, and John.

---

[230]Philo *On the Posterity of Cain and His Exile* (trans. Colson and Whitaker, LCL, 2:345-346). Philo of Alexandria lived approximately between the years 20 B.C.E and 40 C.E.

[231]Philo *Moses* 1.195 (trans. Colson, LCL, 4:376-77).

[232]Philo *Moses* 2.281 (LCL, 6:591).

[233]Philo *The Embassy to Gaius* (trans. Colson and Earp, LCL, 10:122-23).

The Concept Ἀδης in James

The word ἄδης does not occur in the book of James. However, its synonym, γέεννα is used by James. In the context of its occurrence, James speaks of the tongue in a metaphorical language calling it πῦρ (pyr) "fire." James points out that the tongue is a small organ, but it may destroy the whole body by setting it on fire. However, the tongue will be set on fire by γέεννα (ὑπὸ τῆς γεέννης). The preposition ὑπο (hypo) is instrumental dative which means that γέεννα is the instrument by which the tongue is set on fire. Here James gives the notion that γέεννα is a fiery place. Looking at his eschatology, James believes that the wicked rich will be judged by fire; it will consume (φάγεται) their flesh (τὰς σάρκας) not their disembodied souls (5:3b). The judgment will be in the last days (5:3c). Thus, in this context, γέεννα refers to the place of punishment of the wicked people after the *Parousia*[234] (5:7).

The Concept Ἀδης in Pauline Epistles

It is interesting to note that Paul does not explicitly mention the word ἄδης in any of his writings. However, there are significant concepts in Paul which are related to ἄδης. One of the concepts related to ἄδης is θάνατος (death). Paul says, "The last enemy to be destroyed is death" (1 Cor 15:26). The destruction of death has been fully completed through the resurrection of the body (v. 42), when the perishable and mortal will put on imperishable and immortal body (v. 54). Consequently, Paul says, "Death is swallowed up in victory" (v. 54c, NASB).[235] It is very significant to note that, in Paul, given a very popular Greek belief in the consciousness of souls in ἄδης, there is no explicit or clear mention of such belief in any of his epistles. Some scholars think that several passages in the Pauline Epistles support the belief in the consciousness of the soul ἄδης. One

---

[234]This word is used throughout this study instead of "the second coming of Jesus."

[235]This victory over death was wrought by God through the death and resurrection of Jesus. But its final overthrow will be when the believers are resurrected at the *Parousia*. See Gordon D. Fee, *The First Epistles to the Corinthians*, NICNT, 803-04; Craig L. Blomberg, *1 Corinthians*, NIVAC, 317.

such passages, this time in heaven, is 2 Cor 5:8[236] which reads, "To be away from the body and at home with the Lord" (NIV). Some scholars say that this passage refers to the intermediate state of the dead people. For other scholars, the statement "to be at home with the Lord" may mean that, at the moment of death, the souls of the righteous will go to heaven to be with the Lord.[237]

However, if we consider the passage in its immediate context, we are clear of its plausible interpretation. In v. 1, Paul, in a figurative way, calls our earthly mortal body as an "earthly tent"[238] (2 Cor 5:1a, NIV), and the immortal body "a building from God, an eternal house in heaven" (5:1b, 4). He elaborates that when we are clothed by our heavenly dwelling, "what is mortal may be swallowed up by life" (v. 4).[239]

The question is, when will we be clothed by our heavenly dwelling, that is, our immortality? Will that happen the moment the person dies? Actually, this concept is similar to what Paul mentions in 1 Cor 15:51-55, which has already been discussed above. He explains that the changing of the mortal body into an immortal or heavenly body will take place at the time of the resurrection of the body (1 Cor 15:52). This takes place at the time of Christ's second coming (15:23; cf. 1 Thess 4:16-17).[240] Thus, it is clear that the resurrected body is the one to be clothed with immortality at the second coming of Jesus. The soul,

---

[236]The other one similar to this is in Phil 1:23 which says, ". . . to depart and be with Christ."

[237]Paul Barnett insists that Paul here "is speaking of the believer's intermediate state between death and the general resurrection. To die, expressed as 'away, out of the body', also means to be 'at home with the Lord'." Paul Barnett, *The Second Epistle to the Corinthians*, NICNT, 271. Cf. Ralph P. Martin, *2 Corinthians*, WBC, vol. 40, 112; Murray J. Harris, "2 Corinthians," *EBC*, 348; Ernest Best, *Second Corinthians*, Interpretation (Louisville, KY: John Knox, 1987), 47.

[238]Margaret E. Thrall takes note of the three possible backgrounds of Paul's phrase, "earthly tent." The first is the Greek concept that the material body is the dwelling-place of the soul. The second is that, it signifies man's total earthly existence. The third is that, it signifies the earthly-tabernacle symbolism. Paul speaks of the believers' body as the temple of the Holy Spirit. Margaret E. Thrall, *2 Corinthians*, ICC, 360.

[239]To be naked in v. 3 and to be unclothed in v. 5 do not refer to the soul in an intermediate state. These Pauline terms may just be figurative descriptions of death. See for example, Craig S. Keener, *1-2 Corinthians* (New York: Cambridge University Press, 2005), 180-81; Froom, 329; James M. Scott, *2 Corinthians*, NIBC, vol. 8, 113.

[240]Larry Richards, *2 Corinthians*, Abundant Life Bible Amplifier (Nampa, ID: Pacific Press, 1998), 112.

therefore, is not clothed with immortality immediately after the person dies.[241]

Furthermore, Paul is clear as to when the righteous ill be with their Lord (2 Cor 5:8; Phil 1:23). Some scholars say that this will happen immediately after their death.[242] Evidently, however, it does not take place immediately after the death of the righteous.[243] Paul clarifies that the righteous are asleep in Jesus in their grave or in the dust (1 Cor 15:51; 1 Thess 4:13-15).[244] At the *Parousia*, the Lord will raise them and they will be caught up to meet Him in the air (1 Thess 4:16). Then and only then will they be with the Lord (1 Thess 4:17; cf. John 14:1-3).

The Concept Ἅδης in Peter and Jude

The word ἅδης does not occur in Peter's and Jude's writings. However, there are verbal and conceptual imagery

which are synonymous to the concept of ἅδης. One similar concept to that of the going down of the souls of the dead to ἅδης is the popular tradition of Christ's descent into ἅδης. This tradition is elaborated in the NT Apocrypha. Perhaps the biblical sources for this tradition include Acts 2:27[245] and 1 Pet 3:19.

The passage, 1 Pet 3:19,[246] is considered by many scholars as *crux interpretum* or as one of the most perplexing and vexatious texts in all of Holy Scripture.[247]

---

[241]Victor Paul Furnish already notes the issue at hand. He points out that Paul's reference to the new body, which will be given to the believers whether immediately after death, at the resurrection, or at the final transformation, needs further debate. Victory Paul Furnish, *2 Corinthians*, AB, vol. 32A, 294. Scott Hafemann sees that Paul here is not speaking of an interim state of bodiless souls with Christ, but that Paul refers to the resurrection glory that is still to come. Scott Hafemann, *2 Corinthians*, NIVAC, 215-16.

[242]See for example, Murray J. Harris, *The Second Epistle to the Corinthians*, New International Greek Testament Commentary, 400.

[243]Frank J. Matera points out that "though it is possible that Paul may have reckoned with being in an intermediate state of being with the Lord if he should die before the *Parousia*, it does not appear that this intermediate state is the explicit object of this text." Frank J. Matera, *2 Corinthians*, The New Testament Library (Louisville, KY: 2003), 125.

[244]The "death-sleep" concept is common in the NT (cf. John 11:11,12). In fact, it was already common in the time of the OT (see 1 Kgs 11:21; Job 14:12; Dan 12:2). Cf. "Present with the Lord" (2 Cor 5:8), *SDABC*, 6:863.

[245]Acts 2:27 will not be discussed here. It will be discussed in chapter 3.

[246]ἐν ᾧ κα τοῖς ἐν φυλακῇ πνεύμασιν πορευθεὶς ἐκήρυξεν. The translation may be, "through whom also He went and proclaimed to the spirits in prison."

[247]John H. Elliott, *1 Peter*, AB, vol. 37B, 647.

Biblical interpreters have been greatly divided in their interpretations of the text, since the time of the Church Fathers.[248] Many scholars generally believe that when Christ died His soul or spirit descended to the realm of the dead, at the time of His death, prior to His resurrection.[249] Then, He preached to the spirits imprisoned in the lower world.[250]

A short analysis of the text is needed in order to clarify the issue on whether or not Jesus preached to the spirits in a prison in Hades after His death and before His resurrection. The passage seems to start in 3:18 and ends in 4:6. The theme of Peter's discussion is the suffering[251] of the believers for the sake of righteousness. Peter's discussion of their suffering begins in v. 13. He exhorts his audience that naturally no one would harm them if they are zealous in doing good (v. 13). However, even if they could not avoid suffering while doing right, they are still blessed (v. 14). They should also be ready always to give an answer to anyone who would ask them about their faith (v. 15). They should always keep a good conscience and good behavior even in the midst of verbal attacks (v. 16). Peter goes on to say that it is better, if it is God's will, for believers to suffer for doing what is right than doing what is wrong (v. 17). Peter then points out that, in the same manner, Christ also (ὅτι καὶ Χριστὸς) "suffered when he died for our sins" (v. 18a, NLT) to bring us to God (3:18b). Up to this point, Peter's comparison of the lives of his recipients to that of Christ Jesus is clear. However, the problem begins when Peter says, "Having been put to death in the flesh, but made alive in the spirit or by the Spirit" (3:18c). The problem here is the meaning of πνεύματι (pneumati). Is it "in spirit" or "by the Spirit"?

---

[248]Ibid., 648-50.

[249]Ibid.

[250]Scholars are divided regarding the identity of the "spirits in prison." The several views are the following:
    1. They are the fallen angels who instigated the evil that was destroyed in the flood (1 Enoch). Christ announced to them His triumph.
    2. They are the spirits of the deceased of Noah's generation to whom Christ preached so as to convert them and bring them to salvation.
    3. They are the spirits of the converted men in Noah's generation, and to all OT righteous. Ibid., 648-49.

[251]It occurs four times in this context (3:14,17; 4:1).

In the history of interpretation, many interpreters insist that "in spirit" means that it is the spirit of Jesus or His soul that is meant here.[252] If so, "in spirit" becomes the antecedent of "ἐν ᾧ" (by which) of v. 19. Hence, it is the soul of Jesus that preached to the spirits imprisoned in ᾅδης after His death and prior to His resurrection. However, this interpretation is not supported by the immediate context, especially in light of Peter's σάρξπνεῦμα (sarx-pneuma) distinction.[253] It is not also supported by the broader NT context.

J. Ramsey Michaels seems to be more plausible when he argues that the σάρκι and πνεύματι are both datives of respect rather than instrumental dative, since the latter does not fit the idea of σάρκι. Christ was put to death "in the flesh," but hardly "by the flesh."[254] His conclusion that the "flesh" and "spirit" contrast here "is not between the material and immaterial parts of Christ's person (that is, His 'body' and 'soul'), but rather between His earthly existence and His risen state (cf. Rom 1:3-4; 1 Tim 3:16)"[255] is reasonable. If "in spirit" means Christ's post-resurrection state, that is, His original divine state, then the antecedent of "ἐν ᾧ καὶ" (en hô kai) could be Christ's post-resurrection state. Then it would be smooth to say that "by which also" may mean "in that state also."[256] He went and preached to the spirits in prison[257] (3:19) who were disobedient at the time

---

[252]Cf. Norman Hillyer, *1 and 2 Peter, Jude*, NIBC, vol. 16, 117.

[253]See J. Ramsey Michaels, *1 Peter*, WBC, vol. 49, 204.

[254]Ibid.

[255] Ibid. William Joseph Dalton argues that in the flesh-spirit contrast which occurs in the NT (Matt 26:41; Mark 14:38; John 3:6; 6:63; Rom 1:4; 8:4,5,6,9,13; 1 Cor 5:5; 2 Cor 7:1; Gal 3:3; 4:29; 5:16,17,19; 6:8; Col 2:5; 1 Tim 3:16; Heb 12:9; 1 Pet 3:18; 4:6), nothing supports the idea of the distinction of body and soul. William Joseph Dalton, *Christ's Proclamation to the Spirits: A Study of 1 Pet 3:18-4:6*, Analecta Biblica, 2d rev. ed. (Roma: Edtrice Pontificio Istituto Biblico, 1989), 138.

[256]The post-resurrection state of Jesus is much like His pre-incarnate, glorified state. "By Which" (1 Pet 3:19), *SDABC*, 7:574.

[257]The "spirits in prison" here may refer to living human beings who were in a figurative prison of sin, although some scholars say these are the souls in prison in a[[dhj; or the rebellious angels who were in prison as found in 1 En 20. The "spirits" as souls has been already ruled out in the exegetical analysis. The "spirits" as rebellious angels has a strong case in the exegetical analysis. Some scholars argue that Jesus in His post-resurrection state proclaimed His triumph to the rebellious angels. See Dalton, 159. However, there are also evidences that "the spirits in prison" here may mean the living human beings in the time of Noah:
    1. It is evident in v. 20 that the 'disobedient' which refers back to the spirits in prison in v. 19 were the unrepentant contemporaries of Noah. As a result only eight persons were saved in the ark. The Genesis account does not mention angels as recipients of Noah' preaching. The idea that the "sons of God" in Gen 6:2

of Noah (3:20). To be clear, it might be Jesus in His pre-incarnate state that preached to the antediluvian people in the time of Noah. Jesus' preaching could be through the ministry of Noah. The other possible interpretation which is not out of context could be that σάρκι may mean "by the flesh" and πνεύματι could mean "by the Spirit." If this was what Peter meant, then the translation could be, "He was put to death by the flesh (or human beings) but was made alive by the Spirit" (v. 18c). Accordingly, the antecedent of "ἐν ᾧ" (by which, by whom, or though whom) would be the Spirit (the Holy Spirit). This would mean that Jesus preached to the antediluvians at the time of Noah through the Holy Spirit in the ministry of Noah.[258]

This idea is supported by the immediate context (4:6). It also receives support in the wider NT context (John 16). The OT evidence is much more compelling because God said in the context of Noah, "My Spirit shall not strive with men forever" (Gen 6:3, NASB). Either of these two interpretations is plausible as far as the immediate and wider contexts (NT and OT) are concerned. The interpretation that Jesus proclaimed His triumph to the angels (spirits) in prison who were rebellious prior to the flood at His post-resurrection state is also possible as argued by William Joseph Dalton.[259] Definitely, one of these interpretations was meant by Peter. Whatever Peter meant, it is clear that the "spirits-disembodied souls" idea is ruled out by the context.

---

are angels is not supported in the entire Scripture except Job 1:6. The idea is found in the pseudepigraphal book of Enoch.

2. The idea that spirits are human beings is plausible because the word ψυχαί (psychai) in v. 20 does not mean the disembodied souls but human beings, specifically Noah and his family.

3. The word "spirit" may also mean "person" in other NT occurrences (1 Cor 16:18; Gal 6:18; 2 Tim 4:22; Phil 4:23; Heb 12:9,23; cf. Num 16:22; 27:16).

4. 1 Pet 4:6 supports the interpretation that the spirits in prison refers to human beings who were imprisoned in sin (Cf. Isa 47:2; 61:4; Luke 4:18), not to rebellious angels.

[258]See for example Edmund Clowney, *The Message of 1 Peter*, The Bible Speaks Today, ed. John R. Stott (Leicester, England: Inter-Varsity, 1988), 163-64; Robert Leighton, *Commentary on First Peter* (London: Henry Bohn; reprint, Grand Rapids: Kregel, 1972), 355-58.

[259]Dalton, 143-64. Cf. Peter H. Davids, *The First Epistle of Peter*, NICNT, 140-41; Edwin A. Blum, "2 Peter," *EBC*, 242-43; A. M. Stibbs and A. F. Walls, *1 Peter*, TNTC, vol. 17, 142-43; Robert M. Johnston, *Peter and Jude*, Abundant Life Bible Amplifier, 96-97; Daniel J. Harrington, *1 Peter*, Sacra Pagina, vol. 15 (Collegeville, MN: Liturgical Press, 2003), 102-03.

Another word which will be tackled is ταρταρώσας (tartarôsas).[260] This is a participial form of the noun ταρταρος (tartaros). It occurs only here in 2 Pet 2:4 and is synonymous to the word ᾅδης. While ᾅδης, in several occurrences in the NT, may mean "grave" or "the place of the dead beneath the earth," ταρταρος is seen here as the place where the rebellious angels were cast down, awaiting for the final judgment (cf. Jude 6).[261] Peter and the rest of the NT writers do not elaborate further about this place. In extra-biblical literature, ταρταρος is believed to be deeper than ᾅδης; it is a place where divine punishment is meted out.[262] However, here in 2 Pet 2:4, the rebellious angels are not yet punished but are just reserved for the day of judgment. Other passages in the Scripture tell us that Satan and his angels were cast down to the earth when they were defeated by Michael and His angels in heaven (Rev 12:4,9, 13).[263] With the contrasting data between the Scripture and the extra-biblical literature, it seems that Peter used the extra-biblical word ταρταρος which is popular to his Greek audience, though without necessarily transporting its popular meaning.[264] The Scriptural data may still be in Peter's intention, which means that the whole earth, which may include probably the place beneath, is in view.[265]

---

[260]The NASB, NIV, KJV, and NLT translate it as "cast, threw, or sent into hell."

[261]This idea was actually popular among extra-biblical Jewish writers (1 En 20:2; Sib. Or. 4:186; Philo, Mos. 2.433; Praem. 152). However, "Hellenistic Jews were aware that the Greek myth of the Titans had some similarity to the fall of the Watchers (Josephus, Ant. 1.73; cf. LXX Ezek 32:27; Sir 16:7). However, in an apocryphal Christian passage (Sib. Or. 2:231) the Watchers themselves seem to be called τιτάνες (Titans)." Richard J. Bauckham, *Jude, 2 Peter*, WBC, vol. 5, 249.

[262]According to Walter Bauer, it means the "netherworld," thought of by the Greeks as a subterranean place lower than ᾅδης where divine punishment was meted out, and so regarded in Israelite apocalyptic as well: Job 41:24; 1 En 20:2; Philo, Exs. 152; Jos., C. Ap. 2, 240; Sib. Or. 2, 302; 4, 186. Bauer, BAGD, s.v. "tartarow." Scholars also believe this extra-biblical tradition. See Jerome H. Neyrey, *2 Peter, Jude*, AB, vol. 37C, 202; Blum, 278.

[263]Isaiah tells us that Lucifer was cast down to the earth (14:12) or brought down to lAav. (v. 15). The earth in v. 12 is parallel with שְׁאוֹל in v. 15.

[264]*SDABC* says, "Peter employs a Greek term to convey his thought, but does not thereby endorse either Greek idea of ταρταρος or the popular Jewish concept of γέεννα. Here, ταρταρος refers simply to the place of abode to which the evil angels are restricted until the day of judgment." "Cast Them Down to Hell" (2 Pet 2:4), *SDABC*, 7:605.

[265]I think the plausible argument for this is the fact that Satan and his angels are spirits and could not be limited to a certain space beneath the earth. It is also supported by the fact that they are very active in the world (see for example, Eph 6:12; Jas 4:7). One thing more, Peter, definitely, would not adapt the Hellenistic

In Jude 6, the parallel passage of 2 Pet 2:4, the word ταρταρος ιs not used. Nonetheless, the idea that the rebellious angels are kept in darkness for the judgment is still present. The presence of the same idea in Jude 6 is an indication that this idea was very well-known in Hellenistic Jewish tradition and Christian tradition.[266] It is very natural for scholars to conclude that Jude and Peter had the same intended meaning as that found in the book of Enoch. However, the rest of the biblical data do not warrant such conclusion.

῞Αδης in Revelation

Among the writings of John the apostle, only the book of Revelation[267] speaks about ᾅδης. In Revelation, the word ᾅδης appears four times (1:18; 6:8; 20:13,14) and is always associated with θάνατος (death). It seems that in these four occurrences, ὁ θάνατος καὶ ὁ ᾅδης are personified.[268] In Rev 1:18, John speaks of the glorious Son of Man, Jesus Christ, as the one who was dead but was resurrected. He is now holding the keys[269] of ᾅδης signifying His mighty power and authority over the domain of death and the grave for He Himself has conquered death and has Himself come out of ᾅδης.[270]

There is no indication whether John's understanding of ᾅδης is influenced by

Jews' idea because of the fact that it was influenced by the Greek myth of the Titans.

[266]Bauckham notes, "It was still widely known and accepted, especially in those Jewish Christian circles where the Enoch literature remained popular. Perhaps it was largely owing to the influence of those circles and the continuing popularity of the Enoch literature in second-century Christianity that the fall of the Watchers retained its place in the Christian tradition longer than in Judaism." Bauckham, *Jude, 2 Peter*, 51.

[267]Although the authorship of the book is still an issue among biblical scholars, this research, based on external and internal evidences, accepts the view that the book of Revelation was written by apostle John in the Isles of Patmos on ca. A.D. 96.

[268]The personification of "ὁ θάνατος καὶ o᾽ ᾅδης " (death and hades) is very common in biblical times. In the OT, death and lAav. are also often personified (Ps 18:5-6; 116:3; Hab 2:5; Isa 28:15; Hos 13:14). David Aune notes that in extra-biblical literature, o᾽ qa,natoj kai. o᾽ ᾅδης are also personified (*T. Abraham* [Rec. A] 16-20). Death is also personified in Greek and Latin texts (Hesiod *Theog.* 211; *Orphic Hymns* 87; Aristophanes *Frogs* 1392; Euripides *Alcestis*, passim; Cicero *De natura deorum* 3.17.44; Vergil *Aeneid* 11.197). In Christian Literature, ᾅδης is occasionally personified in order to identify it with Death (*Acts of Pilate* 20-24; Melito *Pass.* 22,55, 102). David E. Aune, *Revelation 6-16*, WBC, vol. 52B, 401.

[269]In Greek mythology, the one who possesses the keys of ᾅδης is Hecate, a chthonian goddess. David E. Aune, "The Apocalypse of John and Greco-Roman Magic," *NTS* 33 (1987): 484-89; idem, *Revelation 1-5*, WBC, vol. 52A, 104.

[270]Alan Johnson, "Revelation," *EBC*, 428-29. Cf. Robert Mounce, *The Book of Revelation*, rev. ed. (Grand Rapids: Eerdmans, 1998), 61.

pagan Greek, contemporary Hellenistic Judaism or OT understanding. However, considering John's significant borrowing of OT concepts and imagery,[271] it is probable that ᾅδης here has an OT meaning: "grave," "pit," or a "place of the dead beneath the earth," especially when it is associated with death (see for example Ps 49:14; 55:15; 18:5; Prov 7:27; Isa 28:15; Hos 13:14).

Another occurrence of ᾅδης is in the context of the seven seals in Rev 6. The vision of the seven seals is an apocalyptic vision of John which portrays a very figurative description of the things that will take place after "these things" (Rev 4:1). The seven seals could be a figurative portrayal of the historical events that will happen from the time of John up to the time of the great day of the wrath of Him who sits on the throne and the Lamb (7:16-17). The rider on an ashen horse whose name is ὁ θάνατος καὶ ὁ ᾅδης[272] (6:8a) is just a personification of a historical situation or event. The event would be the death of a portion of humanity through sword, famine, and pestilence.[273]

Up to this point, there is no indication that John's idea of ᾅδης is similar to that of the Greek writers during his day. The "souls" or "lives" (ψυχὰς) that John saw are under the altar, not in ᾅδης (Rev 6:9). The imagery "under the altar" is most likely taken from OT sanctuary ritual wherein the blood of the sacrificial animal was poured out at the base of the altar of burnt offering (Lev 4:7; Exod 29:12).[274] The blood contains the life of the flesh (Lev 17:11). If this description is literal, it may have a similarity with a Rabbinic belief that "the souls of the righteous are kept under the throne of glory" (Shab. 152b).[275] However, the description in Rev 6:9 may still be understood as a figurative description of a historical event in the

---

[271]These imagery are the following: sanctuary or tabernacle and its furniture, fall of Babylon, Lamb, Gog and Magog, twelve tribes, blowing of trumpets, plagues, Exodus Motif, Sodom and Egypt, OT feasts, and many more.

[272]George Eldon Ladd suggests that ᾅδης here may mean "the underworld or the grave, and Hades accompanies Death to swallow up all those who are struck down by famine pestilence and by wild beasts." George Eldon Ladd, *A Commentary on the Revelation of John* (Grand Rapids: Eerdmans, 1972), 101.

[273]This is evident in the clause, "and authority was given to them over the fourth of the earth" (Rev 6:8b).

[274]Mounce, 146.

[275]Ibid., 147.

opening of the fifth seal (Rev 6:9-11). Alan Johnson may be right in saying that
ψυχὰι may stand "here for the actual lives or persons who were killed rather than
for their souls."[276] The case for a figurative interpretation is really very strong as
far as the context is concerned. The highly figurative nature of the seven seals is
already pointed out.[277]

The last two occurrences of ᾅδης are found in Rev 20:13-14. The passage
in which these two occurrences belong begins in v. 11 and ends in v. 15. The
events in this passage will occur after the one thousand years (Rev 20:1-6). The
one thousand years is the period after the *Parousia* (Rev 19:17-21).[278] In this
passage God is pictured sitting upon His throne and before Him all the dead of
the earth who are resurrected[279] stand (v. 12a). These dead include the wicked
people who died at the *Parousia* (19:21; 20:5). They are to be judged according
to what is written in the books (v. 12bc).

The wicked dead will be given up by the sea and by ὁ θάνατος καὶ ὁ ᾅδης
(20:13). The wicked dead will be resurrected out of any place they rest in death
whether at sea or at their graves or out of ᾅδης (cf. 20:5,6). It is significant to note
that if the belief that souls go to ᾅδης were biblical, then the souls of those who
died in the sea should have been in ᾅδης already.[280] Consequently, the statement,
"the sea gave up the dead which were in it" should not have been mentioned if
John believed that the souls of the dead were already in ᾅδης.

---

[276]A. Johnson, 475.

[277]Ladd comments, "Apocalyptic pictures are not meant to be photographs of objective facts; they are
often symbolic representations of almost unimaginable spiritual realities." Ladd, 102.

[278]This means that there is a chronological progression between Rev 19:17-21 and Rev 20:1-10. Some
scholars saw a recapitulation. See Alfredo G. Agustin Jr., "The Locus of the Millennial Reign of Christ and
His Saints in Rev 20:1-10," (M.A. thesis, Adventist International Institute of Advanced Studies, Silang, Cavite,
Philippines), 2002.

[279]This is the second resurrection. The first resurrection is the resurrection of the righteous (20:4).

[280]David Aune notes, "The popular belief that the souls of those who died at sea did not enter
Hades but remained where they died in the water is expressed in Achilles Tatius 5.16.2." David E. Aune,
Revelation 17-22, WBC, vol. 52C, 1103. However, there is no evidence that this belief was adapted by the
biblical Christian writers. There is even no evidence that this was adapted by the Jewish apocryphal and
pseudepigraphal writers.

This statement, then should be an argument against the popular belief that all the souls are detained in ᾅδης.

After the one thousand years subsequent to the *Parousia*, the resurrected wicked will be judged and thrown into the lake of fire (20:13,14). What is noteworthy is that ὁ θάνατος καὶ ὁ ᾅδης that will up the dead will also be thrown into the lake of fire. Obviously, this is once again a figurative way of expressing the final and complete destruction of the wicked and the total eradication of death and the grave.[281] It seems that 20:11-15 is a repetition of 20:7-10, though each of these two has different emphasis. Rev 20:7-10 emphasizes the final battle and the final destruction of the wicked, whereas 20:11-15 seem to emphasize God's final judgment of the wicked and their final destruction. There are several arguments and evidences that 20:7-10 and 20:11-15 refer to the same event with different emphasis.

Firstly, the wicked are killed at the *Parousia* (19:19-21), and they will be resurrected only after the one thousand years (20:5). But in 20:7 they are already alive, implying that the resurrection of 20:5 has already happened. It seems that 20:12-13 contains a detailed description of the resurrection stated in 20:5. If the nations in 20:7 are not the ones who are resurrected in 20:12-13, how come they are alive? It is clear that they are killed at the *Parousia* in 19:19-21, and they will not be resurrected until the one thousand years are past (20:5). Hence it is plausible to conclude that the wicked who are resurrected in 20:12-13 are the wicked who are gathered by Satan in 20:7-8.

Secondly, the Bible speaks only of two resurrections. The first resurrection is the resurrection of the righteous (20:4-6). Definitely, the second resurrection is the resurrection of the wicked after the one thousand years subsequent to the *Parousia* (20:5,12,13). If there is only one second resurrection, then 20:12,13 is the second resurrection. Thus, the wicked in 20:7 who are already alive are the ones whose resurrection takes place 20:12,13. Therefore, it is plausible to say

---

[281]Ranko Stefanovic, *Revelation of Jesus Christ* (Berrien Springs, MI: Andrews University Press, 2002), 570.

that 20:7-10 and 20:11-15 refer to the same event with different emphasis. If the two passages refer to the same event, then the destruction of the wicked including Satan in 20:9-10 is just repeatedly described in 20:14-15. However, it seems that the description of the destruction of Satan in v. 10 and the destruction of the wicked in v. 15 are figurative. There are several arguments to show that these are figurative:

1. The description of a fire coming down from heaven can be the one that is generally literal. The literal raining of fire is not strange in the Scripture. There are several instances where fire rained down from heaven. The first is the Sodom and Gomorrah story (Gen 19). The second is in Job 1:16 where it says, "The fire of God fell from heaven and burned up the sheep and the servants, and consumed them." The third is in 2 Kgs 1:10,12 where the soldiers sent by king Ahab to capture Elijah were consumed by fire that came down from heaven. Apostle Peter, also in literal language, expresses the destruction of the wicked by a literal fire compared to the literal flood of Noah's day (2 Pet 3:6,7,10,12).

2. The expression "lake of fire" may be figurative because the throwing of ὁ᾽ θάνατος καὶ ὁ ᾅδης into it is obviously figurative. If θάνατος καὶ ὁ ᾅδης are figurative, then the "lake of fire" is also figurative. Ranko Stefanovic may be right when he states, "The lake of fire is not a literal everlasting burning hell, but rather a metaphorical expression describing complete destruction of the wicked (Mat 10:28)."[282] This means that the throwing of Satan (20:10), the beast and false prophets (19:20), and anyone whose name is not found in the book of life (20:15) into the lake of fire is figurative which literally may mean total and complete destruction.

3. It is also evident that the portrayal of θάνατος καὶ ὁ ᾅδης is figurative as in Rev 6:8. Hence, when the rest of the dead (wicked) are resurrected (second resurrection) and judged to suffer the second death in the fire, simultaneously, θάνατος καὶ ὁ ᾅδης will be destroyed.[283] It may mean that θάνατος καὶ ὁ ᾅδης

---

[282] Ibid., 570. Cf. Ladd, 274.

[283] Apostle Paul also mentions that the last enemy is death (1 Cor 15:26), and it will be swallowed up in victory when our mortal body will be clothed with immortality (1 Cor 15:54).

will no longer receive the dead to be kept until another time of the judgment (see 2 Pet 3:9), since the final judgment has come and the wicked are finally destroyed.   Besides, the righteous are already raised to life and clothed with immortality.   Although the final and complete destruction of Satan, the beast, the false prophets, and all their wicked adherents is evident (20:9),[284] yet the next verse seems to suggest an eternal torment in the lake of fire (20:10).   However, we already pointed out that the expression "lake of fire" is not literal but figurative.   If this is literal, we are definite that this is not the eternal burning of souls in ᾅδης since θάνατος καὶ ὁ ᾅδης are themselves destroyed by the lake of fire.   Besides, the wicked are not souls but resurrected dead.

Although ᾅδης is always associated with θάνατος in the book of Revelation, it is often expressed in figurative language.   It may mean "grave" or "the place of the dead beneath the earth."   This is evident, as pointed out above, especially when θάνατος καὶ ὁ ᾅδης are said to give up the dead.   It literally signifies the resurrection of the dead.   This is also evident in the figurative statement that θάνατος καὶ ὁ ᾅδης will be thrown into the lake of fire.   The throwing of θάνατος καὶ ὁ ᾅδης may mean the complete destruction of the wicked in the fire (20:14).

ᾅδης in Josephus

Josephus[285] mentions that people in his milieu had a prevalent idea that ᾅδης is located below the earth, and the dead (probably their souls) went down to it.[286]   Josephus, in relating how the Essenes were tortured by the Roman soldiers during the Jewish war with the Romans in approximately A.D. 66-70, tells us that the Essenes believed that the body was corruptible but the soul was immortal and imperishable.[287]   Josephus, however, says that they shared this belief with

---

[284]The Greek word kate,fagen (katephagen) is the 2 aorist third person form of the present first person form of κατεσθίω (katesthiô)which means "to consume" (Rev 11:5), or "to eat up or to devour" (Matt 13:4). Wesley J. Perschbacher, *The New Analytical Greek Lexicon* (*NAGL*) (Peabody, MA: Hendrickson, 1990), s.v. "katesqi,w."

[285]Josephus was born on A.D. 37 and died after A.D. 97.

[286]Josephus *The Jewish War* 1.30.6 (trans. Thackeray, LCL, 1:282-85).

[287]Josephus *The Jewish War* 2.8.11 (LCL, 2:380-83).

the Greeks. He describes further that the Essenes believed that the souls of the righteous would go to an abode beyond the ocean where they would be refreshed by a gentle breath of the west wind. In contrast, the souls of the wicked would be punished forever in a tempestuous dungeon.[288] Similar to this is the belief of the Greeks, says Josephus, that the souls of their demigods[289] would go to the isles of the blessed, while the souls of the wicked would be punished in ᾅδης.[290]

Josephus himself believes that when men die, if they were spotless and obedient according to the Law, their souls "are allotted the most holy place in heaven."[291] But for the wicked and perverse, "the darker regions of the netherworld [ᾅδης] receive their souls."[292] However, in one passage, Josephus relates that Samuel was brought out of ᾅδης by the witch of Endor.[293] Judging from these descriptions, there seems to be a contradiction between the two immediate accounts above. Since Samuel was a righteous man, his soul should have descended from heaven instead of ascending from ᾅδης. Moreover, the idea that Samuel came from ᾅδης may still reflect a Jewish belief reflected in 1 En 22 and in Luke 16:19-31, where the righteous and the wicked reside, but are separated from each other.

---

[288]Ibid., (LCL, 2:382-83). Josephus also notes that the Pharisees also believed that "the souls of the wicked suffer eternal punishment." Ibid., 2.8.14 (LCL, 2:384-85). He also states that the Sadducees did not believe that souls persist after death or suffer punishment in ᾅδης. Ibid., (LCL, 2:386-87).

[289]These are brave men and war heroes.

[290]Josephus *The Jewish War* 2.8.11 (LCL, 2:382-83).

[291]Josephus *The Jewish War* 3.8.5 (LCL, 3:680-81).

[292]Ibid.

[293]Josephus *Jewish Antiquities* 6.14.2 (trans. Thackeray, LCL, 6:332-33).

The Concept of Ἅδης in the Babylonian Talmud

In the Babylonian Talmud,[294] *gehenna* seems to be a general term that has several meanings. It refers to שְׁאוֹל (Er. 19a).[295] Other meanings mentioned are "destruction,"[296] "pit" or "pit of destruction," "tumultuous pit," "miry clay," "shadow of death," and the "underworld" (Er. 131; cf. BB. 79a).[297]

One passage in the Talmud tells of a father advising his son to do well according to his ability, the reason being that in שְׁאוֹל [298] (Er. 54a) there is no more enjoyment (Er. 54a).[299] This may indicate a belief in a continued existence of a person's soul or spirit after death, though it has no joy or happiness. However, in another passage, a Rabbi tells his fellow Rabbi that the world of the dead is like a wedding feast (Er. 54a)[300] indicating a belief in an enjoyment in the afterlife.

Another idea in Talmud that is similar to the OT is that *gehenna*, the generic name for שְׁאוֹל, is described as a deep pit (Shab. 33a).[301] In the immediate subsequent discussions, *gehenna* is portrayed as the place of punishment of the wicked (Git. 7a-7b),[302] but the wicked would be punished only for twelve months (Shab. 33b).[303] *Gehenna* is also portrayed as burning with fire (Shab. 39a),[304] with

---

[294]The Babylonian Talmud was written between the third century C.E. and fifth century C.E. See H. L. Strack and G. Stemberger, *Introduction to the Talmud and Midrash*, trans. Markus Bockmuehl (Edinburgh: T. & T. Clark, 1991), 211-12. However, the Jewish oral tradition began probably in second century B.C.E. See ibid., 70.

[295]Translated as netherworld in this English version of the Talmud. The author, Rabbi Joshua ben Levi, when citing a proof of the netherworld from Scripture, points to a passage in Jonah which tells about the experience of Jonah in the belly of the fish. Israel W. Slotski, *Erubin* (London: Soncino, 1938), 131.

[296]The author cites Ps 88:12. In Ps 88:12, destruction is synonymous with death.

[297]Slotski, *Erubin*, 131. In another passage, lAav. and Gehenna are the same, and are synonymous with Shades (*Refaim*). Israel W. Slotski, *Baba Bathra* (London: Soncino, 1935), 319.

[298]In this context, lAav. may mean grave. The subsequent sentence talks about the grave. Slotski, *Erubin*, 375.

[299]Ibid.

[300]Ibid.

[301]H. Freedman, *Shabbath* (London: Soncino, 1938), 153.

[302]Maurice Simon, *Gittin* (London: Soncino, 1936), 24.

[303]Freedman, *Shabbath*, 157.

[304]Ibid., 182. Cf. Slotski, *Erubin*, 129; H. Freedman, *Baba Mezia* (London: Soncino, 1935), 489.

Satan as its prince (BM. 85a-85b).[305] The Jews of the Talmud also believed that
the wicked descended to *gehenna* (BM. 85a-85b),[306] hence, *gehenna* is the place
for those already judged (Er. 18a-18b).[307]

It seems that the Jews believed that the punishment of the wicked in *gehenna*
would start even before the final day of judgment. The wicked began to suffer
the moment they descend to *gehenna*, but would rest from punishment during
Sabbath.[308] Furthermore, the souls of the wicked would not return to their sheath
or body.[309] They would suffer in the fire of *gehenna* in the world to come, while
the righteous would be enjoying life in the world to come.[310] When the wicked
suffer in the fire of *gehenna* after the judgment at the last day, their souls will melt
away, that is, they would be annihilated.[311]

Gehenna is also called hell, the place for the wicked. It is a place where
Korah and his allies descended to (BB. 172a).[312] One Rabbi taught that the earth
that opened and devoured Korah and his allies was the mouth of *gehenna* (BB.
74a-74b).[313] He explicitly states that *gehenna* existed already in the time of Israel's
sojourn in the wilderness (BB. 172b-173a).[314] It is evident here that *gehenna* is
a place designated for the wicked even before the last-day judgment. This also
indicates that *gehenna* is synonymous to lAav. (HB) or ἅδης (LXX), which occur
in Num 14. Furthermore, *gehenna* is believed to be one of the seven things God

---

[305]Freedman, *Baba Mezia*, 502.

[306]Cf. ibid., 349.

[307]Slotski, 125-26. Gehenna is always associated with the judgment. Cf. Israel W. Slotski, *Yebamoth*
(London: Soncino, 1936), 705-06.

[308]H. Freedman, *Sanhedrin* (London: Soncino, 1935), 446. Cf. ibid., 765; idem, *Kiddushin* (London:
Soncino, 1936), 197.

[309]This is "dualism." It may be an evidence of the influence of Greek philosophy.

[310]Freedman, *Sanhedrin*, 739.

[311]Slotski, *Baba Bathra*, 318.

[312]Ibid., 753.

[313]According to another Talmud passage, Korah and his allies seem to be conscious in *gehenna*. Every
thirty days, *gehenna* causes them to turn back near the top of the pit that swallowed them in order to say,
"Moses and his law are truth and we are liars." Ibid., 294.

[314]Ibid., 757.

created before creating the rest of the world (Pes. 38b).[315] Its fire was created at

the eve of the Sabbath (Pes. 38b).[316] Like the OT, שְׁאוֹל is believed to have a gate

(Yeb. 21b-22a),[317]

and its entrance is believed to be in the valley of Hinnom near Jerusalem (Suk.

32b).[318]

In the Talmud, *gehenna* is also synonymous with the grave. This is evident

when it suggests that the corrupt judges (Exod 21:22) are consigned to *gehenna*,

and that they will not ascend from their grave in the future world.[319] The passage

again implies that *gehenna* already exists before the last-day judgment.

It is observed that in some occurrences in the Talmud, *gehenna* is often

associated with the wicked. The wicked descend to *gehenna* when they die.[320]

However, in one passage, the idea emerges that the souls of the righteous also

descend to *gehenna* but they will be delivered by God from the fiery furnace of

gehenna.

Ἅδης in Other Greco-Roman Writers

According to Dio Chrysostom,[321] a man named Heracles who was sent to

Ἅιδης.[322] He also tells the story of Odysseus who went to Ἅιδης.[323] Odysseus met

---

[315]The other six are the following: (1) the Torah, (2) Repentance, (3) Garden of Eden, (4) the Throne of Glory, (5) the Temple, and (6) the name Messiah. H. Freedman, *Pesahim* (London: Soncino, 1938), 265.

[316]Ibid.

[317]Slotski, *Yebamoth*, 129. See idem, *Baba Bathra*, 343.

[318]Israel W. Slotski, *Sukkah* (London: Soncino, 1938), 142.

[319]Freedman, *Sanhedrin*, 765.

[320]Cf. Freedman, *Baba Mezia*, 349, 351, 477; idem, *Sanhedrin*, 749; idem, *Kiddushin*, 423.

[321]He lived between c. A.D. 40-c. A.D. 120.

[322]Dio Chrysostom *Discourses* 4.47.4 (trans. Crosby, LCL, 4:248-49). Here, Dio Chrysostom used the word Ἅidhj.

[323]Dio Chrysostom most likely had Homer's story in mind. Dio Chrysostom *Discourses* 1.4.37 (LCL, 1:184-85). The form that occurs here is ᾅδου. This form is genitive case in Koine Greek (the Greek of the NT) but here the context shows that this is a dative case. This form is already similar with the NT and LXX forms. Chrysostom uses the word ᾅδης instead of Ἅιδης which is used by Plato. Apparently, this is a contract form of

Agamemnon, the hero in Trojan war at the gates of ῞Αιδης.[324]   Dio Chrysostom also describes the suffering of the wicked in ῞Αιδης.   He mentions Tantalus who dreads of a rock which sways over his head in ῞Αιδης.[325]   Plutarch mentions the descent of Odysseus to the house of ῞Αιδης in the underworld to consult the seer (cf. Homer *Odyssey*, 4.37).[326] He also mentions several significant beliefs and practices in relation to ῞Αιδης.   Plutarch[327] recounts that people put white robes on the dead and mourners also wore white dresses,[328] the purpose being to array themselves against the powers of darkness and ῞Αιδης.[329] They also clothed the dead in white in order to send forth his soul to ῞Αιδης pure and bright.[330]   In Plutarch, it is also noted that ῞Ερως (Eros) "love" is the only thing that ῞Αιδης obeys, so that "celebrants of Love's mysteries have a higher place in Hades."[331] It was even believed that "lovers are able to return to the light even from ῞Αιδης."[332] It is clear that ῞Αιδης and Tartaroj[333] are associated with each other and may refer to the same place.[334]   It is also to be noted that the good were believed to be conveyed to Elysium's plain after death and "there continue to lead a life most easy to be sure though not blessed or divine until their second death."[335] They would

---

῞Αιδης.

[324]Dio Crysostom *Discourses* 5.74.18-19 (LCL, 5:227).

[325]Dio Crysostom *Discourses* 1.6.55 (LCL, 1:278). Here, Chrysostom uses the word ῞Aidhj.

[326]Plutarch *Moralia* (On Being Busy Body) 516 (trans. Helmbold, LCL, 6:476). The form that occurs here is ῞Aidouj; this is a dative case. Plutarch uses this word to refer to the god of the underworld but is always associated with the word "house" which may refer to the "underworld."

[327]He lived between c. A.D. 45-A.D. 120.

[328]Plutarch *Moralia* (The Roman Questions) 270 (trans. Babbit, LCL, 4:47).

[329]Ibid.

[330]Ibid.

[331]Plutarch *Moralia* (The Dialogue on Love) 761 (trans. Minar, Sandbach, Helmbold, LCL, 9.383). ῞Aidou in this context refers to the underworld.

[332]Ibid.

[333]It has been called Tartaroj because of its coldness. Plutarch *Moralia* (The Principle of Cold) 948 (trans. Cherniss and Helmbold, LCL, 12:247).

[334]Plutarch *Moralia* (The Face of the Moon) 940 (LCL, 12:181).

[335]Ibid., 942 (LCL, 12:189).

enjoy the gentlest part of the air, known as "the meads of Hades," which would eventually blow away their impurities accumulated from the body.[336] However, the "unjust and licentious souls pay penalties for their offences."[337] Furthermore, there is a conflicting belief in that the side of the moon that faces heaven is called "Elysian Plain," while the side that faces the earth is called "House of counter-terrestrial Persephone."[338] Plutarch also relates a fabulous story of two gods who fight and make war with each other for thousands of years but finally tells of the annihilation of Ἀιδης.[339] This annihilation of Ἀιδης enables human beings to live happily and peacefully.[340] In this mythology, Zeus and his allies are considered the good gods, while Ἀιδης and his allies are the evil gods.[341] It is to be noted that "Osiris" is the Egyptian name of Ἀιδης, the king of the underworld.[342] The souls who are set free migrate into the realm of Ἀιδης,[343] who then becomes their king.[344] Furthermore, it is evident in Plutarch that the Greeks believed that if the dead did not have a burial, their souls would not join with those in Ἀιδης but would wander around in a no-man's land.[345] Plutarch also cites Homer's literary work as a basis for a belief in the consciousness of souls in Ἀιδης. Hence, it is evident that Homer became the basis for several Greek writers especially

---

[336]Ibid., 943 (LCL, 12:201).

[337]Ibid.

[338] Ibid., 944 (LCL, 12:207-11).

[339]This story is similar to the one mentioned in Rev 20:14-15.

[340]Plutarch *Moralia* (Isis and Osiris) 370 (trans. Babbit, LCL, 5:115). Plutarch used the form Ἀidhj to refer to the underworld.

[341]Ibid., (LCL, 5:116-17). The form used by Plutarch in reference to the underworld is the same as the name of the god of the underworld. Both usages are in the same context which means that this form is used by Plutarch interchangeably.

[342]Ibid., 382 (LCL, 5:183).

[343]See Plutarch *Moralia* (Table-Talk) 745 (LCL, 9:279); idem, *Moralia* (Dialogue on Love) 765 (LCL, 9:403). It is also translated as the "realm of death." It is the same as "the realm of Pluto." Ibid., 758 (LCL, 9:359).

[344]Plutarch *Moralia* (Isis and Osiris) 383 (LCL, 5:183).

[345]Plutarch *Moralia* (Table-Talk) 740 (LCL, 9:247).

regarding the description of "Αιδης.[346]

Several thematic and conceptual parallels seem to exist between the descriptions of "Αιδης in both the parable of the rich man and Lazarus in Luke (16:19-31) and the story of Micyllus and Megapenthes in the writings of Lucian of Samosata.[347] First, both stories describe the contrast in the lives of the poor and that of the rich on earth and in "Αιδης. On earth, the rich man and Megapenthes were enjoying a very luxurious life (Luke 16:19; Lucian *Cat.*16-17), while the poor men, Lazarus and Micyllus, were suffering from hunger (Luke 16:20-21; Lucian *Cat.*15). Second, both Lazarus and Micyllus were desiring just to taste a very sumptuous food of the rich men (Luke 16:21; Lucian *Cat.*16). Third, in both stories, there is a reversal of their situations in "Αιδης. Contrary to their situations on earth, here, both the poor men were enjoying the afterlife in "Αιδης, while rich men were suffering. Micyllus was laughing on the journey to "Αιδης (Lucian *Cat.*17) and finally resided in the island of the blest (Lucian *Cat.*25). On the other hand, Megapenthes was lamenting on the journey to "Αιδης (Lucian *Cat.*20), and finally was punished by refusing him a drink of the water from Lethe and by binding him with fetters for his wickedness on earth (Lucian *Cat.*28). Similarly, Lazarus was enjoying a blessed rest in the bosom of Abraham (Luke 16:22) while the rich man was agonizing in the flame, and was also refused the cooling of his tongue by the finger of Lazarus dipped in the water (Luke 16:23-24). In both stories, the requests of both rich men were refused. Megapenthes wanted to personally return to earth to finish some unfinished business (Lucian *Cat.*8-13), while the rich man requested Abraham to let Lazarus return to earth to warn his five brothers (Luke 16:27-28).

However, there are conceptual and thematic contrasts between these two stories. First, in Lucian, the souls of the dead are transported by Hermes to "Αιδης, riding in a boat across a river (Lucian *Cat.* 17-21). In Luke, Lazarus is carried away by the angels to the bosom of Abraham and the rich man immediately finds himself in "Αιδης (Luke 16:22-23). Second, in Lucian, the souls of the dead are

[346]Cf. Ibid., 743 (LCL, 9:269).

[347]Lucian *Cataplous—The Downward Journey or the Tyrant* (trans. Harmon, LCL, 2:3-49).

judged upon arrival in Ἅιδης. The soul of the rich man is punished while that of the poor is rewarded (Lucian *Cat.* 23-29). In Luke, however, the rich man already suffers punishment in the fire without any explicit judgment (Luke 16:23-24). Third, the punishments in both stories are different. In Lucian, Megapenthes is simply bound with fetters, and is not allowed to drink water (Lucian *Cat.* 28-29). In Luke, the rich man is tortured in the fire (Luke 16:23).

In another writing, Lucian tells of some men who testify to those who do not believe that the souls of people really exist in Ἅιδης. Lucian tells of a man who once in his life saw a giant creature in the woods who, by stamping on the ground, made a great and deep chasm into the ground. Immediately after that, the man saw Ἅιδης at the bottom of the deep chasm. In Ἅιδης, the man saw the river of blazing fire, the lake, and the souls of the dead who lay in the asphodel to let the time pass away with their friends and kinsmen.[348] Another man testifies that when he was sick, he was taken to Ἅιδης and there he saw some known figures like Tantalus and Pluto. He was allowed to return to earth because his time to die had not yet come.[349] In addition, another man testifies that the soul of his wife came back from Ἅιδης and appeared to him.[350] All these men testify in order to persuade some men who do not believe on the existence of spirits and souls of the dead.[351]

In another writing, Lucian relates the story of a man named Mennipus who, by the help of a Babylonian magician, descended to Ἅιδης alive and returned to the earth. Ἅιδης, as described by Mennipus, has gates with guards.[352] The

---

[348]Lucian *The Lover of Lies* 24 (LCL, 3:354-57). In this passage the form that occurs is Ἅιδου which is a dative case in the context. It refers to the underworld. See also idem, *Menippus or the Descent into* Ἅιδης 8 (LCL, 4:86) for another dative case of this form.

[349]Lucian *The Lover of Lies* 25 (LCL, 3:359). The form that occurs here is Ἅιδην which seems to be in the dative case. Again it speaks of the underworld.

[350]Ibid., 27 (LCL, 3:361, 363).

[351]Ibid., 29 (LCL, 3:365).

[352]Lucian *Menippus* 6,8 (LCL, 4:82-87). The form that occurs in this passage is Ἅιδου in the genitive case. In some passages in Lucian, this form is dative as noted above. In this context, it speaks of the underworld.

king of the underworld is called *Aïdoneus*.[353] He also saw the Lake, the river of burning fire, and the palace of Pluto.[354] He also rode in the ferry boat carrying the dead who were groaning.[355] He even saw the souls of the dead lining up the court of Minos waiting to be prosecuted.[356] After judging the dead, Minos would send them to the place of the wicked to be punished in proportion to their crimes.[357] Mennipus and the magician went to the place of punishment and saw people small and great being roasted in the fire.[358] At last they came to a plain called Acherusian[359] where the demigods live together with the dead.[360]

Ἅδης in the Apocryphal New Testament

In the apocryphal book "The Pilate Cycle," a story is told about Christ's descent to Hades. In the story, Joseph, probably of Arimathaea, tells the high priests that what is marvelous with Jesus' resurrection is that He was not raised alone, but with the other dead men who appeared in Jerusalem. Two of these men tell the details of how Jesus raised the dead from the realm of Hades. According to the testimony, when Jesus descended to Hades between His death on Friday and His resurrection on Sunday, He broke the gates and bars of Hades and resurrected Adam, Abraham, John the Baptist, and all the souls of the saints. Furthermore, there is a detailed description of the conversation between saints like Isaiah and David concerning their prophecies whose fulfillment is evident already in Hades. There is also a detailed conversation between Satan and Hades on how to prevent Jesus from entering the realm of Hades. However, they find out that they are unable to resist the power of the King of Glory who invaded Hades. Christ was

---

[353]Ibid., 10 (LCL, 4:89). This is probably another version of the name Ἀϊδης, the god of the underworld. Here he is called the king of the dead.

[354]Ibid.

[355]Ibid., 10-11 (LCL, 4:89-90).

[356]Ibid., 11 (LCL, 4:90).

[357]Ibid., 12 (LCL, 4:93).

[358]Ibid., 14 (LCL, 4:95).

[359]This is probably the place of the virtuous dead.

[360]Lucian *Menippus* 15 (LCL, 4:97).

able to set the prisoners of Hades free because of His death on the cross.[361]

It is evident that many, if not all, of the early Christians believed that the souls of the dead saints were also imprisoned in Hades. They further held the belief that when Jesus died and descended to Hades, He sets those saints free by resurrecting them.

In the apocryphal Apocalypse of Paul,[362] apostle Paul is said to have been caught up to the third heaven, where he was shown many things. Paul was shown that the souls of both the just and the sinners depart from their bodies when they die. At death, the soul of a person was led by an angel into the presence of God in heaven for judgment. When God found him to be just, He would command an angel to hand over the soul to Michael, the angel of the Covenant, and the soul was led into Paradise of joy. This soul would return to his body at the resurrection (v. 14).[363] Moreover, the fate of the soul of the sinner was also shown to Paul. When the soul of the sinner entered heaven, he was brought into the presence of God for judgment. When God found him to be wicked and unrepentant, the soul would be handed over to the angel Tartaruchus, the angel in charge of the punishment of the sinner, who would then cast the sinful soul into utter darkness where there is weeping and gnashing of teeth. This soul would stay there until the great day of judgment (v. 16). In the subsequent passage, the soul of a sinner after facing God in His judgment throne was delivered to Tartarus, who led the soul down into hell, into the lower prison. The soul will be put in torments till the great day of judgment (vv. 17-18). An angel led Paul to the different places of souls. The place of punishment was also shown to him. The souls of the wicked are already being punished in the fire in deep pits called Abyss while waiting for the great day of judgment in the last days (vv. 31-44).

---

[361]J. K. Elliott, *The Apocryphal New Testament,* trans. M. R. James (Oxford: Clarendon, 1993), 185-90.

[362]The origin of this literature was likely in Greek written about mid-third century. This was responsible for the spread of many popular ideas about heaven and hell throughout Christianity. Ibid., 616. Hugo Duensing and Aurelio de Santos Otero suggest that this work is to be dated between the end of the fourth century and the beginning of the fifth century. Hugo Duensing and Aurelio de Santos Otero, "Apocalypse of Paul," in *New Testament Apocrypha,* ed. Wilhelm Schneemelcher and R. McL. Wilson (Louisville, KY: Westminster John Knox, 2003), 696.

[363]J. K. Elliott, 624-25.

῾Ἅδης **in the Early Church Fathers**

Clement of Alexandria,[364] in his writings *The Stromata*, states that Jesus Christ at His death descended to Hades. There, He preached the Gospel to all the souls of men, both the Hebrews and the Gentiles, especially to those who died before the first advent of the Lord.[365] Clements cites 1 Pet 3:19,20; Ps 16:9-11; Acts 2:26-28 in support of his view.

Hippolytus[366] seems to associate שְׁאוֹל, which he refers to as ᾅδης in the context, with Τάρταρος, a dark place which is located in a doleful locality.[367] Furthermore, he seems to equate "grave" with ᾅδης when he says that the latter does not cease to receive the souls of unrighteous men.[368] He also argues in his commentary on Luke 23 that Jesus' soul entered Hades at His death, and that the warders trembled upon seeing Him.[369] In his discourse against Plato, he likewise describes Hades as a place where the souls of both the righteous and the unrighteous are detained. It is located beneath the earth. It is a dark place, and angels are stationed as guards punishing the wicked according to their deeds. Within ᾅδης, there is a lake of unquenchable fire, a place where the wicked, who will be sentenced in the day of judgment, will suffer endless punishment.[370] The righteous, however, are not in the same place with the unrighteous in Hades. The righteous are led by an angel to the place in Hades which is full of light. There, the righteous souls dwell from the beginning. That locality is neither so hot nor cold. It is called the bosom of Abraham. However, to the left, angels in charge of punishment drag the wicked to their own place where they are punished.[371]

Arnobius also assumes that ᾅδης is the place of punishment for the wicked.

[364]He lived between A.D. 153-217.

[365]Clement of Alexandria *Stromata* 6.6 (ANF, 2:490-91).

[366]Hippolytus wrote from the third century.

[367]Hippolytus *Fragments from Commentaries* (trans. Salmond, ANF, 5:174).

[368]Ibid.

[369]Ibid., (ANF, 5:194).

[370]Hippolytus *The Extant Works and Fragments* (ANF, 5:221).

[371]Ibid., (ANF, 5:222).

He also calls it Tartarus, a place of darkness, of rivers of fire, and of marshes with miry abysses. He also believes that the souls or spirits of men are imperishable.[372] In the late third and early fourth century, Victorinus, in his commentary on the Apocalypse of John 6:9, said that the souls under the altar are the souls in Hades, which is beneath the earth. It is a place where the souls of the wicked are punished in the fire and where the souls of the saints repose.[373]

Summary

This summary section first highlights the commonalities between *ANET*, Homer, Plato, OT–LXX version, OT Apocrypha, OT Pseudepigrapha, Dead Sea Scrolls, Philo, NT (aside from Synoptic Gospels and Acts), Josephus, Babylonian Talmud, Other Greco-Roman writers, NT Apocrypha, and Early Church Fathers. The second section highlights their differences.

Commonalities

There are several commonalities among these literature which range from the second millennium B.C. up to the third or fourth centuries of the Christian era. These commonalities are the following:

1. Overwhelmingly, all these literature agree that ᾅδης or שְׁאוֹל is located beneath the earth. It is also called "death," "grave," "pit," or "deep pit."

2. It is described as dark and gloomy. It has gates with gatekeepers. It is the place where the souls of the dead are imprisoned.

3. All these literature concur, except for the OT–LXX and NT, that some gods are in charge of the underworld. In *ANET,* these are *Gilgamesh, Ereskigal,* and Osiris. In Greek literature these are Ἅιδης or ᾅδης who is also called Pluto and Περσεφονείης (Persephone).

4. Many of these literature also are in unison in stating that the dead are conscious in ᾅδης.

---

[372]Arnobius *Against the Heathen* 2.29 (trans. Bryce, ANF, 6:445).

[373]Victorinus *Commentary on the Apocalypse of John* (trans. Wallis, ANF, 7:351).

5. Majority of these literature also indicate that immediately after death the souls of the dead are transported to ᾅδης and there face the judge in the underworld. After their judgment, the souls will be separated spatially in ᾅδης. The wicked will suffer some sort of punishment, while the righteous will enjoy the afterlife in a place of blissfulness.

6. The most common agent of punishment in ᾅδης among these literature is fire. The idea of a burning ᾅδης is the most common concept among these literature except for the OT and NT.

7. Majority of these literature show that both the righteous and the wicked are held in ᾅδης at death. Nevertheless, they are separated from each other.

8. In majority of these literature, there is always a story about a human being or a goddess (in *ANET*) who entered ᾅδης but was able to escape it and return to the land of the living. According to NT Apocrypha, Jesus Christ entered ᾅδης at His death and delivered some righteous individuals from it and brought them to life with Him.

Differences

1. The form ᾅδης is used in LXX, OT Apocrypha and Pseudepigrapha, NT and, most likely also, in NT Apocrypha and Early Church Fathers, whereas in Greco-Roman literature, the form Ἅιδης is commonly used. In the Babylonian Talmud, the term most frequently used is *gehenna* instead of ᾅδης.

2. *ANET* and Greco-Roman literature always describe ᾅδης as being ruled by an evil god. In the OT, there is no such god who rules שְׁאוֹל or ᾅδης.

3. In all Jewish and Christian literature, including the OT, there is a uniform belief that ᾅδης or שְׁאוֹל is just a temporary place for the righteous dead. It is reflected in the lexical meaning of the word שְׁאוֹל and in the contexts of its occurrences. There is an overwhelming idea that God will deliver them from ᾅδης or שְׁאוֹל. They will be resurrected in the last day and will receive eternal life. They will also live in the new heaven and new earth with a glorified body.

In all Greco-Roman literature, however, ᾄδης is a permanent place both for the good souls and for the bad souls. They are immediately judged and separated from each other. The good souls reside in a blissful and peaceful place, whereas the bad souls are punished in the fiery place.

4. In extra-biblical Jewish literature, the wicked also suffer in a fire before the day of judgment. After the judgment in the last day, they will suffer for eternity in ᾄδης or γέεννα, whereas in the OT and NT (except Luke 16:19-31), the righteous and the wicked remain silent in ᾄδης. The OT even explicitly say that the dead are unconscious in שְׁאוֹל. There is no explicit description in OT and NT about the suffering of the wicked souls in the fire or the enjoyment of the righteous souls in a blissful place in ᾄδης. In the NT, the judgment will be at the last day. After the judgment the wicked will suffer in the fire of γέεννα rather than ᾄδης because ᾄδης itself will be burned in the lake of fire. The wicked will not suffer in the fire for eternity.

5. Unlike the Greco-Roman literature, the OT, NT, extra-biblical Jewish and Christian literature agree that the judgment will take place in the last day. In Greco-Roman literature, the souls of the dead are judged immediately upon arrival in ᾄδης. In Jewish and Christian literature, the judgment takes place at the last day.

6. Both the Greco-Roman literature and extra-biblical Jewish and Christian literature overwhelmingly indicate that souls are conscious in ᾄδης, whereas the OT and NT, except for some figurative and metaphorical portrayal, show that souls are unconscious in ᾄδης or שְׁאוֹל.

7. Unlike Greco-Roman, and extra-biblical Jewish and Christian literature, OT and NT (except Luke 16:19-31) do not literally indicate a fire burning in שְׁאוֹל or ᾄδης which tortures the souls of the wicked. OT and NT also do not say that the wicked are already enjoying in a blissful place in ᾄδης.

8. Unlike in Greco-Roman literature, OT, NT, and some Jewish extra-biblical literature express the idea that ᾄδης or שְׁאוֹל is synonymous with θάνατος or מָוֶת.

9. Ἅδης also parallels grave in the OT and in some Jewish extra-biblical literature, unlike the Greco-Roman literature.

10. In the OT and NT (except Luke 16:19-31), there is no mention of separation between the righteous and the wicked in ἅδης. On the contrary,

Greco-Roman and Jewish-Christian extra-biblical literature uniformly refer to a separation between them.

11. In majority of these literature, both Greco-Romans and Jewish-Christians describe the place of punishment and the place of refreshment which are just adjacent to each other in ἅδης. However, the OT and NT (except Luke 16:19-31) do not say anything about these places in ἅδης. The wicked and righteous souls are not separated; rather, both are asleep in the dust or in the grave and are unconscious.

12. The OT and other Jewish literature often describe שְׁאוֹל or ἅδης in a figurative way. They describe the separation of a righteous man from his God as a שְׁאוֹל -like experience. They both describe a troubled life of the righteous person as a שְׁאוֹל -like experience. This idea is not found in Greco-Roman literature.

13. In some Jewish extra-biblical literature in the NT period, there is already a belief that the souls of the righteous go to heaven. This belief is absent from the OT, inter-testamental Jewish literature, and from NT.

14. Chronologically, in the pagan literature of *ANET* and Greco-Romans from the second millennium B.C. up to the fourth century A.D., the idea is always consistent that the souls of men are conscious at death. They are carried into the underworld or ἅδης. In the OT, NT, and Jewish-Christian literature, a different picture obtains. The OT speaks of the whole person going down to שְׁאוֹל at death. When the OT speaks of a dead person in שְׁאוֹל, it does not speak of him as soul but as dead. In the inter-testamental period, contrary to the OT, the Jews, like the Greeks, began to believe that souls are conscious in שְׁאוֹל or ἅδης. At the time of the NT, the Jews continued to hold the belief that the souls of the righteous and

the wicked are detained in ᾅδης before the final judgment. In the NT biblical literature (except Luke 16:19-31), there are no explicit statements or teachings from Jesus and the apostles that souls are conscious in ᾅδης. The rest of the NT is clear that the punishment and reward of the wicked and righteous will be given at the last day.

THE GENERAL BACKGROUND AND THE STRUCTURAL-THEMATIC ANALYSIS OF LUKE'S GOSPEL AND ACTS

THIS chapter discusses (1) the general historical background of the book of Luke, and (2) the structural-thematic analysis of the book, Luke's travel narrative, and Luke 16. In the section on the general historical background of the book of Luke, the issues on authorship, date, purpose, general theme, provenance, and recipients will be discussed.[374] In the structural-thematic analysis, the general structure and theme of the book will also be dealt with. Finally, the structures and themes of Luke's travel narrative and Luke 16 will be considered.[375]

The General Historical Background of the Gospel of Luke

In this section, the general historical backgrounds will be discussed. It includes the author and recipients, date and provenance, genre, purpose, and general themes of Luke.

---

[374]It is very important to establish the genuineness of the apostolicity of the author because of the proliferation of pseudo-gospels especially the gnostic gospels. The demand to establish these historical data is even increased because of the challenge of the historical-critical method especially in the history of the writing of the document.

[375]These steps are taken in this study because of the presupposition that the author, though writing the history of Jesus' life, has an authorial intent and theological focus in portraying Jesus' life to his audience. This means that the book may have structural-thematic patterns that would give hint to the author's theological emphases.

Author and Recipient(s)

The author of the gospel of Luke, like the other gospel writers, does not provide us with the details about himself. However, in the introduction of the book, the author claims to have received an account of the story of the life of Jesus from the disciples.[376] In other words, the author is a contemporary of the disciples (v. 1). He is a first century believer who has a direct or firsthand access to the eyewitnesses or to the account of Jesus' life (v. 2). This account, according to the author, is being circulated in the first community of believers who have a firsthand access with the disciples (v. 2).

Furthermore, the mention of the name of the recipient—Theophilus (Luke 1:1)—has led many scholars to conclude that the author of this gospel narrative and the book of Acts is one and the same person. It is also indicated that the book of Acts was written to Theophilus (Acts 1:1).[377] The author also mentions to Theophilus his "prw/ton lo,gon" (first book, NIV) which he had already probably sent to Theophilus (Acts 1:1-2). Many biblical scholars,[378]

---

[376]These disciples were eyewitnesses of "the things which have been fulfilled among us" (Luke 1:1-4).

[377]Theophilus is the primary recipient of Luke-Acts. However, it is also probable that Luke has in mind the rest of the believers in Theophilus' local congregation as is usually the case in other NT books. Theophilus was probably a Gentile convert as his name indicates. He was probably a government official as indicated in Luke's use of the word kra,tistoj (kratistos). We may also surmise that Luke's secondary recipients are largely Gentile believers in Rome or Caesarea. Knowing the probable recipients of Luke-Acts may also contribute to this study. If the recipients were mostly Gentile converts, then we may understand why Luke includes Jesus' parable of the rich man and Lazarus. The Gentile believers, having their former understanding of ᾅδης could relate with the parable of Jesus.

[378]For example, see Donald A. Carson, Douglas J. Moo, and Leon Morris, *An Introduction to the New Testament* (Grand Rapids: Zondervan, 1992), 113; Donald Guthrie, *New Testament Introduction*, 4th rev. ed. (Downers Grove, IL: InterVarsity, 1990), 117; Everett F. Harrison, *Introduction to the New Testament*, new rev. ed. (Grand Rapids: Eerdmans, 1971), 199-200; Ralph Martin, *New Testament Foundations: A Guide for Christian Students*, vol. 1 (Grand Rapids: Eerdmans, 1975), 244; Werner George Kümmel, *Introduction to the New Testament*, rev. ed., trans. Howard Clark Kee (Nashville, TN: Abingdon, 1975), 147; Eduard Lohse, *The Formation of the New Testament*, trans. M. Eugene Boring (Nashville, TN: Abingdon, 1981), 151-52; Luke Timothy Johnson, *The Writings of the New Testament: An Interpretation*, rev. ed. (Minneapolis, MN: Fortress, 1999), 214; Walter A. Elwell and Robert Yarbrough, *Encountering the New Testament: A Historical and Theological Survey*, 2d ed. (Grand Rapids: Baker Academic, 2005), 98-99; John Drane, *Introducing the New Testament*, rev. ed. (Oxford, England: Lion Publishing, 1999), 200; Irenaeus *Against Heresies* 3.1.1 (ANF, 1:414). Thomas D. Lea, *The New Testament: Its Background and Message* (Nashville, TN: Broadman & Holman, 1996), 144; Robert G. Gromacki, *New Testament Survey* (Grand Rapids: Baker, 1974), 109-11; Paul J. Achtemeier, Joel B. Green, and Marianne Meye Thompson, *Introducing the New Testament: Its Literature and Theology* (Grand Rapids: Eerdmans, 2001), 154-55.

based on external and internal evidences, conclude that Luke is the author[379] of
the third book in the Synoptic Gospels and the book of Acts.[380]

Date and Provenance

The most popular date of Luke is A.D. 80-90, a date after the fall of
Jerusalem.[381] However, this date has been contested by several scholars because
those who propose this date have the reference to the fall of Jerusalem as their
major argument. This argument downplays Jesus' ability to see the future.[382]
The alternative dates are either shortly before Luke finished writing Acts in A.D.
60[383] or early sixties to mid-sixties.[384] This study may accept a date between
Paul's imprisonment in Caesarea (ca. A.D. 56-58) prior to the death of James

---

[379]The importance of knowing the author is relevant in this study. If the author is Luke, one of
Paul's companions in his missionary journeys and Roman imprisonment (Col 4:14; 2 Tim 4:11; Phlm 1:24),
then it is not difficult to guess why he puts so much interest on common people. Being a Gentile may have
also influenced his theological focus. He seems to focus more on the inclusiveness of the gospel. For him,
salvation is for all men (Luke 2:30-32). It is for the Jews and Gentiles, for the rich and the poor, and for
the sinners and the righteous. It is for all kinds of people in the community. His focus on the poor in his
Gospel may also be a very significant point of emphasis to his significantly rich addressee—most excellent
Theophilus (1:3). Theophilus may be a government official, κράτιστος, an honorary form of address to a high
official converted to Christianity.

[380]As early as second century, church tradition already associated the third Gospel with a person called
Luke. The Muratorian Canon, the anti-Marcionite prologue, Irenaeus, Clement of Alexandria, Origen, and
Tertullian identify Luke as the author of this gospel account. See Drane, 200; Irenaeus *Against Heresies* 3.1.1;
Lea, 144.
    The book of Acts gives us data for identifying the author of Luke-Acts since in both books the author
wrote to Theophilus, and Acts mentions a former treatise (Luke 1:3; Acts 1:1). The "we" and "us" passages (Acts
16:10-17; 20:5-28:31) indicate that the author is one of Paul's companions in his missionary journeys. He was
with Paul in his journey to Rome as a prisoner. He was also with Paul during his imprisonment in Rome. The
process of elimination of who is the author among Paul's companion leads scholars to conclude that Luke is
most likely the author. See Gromacki, 109-11; Achtemeier, Green, and Thompson, 154-55.

[381]Bock notes that one of the arguments of scholars favoring this date is that "the Lucan apocalyptic
discourses with their description of siege and their focus on the city presuppose the fall and require a period
after A.D. 70." Darrell L. Bock, *Luke 1:1-9:50*, Baker Exegetical Commentary on the New Testament (Grand
Rapids: Baker, 1999), 16.

[382]They argue "that Jesus was capable of making solely [the prediction of Jerusalem's fall] on the basis
of his knowledge of how God acts to judge covenant unfaithfulness. Luke makes no effort to 'update' remarks
here, he only clarifies that in the temple's collapse the city is not spared either." Ibid., 17-18.

[383]Robert Gromacki argues that the best time Luke wrote his first book is between 56-58 during
Paul's imprisonment in Caesarea, or it took place during the voyage to Rome or in the early months of Paul's
imprisonment. Gromacki, 111.

[384]Some reasons for this date are (1) the failure to note the death of James (ca. 62) and of Paul (ca. late
60s) in Acts, and (2) the silence about the destruction of Jerusalem in Acts. Bock, *Luke 1:1-9:50*, 18.

and the release of Paul from Roman imprisonment which means before A.D. 62.
The provenance could be Caesarea or Rome during Paul's imprisonment in both
cities.[385]

Genre, Purpose, and General Themes

The genre of Luke can be explicitly deduced from his introduction (Luke
1:1). The word διήγησις (diēgēsis) means "narrative, account, or story."[386] Luke
Timothy Johnson suggests that "Luke shares the perception of Hellenistic
rhetoric that the *narratio* (narration) is critical to historical argument or personal
defense."[387] Joel B. Green points out that there is a broad consensus that some
portions in Luke belong to an ancient literary tradition called "historiography,"
proving that Luke's work shares many features of Greco-Roman historiography.[388]

These features are evident in the book itself when it is compared with other
gospel accounts. For example, when Matthew relates the birth of Jesus, he is not
so particular about specific historical landmarks. He just mentions a very loose
historical fact that could be misunderstood (Matt 2:1);[389] on the contrary, Luke's
account shows a natural characteristic of a historical narrative. He mentions the
reigning Roman emperor—Caesar Augustus (2:1a). He cites a very significant
imperial decree—taxing (2:1b). In addition, he notes the regional ruler of
Syria—Cyrenius (2:2). He is also concerned with thorough historical data.[390]
For example, while Matthew does not give the reason why Jesus was born in

---

[385]Establishing the most probable date and provenance is significant in this study in the sense that
it tells us why Luke, in his gospel account, puts so much emphasis on caring for the poor of society. If the
provenance is Rome or Caesarea, then his theological focus fits in the socio-economic situation of the time
since in these large cities existed the poorest of the poor. The date is also significant because approximately
during this period there was a tension between the Jews and the Christians in Rome and elsewhere regarding
the inclusiveness of salvation (Rom 2,3). Salvation is for all men, for the Jews and for the Greeks, for the rich
and the poor, for the free and the slaves, and for male and female. This seems to be the theme of Luke, and this
fits in the date and the provenance.

[386]Bauer, BAGD, s.v. " διήγησις."

[387]Luke Timothy Johnson, *The Gospel of Luke*, Sacra Pagina, vol. 3, 4.

[388]Green, 2-3.

[389]He just mentions one historical figure—Herod the king. This is subject to misunderstanding
because the name Herod is seen to be a family name.

[390]Other historical data could be found in the book (Luke 3:1-2. For example, see Acts 18:2).

Bethlehem, Luke gives more historical details on the birth of Jesus. He relates that Joseph and Mary were residents of Nazareth of Galilee (2:4) before they came to Bethlehem to be registered for a census (2:3-5).

The purpose of Luke-Acts[391] is also explicitly laid out in his introduction (Luke 1:1-4).[392] His purpose is to write an orderly (καθεξῆς)[393] account to Theophilus, "ἵνα ἐπιγνῷς περὶ ὧν κατηχήθης λόγων τὴν ἀσφάλειαν" (so that you may know the full truth about the message you were taught of, 1:4). Primarily, his purpose is to write a chronological sequence of "what has been fulfilled among them" in order to secure or establish the certainty of these things (1:1) in the mind of his prominent recipient, Theophilus, who already received instructions about the Gospel of Jesus Christ.[394] But why does Theophilus need a knowledge of the historical certainty of the things which he was told have been fulfilled among them? L. T. Johnson has this to say,

> If that historical people was not now in possession of the promised blessings, and someone else was, what did that signify for God's reliability? Did God keep his word, or did he utterly betray Israel? And what were the implications for gentile believers in this God? Could they rely on 'the things fulfilled among them' any more that the Jews could? If God's word failed Israel, could it not fail the Gentiles as well?[395]

Furthermore, L. T. Johnson asserts that Luke's purpose in writing to Theophilus is to defend God's work in history. He wants to show how things happened in the exact way they were prophesied. God fulfilled His promises to His people Israel and also extended His blessing to the

---

[391]This study intends not to separate Acts because it is seen in this study as the wider literary context of the Gospel of Luke.

[392]Joseph Fitzmyer stresses that the aim of Luke-Acts has to be the stated purpose of Luke 1:4. It has been generally recognized by many scholars today. Joseph Fitzmyer, *Luke I-IX*, AB, vol. 28, 9. For example, Luke's usual reference to time and historical events in his gospel account may reflect his purpose in writing an orderly or chronological account (1:5; 26; 2:1-3; 3:1-2).

[393]It denotes sequence in time, space, or logic. Bauer, BAGD, s.v. "καθεξῆς." Here, it may mean "chronological sequence." See Guthrie, 106.

[394]Although Luke explicitly states his purpose in the prologue, yet, some scholars see secondary purposes in Luke. See Stein, *Luke*, 35-44.

[395]L. T. Johnson, *The Writings*, 219.

Gentiles. Thus, the things taught to the Gentiles are trustworthy.[396]

Although it is apparent in Luke's introduction that he is writing a historical account, yet Donald Guthrie points out that there is "an important distinction between this writing and history pure and simple."[397] The reason is that "the history concerned a unique person."[398] Guthrie also adds that there have been claims that Luke's purpose in writing the history of Jesus is dominated by a theological motive.[399] Marshall wants to make it clear that it is possible for Luke to be both a historian and a theologian at the same time.[400]

At this juncture, it is also important to point out that, in relation to his having a theological motive, Luke has several important themes in view. The distinctive major theme of Luke-Acts that scholars point out is "the plan of God" (ἡ βουλὴ τοῦ θεοῦ, Luke 7:30; Acts 2:23; 4:28; 5:38; 13:36; 20:27).[401] John T. Squires further states that this theme braces the whole of Luke-Acts.[402] He adds,

> A variety of thematic strands are woven together to emphasize the certainty and consistency of the plan of God as it is worked in the life of Jesus and the history of the early church.[403]

Helmut Flender also notes, "For in the community, under the guidance of the Spirit the divine plan of salvation becomes a reality."[404] Fitzmyer emphasizes that Luke works in a conceptual construct of "salvation history," that is, human history is guided by God's salvific activity. Hence, Luke's statement, "The events that have come to fulfillment among us" (Luke 1:1),

---

[396]Ibid.

[397]Guthrie, 106.

[398]Ibid.

[399]Ibid., 107. Cf. I. Howard Marshall, *Luke: Historian Theologian* (Downers Grove, IL: InterVarsity, 1970), 52.

[400]Marshall, *Luke: Historian*, 19.

[401]John T. Squires, *The Plan of God in Luke-Acts* (Cambridge, UK: Cambridge, 1993), 1-3.

[402]Ibid., 1.

[403]Ibid.

[404]Helmut Flender, *St. Luke: Theologian of Redemptive History*, trans. Reginald H. and Ilse Fuller (London, SPCK, 1967), 143. He further notes, "The whole divine economy of salvation is designated by the term boulh. (Luke 7:30; Acts 20:27; and, in reference to Christ only, Acts 2:23; 4:28; 5:38)." Ibid.

relates to OT history and realizations of God's direction of history.[405]

Guy Nave Jr. delineates that the divine plan is that ὄψεται πᾶσα σὰρξ τὸ σωτήριον τοῦ θεοῦ (all flesh will see the salvation of God, Luke 3:6). He also notes, "ὅτι τοῖς ἔθνεσιν ἀπεστάλη τοῦτο τὸ σωτήριον τοῦ θεοῦ" (that this salvation of God has been sent to the Gentiles, Acts 28:28).[406] At this point, we may agree with the scholars that the major theme of Luke which undergirds all the other themes is the plan of God, which is the salvation for all flesh.[407] This divine plan which was carried out as divine activity in human history is called salvation history which, in part, is taken into account by Luke in Luke-Acts. This plan of God begins with the Jews but ultimately embraces all nations, kindreds, and people. This is shown in the structural analysis below.

Structural-Thematic Analysis

In this section, the structure of the book of Luke will be dealt with. The structure of Luke's travel narrative will also be considered. The discussion will then narrow down to the structure of Luke 16. The themes of the book, the travel narrative, and Luke 16, specifically 16:19-31, will be drawn from the structural analysis.

The Structure of Luke-Acts

Several biblical scholars see a literary unity, continuity, and parallelism between Luke and Acts.[408] L. T. Johnson notes that the "events in Acts clearly

---

[405]Joseph Fitzmyer, *Luke the Theologian: Aspects of His Teaching* (London: Geoffrey Chapman, 1989), 59-61. Cf. Elwell and Yarbrough, 105. Hans Conzelmann originally proposed the idea of "salvation history" in Luke-Acts. See Hans Conzelmann, *The Theology of St. Luke* (New York: Harper & Row, 1961), 137-69.

[406]Guy Nave Jr., *The Role and Function of Repentance in Luke-Acts* (Atlanta: SBL, 2002), 25.

[407]This major theme of Luke is significant as far as the parable of the rich man and Lazarus is concerned. Luke, as he describes Jesus' ministry, wants to stress that the gospel of salvation should be preached to all kinds of people even to the poor, the prisoners, the blind, and the oppressed sectors of the community (Luke 4:18). Luke wants also to show that, in the ministry of Jesus, the plan of God is the salvation of all flesh. It does not involve only the spiritual restoration of humanity but also the restoration of the society where the rich care for the needs of their less fortunate neighbors in the community of faith (Luke 14; Luke 16). This was His original plan for Israel (Exod 22:22,25; Isa 58:7). He wants also to emphasize this once again to the New Israel.

[408]See Robert C. Tannehill, *The Narrative Unity of Luke-Acts: A Literary Interpretation*—The Gospel According to Luke, vol. 1 (Philadelphia: Fortress, 1986), 1-12.

parallel those of the Gospel."[409] Charles Talbert, for example, underscores and synthesizes the works of several scholars for more than half a century.[410] A sample of literary parallelisms noted by Talbert is shown in table 2 below.[411]

TABLE 2

LITERARY PARALLELISM BETWEEN LUKE 1-8
AND ACTS 1-12

Luke	Acts
1:1-4—A preface dedicates the book to Theophilus.	1:1-5—A preface dedicates the book to Theophilus.
3:21—Jesus is praying at His baptism.	1:14,24—The disciples are praying as they await their baptism of the Holy Spirit.
3:22—The Spirit descends after Jesus' prayer and in a physical form.	2:1-13—The Spirit fills the disciples after their prayers with accompanying physical manifestations.
4:16-30—Jesus' ministry opens with a sermon which gives the theme for what follows, fulfillment of a prophecy and rejection of Jesus.	2:14-40—The church's ministry opens with a sermon that gives the theme for what follows, fulfillment of a prophecy and the rejection of Jesus.
4:31-8:56—The theme of fulfillment mentioned in 4:16-30 is illustrated by examples of preaching and healing. Conflicts illustrate the note of rejections.	2:41-12:17—The theme of fulfillment is illustrated by examples of prophesying and wonders. Persecutions illustrate the note of unbelief.

Talbert continues that "within this last general section there are several

---

[409]L. T. Johnson, *The Writings*, 220. For example, Mary "appears at the beginning of each volume, the apostles work wonders remarkably similar to those of Jesus, and Paul's final journey to suffering resembles Jesus' journey to suffering." Ibid.

[410]Talbert, 15.

[411]Ibid., 16. For the rest of the literary parallels between Luke and Acts see ibid., 16-143.

specific correspondences that need to be mentioned."[412] Another literary
parallelism between Luke and Acts is shown in table 3 below.

TABLE 3

LITERARY PARALLELISM BETWEEN LUKE 5-7
AND ACT 3-11

5:17-26—A lame man is healed by the authority of Jesus.	3:1-10—A lame man is healed by the name of Jesus (cf. 9:32-35).
5:29-6:11—Conflicts with the religious leaders.	4:1-8:3—Conflicts with the religious leaders.
7:1-10—A centurion, well-spoken of by the Jews, sends men to Jesus to ask Him to come to his house.	Ch. 10—A centurion, well-spoken of by the whole Jewish nation, sends men to Peter to ask him to come to his house.
7:36-50—A Pharisee criticizes Jesus for being touched by the wrong kind of woman.	11:1-18—The Pharisaic party criticizes Peter for his association with Gentiles.
7:36-50—A Pharisee criticizes Jesus for being touched by the wrong kind of woman.	11:1-18—The Pharisaic party criticizes Peter for his association with Gentiles.

Furthermore, scholars see parallelism within each of the two-volume books. Frederick Danker
sees overt parallelism within Luke's Gospel. He observes,

> Prominent in Luke 1 and 2 are the annunciations by the angel regarding John
> and Jesus, the recitals of their births, and the psalms uttered by Elizabeth
> (or by Mary?) and Zechariah. Simeon (2:25-35) and Anna (vv. 36-38)
> offer a twofold testimony to the redemptive significance of Jesus.[413]

Paul Achtemeier, Joel Green, and Marianne Meye Thompson see "two features
to structure the narrative and give it meaning. The first is the movement from

---

[412]Ibid., 16.

[413]Frederick W. Danker, *Luke*, Proclamation Commentaries, ed. Gerhard Krodel (Philadelphia:
Fortress, 1976), 91.

divine promise to evidence of fulfillment to responses of praise."[414] The second
is the point-by-point parallelism between John and Jesus in chaps. 1 and 2. The
two features are shown in tables 4 and 5 below.

TABLE 4

FIRST FEATURE: DIVINE PROMISE AND FULFILLMENT

Character	Promise	Evidence of Fulfillment	Response of Praise
Zechariah	His wife would bear a son.	John is born	Song of Zechariah
Mary	She would conceive a son.	Unborn John bears witness to Jesus in the womb; Elizabeth blesses Mary.	Song of Mary
Simeon	He would see the Messiah.	He encounters Jesus in the temple.	Song of Simeon

TABLE 5

SECOND FEATURE: PARALLELISM BETWEEN JOHN AND JESUS

John	Event	Jesus
1:5-7	The introduction of parents	1:26-27
1:8-23	The annunciation of birth	1:28-38

---

[414]Achtemeier, et al., 159.

Table 5- *Continued*

1:24-25	The mother's response	1:39-56
1:57-58	The birth	2:1-20
1:59-66	Circumcision and naming	2:21-24
1:67-79	Prophetic Response	2:25-39
1:80	The Growth of Child	2:40-52

In relation to the second feature (table 5),[415] Talbert also highlights very exhaustively the parallel patterns in Luke. For example, Luke 4:16-8:56 falls into two parts, 4:16-7:17 and 7:18-8:56, which begin and end in similar ways. Both Luke 4:16-30—the beginning of the first part— and 7:18-30—the beginning of the second part—stress that Jesus' preaching and healing are fulfillment of Isaianic prophecies. Interestingly enough, the end of the first part (Luke 7:1-10; 11-17) and the end of the second part (Luke 8:43-48; 49-56) show parallelism. The end of the first part recounts a healing story (7:1-10) that emphasizes the faith of the person who came to Jesus. Then it is followed by a resurrection story (7:11-17). The end of the second part also relates a healing story (8:43-48) that emphasizes the faith of the woman who came to Jesus. Then it is followed by a resurrection story (8:49-56).[416] Another literary pattern that scholars see in Luke-Acts is that the arrangement of Luke-Acts makes Jerusalem as the central point of its geographical and narrative structures of Jesus and the Church's ministry and mission. For example, Fitzmyer asserts,

> The overarching geographical perspective in Luke-Acts can be seen in the author's preoccupation with Jerusalem as the city of destiny for Jesus and the pivot for the salvation of mankind. Luke establishes a special

[415]Ibid., 160. Cf. John Nolland, *Luke 1-9:20*, WBC, vol. 35A, 17.

[416]Talbert, 39. Talbert also notes that "much of the materials between the similar beginnings and endings seem to correspond, though not always in order." Ibid., 40. For example, Luke 4:31-41 and 8:26-39 talk about Jesus in conflict with demons. Luke 5:1-11 and Luke 8:22-25 speak about Jesus in a boat with Simon or His disciples with a nature miracle taking place. Luke 5:17-26 and 7:36-50 tell us about Jesus eating with the Pharisees and the issue of forgiveness of sin arises. Luke 5:27-6:5 and 7:31-35 contrast Jesus and His disciples who eat and drink with John and his disciples who fast often. Luke 6:12-16 and 8:1-3 talk about Jesus with the disciples whom He has chosen; this precedes Jesus' teaching of the crowd. Luke 6:17-49 and 8:4-8, 16-21 tell us about Jesus' teaching the multitude; the conclusion concerns "hearing" and "doing" His teaching. Ibid., 40.

relationship between Jesus' person and ministry and that city of David's
throne. He depicts Jesus making his way thither as his goal (13:32). From
there too the word of God's salvation must spread to the end of the earth in
Acts. . . . Thus the geographical perspective becomes a factor in the divine
plan of salvation.[417]

Furthermore, Fitzmyer points out the pivotal role of Jerusalem in Luke's

two-volume work. It is not only a destination of what "Jesus began to do and

teach" (Luke 1:1), but also the starting point of the spread of the word of God;

the apostles were to go from Jerusalem to Judea, Samaria, and to the uttermost

part of the earth (Acts 1:8; 23:11; 28:14).[418] This study proposes a geographical

structure of Luke-Acts as shown in table 6 below.

TABLE 6

GEOGRAPHICAL STRUCTURE OF LUKE-ACTS[419]

Luke 1:1-4——Prologue
1:5-2:52——The infancy and childhood narrative begins and ends at Jerusalem——in the Temple.
3:1-4:13——The preparation for Jesus' public ministry. He receives the Holy Spirit. Jesus' temptation ends at the temple.
4:14-9:50——The Galilean ministry
9:51-19:48——Jesus' journey to Jerusalem, the end of travel narrative——Jesus goes into the temple in Jerusalem.
20:1-21:38——Jesus' ministry in Jerusalem
22:1-23:56a——The passion narrative——Jerusalem
24:45-53——JERUSALEM (Yahweh/Temple)——God's salvation flows   to all. The disciples praise God at the temple.
24:45-53——JERUSALEM (Yahweh/Temple)——God's salvation flows   to all. The disciples praise God at the temple.

---

[417]Fitzmyer, *Luke I-IX*, 164-65.

[418]Ibid., 168.

[419]This geographical structure of Luke-Acts is based on the idea of scholars that there is a geographical-structural pattern in Luke-Acts.

Table 6——*Continued*

Acts 1:1-2——Prologue
1:3-26——Infancy and preparation of the Church for public ministry——begins in Jerusalem.
2:1-7:60-The Church received the Holy Spirit. The Church begins her ministry in Jerusalem. They prayed and ministered at the temple. End of Jerusalem ministry, Stephen's vision of heaven——saw Jesus at the right hand of God.
8:1-11:18——Witness in Judea and Samaria, beginning of Gentile mission.
11:19-28:31——Witness to the ends of the earth.

From the above table,[420] it is clear, as already noted by several scholars, that the center of Luke-Acts's geographical structure is Jerusalem. It shows that Luke's gospel narrative begins and ends in Jerusalem. It also shows that the book of Acts begins its narrative in Jerusalem. Thus, Jerusalem is the focal point of Luke–Acts. The structure shows the overall theme: Jerusalem/temple is the locus on earth where salvation was achieved and was first proclaimed before it reached the ends of the earth.[421]

However, aside from this widely accepted thematic perspective in Luke-Acts' structure, there is another thematic idea that is noticed in this geographical structure of Luke-Acts. Luke seems to also emphasize the centrality of the temple in Jerusalem in his geographical structure. This may also have an important role in his theology, especially in the theology of salvation in Luke-Acts. Cyprian Robert Hutcheon asserts that the "temple is a 'sign' of critical importance for trying to understand Luke's theology."[422] He also notes that Luke's gospel begins and ends in the temple of Jerusalem.[423] It is very noticeable that the infancy and childhood narrative of John and Jesus begins and ends in the temple (1:5-2:52).

---

[420]Liefeld also suggests that "the central theme in the writings of Luke is that Jesus offers salvation to men." Liefeld, 811. Cf. Marshall, *Historian and Theologian*, 116.

[421]In the OT, salvation also begins in Jerusalem/Zion (Isa 46:13), and will reach the ends of the earth (Isa 49:6).

[422]Cyprian Robert Hutcheon, "'God with Us': The Temple in Luke-Acts, *St. Vladimir's Theological Quarterly* 44 (2000): 3 [journal on-line]; available from Academic Search Premier database; Internet; accessed 4 December 2007.

[423]Ibid., 4.

It begins with the annunciation of the birth of John by angel Gabriel. It ends with the visit of Jesus to the temple in Jerusalem. The temptation of Jesus also ends at the temple in Jerusalem (4:1-13). In its Matthean parallel, the temptation at the temple is in the middle of the narrative (4:1-11). Luke's travel narrative also ends with Jesus entering the temple in Jerusalem (9:51-19:48). As already noted by Hutcheon, the Gospel of Luke ends at the temple with the disciples praising God for all the wonderful things they have witnessed (24:53).

The book of Acts begins at Jerusalem. It begins with the birth of the Church (1:3-26). The Church also begins her ministry in Jerusalem, especially at the temple. However, there is a slight difference between Luke and Acts. First, in Luke the narrative begins and ends in Jerusalem (1:5-24:53), whereas in Acts the narrative begins in Jerusalem but ends in Rome, the capital of the then Roman world empire (1:3-28:31). Second, in Luke, Jesus' life and ministry begin in the temple and end in the temple (2:21-19:48). In Acts, the birth and ministry of the Church begin in Jerusalem/temple, but the narrative shifts its focus. From the ministry of the Church in earthly Jerusalem/temple, it shifts to Stephen's vision of the glory of God and Jesus in the heavenly Jerusalem/temple (2:1-7:60).[424] We may suggest then that, in the Gospel, the temple is central to Luke-Acts' theology of salvation.[425] How do these insights from structural analysis contribute to this study? The contributions are the following:

1. Luke's shift from a local place (earthly Jewish temple) to the heavenly temple helps us understand his theological focus. He wants to emphasize the universality of salvation. It is not limited only to the Jews. It is inclusive; it includes all people of the earth. Salvation is not only for the Jews but also for the Gentiles. It is not only for the rich but also for the poor. It is not only for the so

---

[424]In the OT imagery, aside from the familiar belief that God dwells with His people in Jerusalem temple/ sanctuary (Ps 5:7; 48:9; 65:4; 68:29; 79:1; 138:2), He was also sometimes seen in His temple in heaven (Ps 11:4).

[425]It seems that in Luke-Acts, salvation proceeds from the temple where God dwells, as in the OT. In Luke-Acts, there seems to be a paradigm shift of the locus of salvation, that is, from the earthly temple in Jerusalem (in Luke) to the heavenly temple (in Acts 7) where Jesus sits at the right hand of God. Cf. Davidson Razafiarivony, "The Meaning of the Temple in Stephen's Speech," (M.A. thesis, Adventist International Institute of Advanced Studies, Silang, Cavite, Philippines, October 1996), 122.

called 'righteous' but also for sinners.

2. Luke also stresses mission in Luke-Acts. He starts with Jesus who proclaimed the gospel to the poor, to the prisoners, to the blind, and to the oppressed. This proclamation was passed on to the disciples and the Church. In Luke, mission involves caring for others, especially the poor. This is a very significant theme that is also emphasized in the two parables of Luke 16—the shrewd steward showed concern for his master's debtors while the rich man in 16:19-31 did not reach out for Lazarus outside his gates. The rich man did not have a sense of mission, and Christ highlights this negative aspect in Luke 16.

The Structure of the Travel Narrative

Scholars almost unanimously agree that the travel narrative begins in 9:51. However, they are very divided as to where the travel narrative ends. Some scholars, in their outline of Luke's Gospel, end the travel narrative in 19:27.[426] Others end it in 19:44,[427] while the rest end it in 19:48.[428] This study considers 9:51-19:48 as the section which covers the travel narrative of Jesus[429] based on few reasons:

1. In this travel, one would expect Jesus to reach His destination. His destination, as indicated in 9:51 and 13:22, is Jerusalem.

2. The context of v. 44 suggests that Jesus is not yet in Jerusalem, though He approaches it (v. 41). When He gets closer to Jerusalem, He laments over its impending doom (vv. 42-44).

3. The literary structure of Luke, as shown above, favors this ending. The infancy and childhood narrative ends in Jerusalem/ temple. The temptation of Jesus ends in Jerusalem/temple. The ministry of Jesus also ends in Jerusalem/temple. The book itself ends in Jerusalem/ temple.

---

[426]Stein, *Luke*, 32-33; L. T. Johnson, *Luke*, vi-v;   C. A. Evans, *Luke*, 16.

[427]Bock, *Luke*, 30; Liefeld, 819-20; Carson, Moo, and Morris, 112; Morris, 62.

[428]Green, 27-28; Kenneth Bailey, *Poet and Peasant: A Literary-Cultural Approach to the Parables in Luke*, combined Edition (Grand Rapids: Eerdmans, 1983), 79.

[429]Cf. Bailey, 79-82.

As far as the literary analysis is concerned, Bailey's literary structure of the travel narrative is helpful.[430] He calls the "Travel Narrative" as "Jerusalem Document," arguing that there was no "traveling" done at all.[431] In his literary analysis of the so called "Travel Narrative," he proposes "a carefully constructed inverted outline."[432] Here is his proposed chiastic structure:[433]

1. JERUSALEM: ESCHATOLOGICAL EVENTS——9:51-56

2. FOLLOW ME——9:57-10:12
        HIDDEN FROM THE WISE——10:21
          ONLY THE SON KNOWS THE FATHER——10:22
            BLESSED ARE YOUR EARS——10:23-24[434]

3. WHAT SHALL I DO TO INHERIT ETERNAL LIFE?——10:25-41

4. PRAYER——11:1-13

5. SIGNS AND THE PRESENT KINGDOM——11:14-32

6. CONFLICT WITH THE PHARISEES: MONEY——11:37–12:34

7. THE KINGDOM IS NOT YET AND IS NOW——12:35-59

8. THE CALL OF THE KINGDOM TO ISRAEL——13:1-9
9. THE NATURE OF THE KINGDOM——13:10-20
    (a) Love and not Law——vv.10-14
    (b) Humility——the kingdom is like mustard seed——
    vv. 18-20

10. JERUSALEM: ESCHATOLOGICAL EVENTS——13:22-35

9' THE NATURE OF THE KINGDOM——14:1-11
    (a) Love and not law——a healing on the Sabbath——vv. 1-4
    (b) Humility——he who humbles himself will be exalted——vv. 7-11

8' THE CALL OF THE KINGDOM TO ISRAEL AND TO THE
    OUTCASTS——14:12-15:32

---

[430]Kenneth Bailey's structure of Luke's travel narrative seems evident in the literary and thematic contexts.

[431]Bailey, 82.

[432]Ibid., 79.

[433]This is just a summary of his proposed structure. Only the portions that deal with humility are shown. See ibid., 80-82 for the detailed literary structure of the travel narrative. Talbert also sees a chiastic structure in Luke's travel narrative. He proposes that the chiastic structure starts from Luke 10:21 to 18:30. See Talbert, 51-52.

[434]Bailey considers this portion (10:21-24) as an extra material inserted between sections. Bailey, 80.

7' THE KINGDOM IS NOT YET AND IS NOW—16:1-8,16

6' CONFLICT WITH THE PHARISEES: MONEY—16:9-31

5' SIGNS AND THE COMING KINGDOM—17:11-37

4' PRAYER—18:1-14

      CHILDREN AND ETERNAL LIFE—vv. 15-17

3' WHAT SHALL I DO TO INHERIT ETERNAL LIFE?—18:18-30

      PREDICTION OF THE PASSION—vv. 31-34

2' FOLLOW ME—v. 35-19:9

1' JERUSALEM: ESCHATOLOGICAL EVENTS—v. 10, vv. 28-48

Bailey asserts that this literary pattern was arranged by a pre-Lucan Jewish-Christian theologian. He then conjectures that Luke had this document available since he claims that he used written sources.[435] Although, generally, Bailey's work seems fancy and more on conjectures, yet, in his structural analysis, there are significant thematic insights which are also evident in the literary context of the whole book. Specifically, these thematic insights are in his structural analysis of Luke's travel narrative. One of these themes is Luke's emphasis on "Jerusalem" which has already been noted in the analysis of the general structure above.

Another theme that is emphasized in Luke's travel narrative is the exaltation of the poor, the humble, the outcasts, and the marginalized of society on the one hand, and the abasement of the selfish rich, the proud, and the socially and religiously prominent Jews on the other hand. Significantly, this is not given much emphasis in the rest of the Synoptics. Bailey notes that the theme of "humilitis" seen in Luke 14:25-33; 15:11-32; 16:1-8a; 16:19-31; 17:7-10; 18:9-14; 19:1-10.[436]

Humility is not only prominent in Luke's travel narrative, but also in other parts of the book. Luke explicitly highlights this theme in 1:46-56. It tells us about the song of Mary who exalts the Lord (v. 46). In this song, Mary rejoices (v. 47) and acknowledges her humble state (v. 48). She also acknowledges the mighty acts of God (v. 49) in scattering the proud (v. 51), in bringing down rulers (v. 52a) and exalting the humble (v. 52b), in filling the hungry (v. 53a) and in

---

[435]Ibid., 83.

[436]Ibid.

sending away the rich empty-handed (v. 53b).

In another passage (Luke 3:5), John the Baptist emphasizes this theme. In a figurative way, quoting from the OT (Isa 40:3-5), John emphasizes the need for humility before God and for repentance as both elements are requisites for those who wait for the coming of the Messiah. It is significant to note that the clause, "And every mountain and hill will be brought low" appears only here in Luke. It does not occur in its parallel passages (Matt 3:3; Mark 1:3).

This theme is also related to one of Luke's emphasis: God's concern and plan for the poor as far as salvation is concerned. This is clearly evident from the fact that of the twenty-one occurrences of the word πτωχός (poor) in the Synoptic Gospels, ten occur in Luke (4:18; 6:20; 7:22; 14:13,21; 16:20,22; 18:22; 19:8; 21:3), six in Matthew (5:3; 11:5; 19:21; 26:9,11), and five in Mark (10:21; 12:42,43; 14:5,7). In Luke 4:16-30, Jesus' Jubilee's proclamation, Luke stresses specifically that the message of the gospel of the kingdom of God is primarily for the poor (v. 18),[437] the captives (v. 18b), the blind   (v. 18c), and the oppressed (v. 18d). This is significant because in its parallels in Matthew (13:53-58), Mark (6:1-6), and John (4:44; 1:45; 6:42; 8:59), this statement is lacking.

Furthermore, Luke's emphasis on God's concern for the poor is highlighted in his version of the beatitudes of Jesus (6:20). In Matthew, the emphasis is specifically on spiritual poverty, Μακάριοι οἱ πτωχοὶ τῷ πνεύματι (Blessed are the poor in spirit, 5:3). In Luke, however, the emphasis may include physical poverty, Μακάριοι οἱ πτωχοι, (Blessed are you poor).[438]

The other passages are 14:13,21 and 16:20,22. These passages have no parallels in the rest of the Synoptic Gospels and John. The passages in chap.

---

[437]Bock points out that "it cannot be denied that 'poor' here refers to those who live in a socially and economically limited environment. But according to the use of this term in the OT and in Luke, that is not all that is intended here. The OT background points to the *anawim*, the 'pious poor,' the afflicted (2 Sam 22:28; Ps 14:6; 22:24; 25:16; 34:6; 40:17; 69:29; Amos 8:4; Isa 3:14-15). These are the humble whom God will exalt (Luke 1:51-53) and who, like the prophets, suffer for being open to God (6:20-23; cf. the description in 1 Cor 1:26-29; Jas 2:5)." Bock, *Luke*, 136. Cf. Paul Hertig, "The Jubilee Mission of Jesus in the Gospel of Luke: Reversals of Fortunes," *Missiology* 26 (1998): 173.

[438]This passage should not be taken out of context. The passage does not say that automatically if you are poor you can enter the kingdom of God, or if you are rich you are excluded from the kingdom of God. The text is specifically intended for the disciples of Jesus (6:20a). This is evident in the use of the second person in Luke, while Matthew uses the third person. Cf. Nolland, *Luke 1-9:20*, 283.

14 talk about dinner invitations. Jesus emphasizes that when a person holds a dinner, he/she has to invite the poor, the crippled, the lame, and the blind. Verse 13 is clearly literal, while v. 21 could be figurative because it is set in the context of the parable of the "Great Feast" which may symbolize the "Messianic Banquet" (v. 15). Generally, in these passages, Jesus is emphasizing the need of humility even in inviting guests for dinner. This is shown by inviting the marginalized of society, the crippled, the blind, and the lame. In this way, the one who does this opens himself for an invitation to the feast in the Kingdom of God.

Verses 20 and 22 of Luke 16 are interestingly part of the problem passage of this study. This passage talks about the poor Lazarus, who was longing to feed on the crumbs from the rich man's table (vv. 20,21), and the rich man who was living a luxurious life, neglecting the poor Lazarus at his gate (v. 20). In the context of the parable,[439] Jesus rebukes the Pharisees for not being prudent stewards of earthly riches as the Law teaches (16:14,15). Prudent stewardship involves caring for the need of the poor, the widows, and the orphans in the Jewish covenant community. Another theme which is emphasized in this parable and elsewhere in Luke is the reversal of situation. The proud in heart, rulers (1:51,52), selfish rich (16:23), and spiritually proud Pharisees (18:9-17) are humbled before God, whereas the faithful women, the pious poor, and the penitent tax collectors are exalted before Him.

Another theme which is prominent in the structural arrangement of Luke's travel narrative is the breaking in of the kingdom of God.[440] Looking at the structure, the kingdom motif in the travel narrative is very vital. It is evident in "5" (11:14-32) and "5'" (17:11-37). It deals with the signs of God's kingdom which were already present, and yet still coming. The two passages, "7" (12:35-59) and "7'" (16:1-8,16) emphasize the already-and-not yet aspect of the kingdom. Furthermore, "8" (13:1-9) and "8'" (14:12-15:32) speak about the call of the kingdom to Israel and to the outcasts. In addition, "9" (13:10-20) and "9'" (14:1-

---

[439]Detailed discussion of this parable will be in the literary analysis.

[440]Talbert also notices the kingdom motif in his chiastic structure of Luke's travel narrative. See Talbert, 53.

11) focus on the nature of the kingdom. What Luke seems to emphasize here is that, it was in the context of the kingdom God (which had already arrived) that Jesus taught His disciples the principles or ethics of His kingdom: (1) love your neighbor (10:29-37), (2) love the Lord (10:38-42; 18:28-30), (3) the importance of prayer (10:1-8; 18:1-14), (4) prudent stewardship (12:13-21; 16:1-8; 19-31), (5) humbleness (13:18-20; 14:7-11), and (6) care for the marginalized of society (14:12-14; 16:19-31; 18:22-28).

The Structure of Luke 16:1-31

Luke 16:1-31 consists of two parables: (1) the parable of the shrewd manager (vv. 1-8), and (2) the parable of the rich man and Lazarus (vv. 19-31). In between the two parables (vv. 9-18), Jesus is seen confronting the Pharisees. Looking at Bailey's structure, Luke 16:1-8,16 is summarized as "the Kingdom is not yet and is now," and 16:9-31 is labeled "conflict with the Pharisees: Money." Bailey's label for 16:1-8 seems out of context. However, v. 16 speaks of the arrival of God's kingdom. In the first place, this is a parable. It is clear that Jesus' emphasis is not on the presence of His kingdom; rather, the emphasis is primarily on being shrewd with the temporary material things that God entrusts to us (v. 8b). In v. 9, Jesus explains his statement in v. 8b on how to be prudent in dealing with the temporary, unrighteous wealth the disciples possess. In vv. 10-13, in connection with the preceding parable, Jesus also stresses the need to be faithful with the little things (v. 10) and unrighteous wealth (v. 11) as well as the need to be faithful to God by serving only one master, not two——God and wealth (v. 13). The Pharisees react to this teaching by scoffing at Him (v. 14). Luke states the reason why they react like this, "Because they were lovers of money." In v. 15, Jesus counteracts and rebukes the Pharisees, exposing their real standing before God. Then, Jesus reveals the truth concerning the breaking in of the kingdom of God and the perpetuity of the Law and The Prophets even at the era of the kingdom of God (vv. 16-18). John Nolland suggests that

> until John, there were only the law and the prophets; now the ministries
> of John and Jesus, involved as they were with the coming of the kingdom

of God, both confirm the demands of the law and make yet more radical demands upon those who wish to come to terms with what God is now doing.[441]

To uphold the permanence and authority of the Law, Jesus cites the OT law on adultery (Exod 20:14; Lev 18:20; Deut 5:18) and adds that a man who divorces his wife and marries another commits adultery.[442] He also uses a parable (the rich man and Lazarus) to further stress the authority of the Law and the Prophets (vv. 16-31), especially in properly dealing with the temporary, earthly wealth.

Here is a suggested structure of Luke 16:1-31:

A. Jesus' Action——Teaching His disciples to be faithful stewards of unrighteous wealth

Luke 16:1-8a——Jesus' parable of a shrewd
steward——intended audience: Disciples

16:8b-13——Jesus teaches several lessons from the
parable stressing prudence and faithfulness to God
especially in dealing with unrighteous wealth.

B. Pharisees' Reaction to Jesus' Teaching on Wealth

Luke 16:14——Scoffing at Jesus' teaching

B' Jesus' Counteraction Against the Pharisees

Luke 16:15——Rebuking the Pharisees and exposing their inner motives
and real standing before God.

Luke 16:16——Jesus announces the arrival of the kingdom of God.
Luke 16:17-18——The Law and the Prophets are still the source of
authority in the kingdom of God.

A' Jesus' Action——Teaching concerning unwise
stewardship——intended recipients: Pharisees

Luke 16:19-31——Jesus tells this parable stressing the authority of the Law
in matters of dealing with unrighteous wealth.

---

[441]Nolland, *Luke 9:21-18:34*, 822.

[442]During the time of Jesus, the School of Shamai would allow divorce only on grounds of fornication. However, the School of Hillel would allow divorce simply because the husband found another woman more attractive.   L. T. Johnson, *Luke*, 251.

This structure shows that the theme of Luke 16:1-31 is the wise and unwise use of the temporary, unrighteous wealth that men have acquired in this life.[443] Jesus' purpose in the first place is to teach His disciples to be wise in dealing with unrighteous wealth and to be faithful in dealing with what is entrusted to them (vv. 1-13). When confronted by the Pharisees on this teaching, Jesus stresses the authority of the Law and the Prophets (vv. 14-18), especially the rules on the proper use of wealth. Finally, Jesus tells the parable of the rich man and Lazarus (vv. 16-31). The theme is still on wealth, though here the emphasis is on the unwise use of wealth. The Law is still valid and is the ultimate source of ethical authority in man's life. Fitzmyer asserts that the continuing or abiding validity of the Law is emphasized in Jesus' words at the end of the parable: "If they listen not to Moses and the prophets (v. 31)."[444] In view of the bigger picture——Luke's travel narrative——it should be noted that Jesus' teaching here is a part of His ethical and moral teachings to His disciples as citizens of the kingdom of God that has already broken into the world with the first coming of Jesus.

Summary and Conclusion

In summary, the analysis of the general historical background of the Gospel of Luke shows that Luke, one of the companions of apostle Paul in his missionary journeys, is the author of Luke-Acts. The explicit recipient is Theophilus. The date of writing might be between Paul's imprisonment in Caesarea (A.D. 56-58), and prior to the death of James and release of Paul, which means before   A.D. 62. The provenance could be Caesarea or Rome.

The genre of the gospel of Luke generally may be classified as "narrative" or "story." Some portions in Luke belong to an ancient literary tradition called "historiography." The purpose of Luke-Acts is to write an orderly (chronological) account to Theophilus in order to affirm the truthfulness of what has been taught to him. Another purpose is to defend God's purpose in history. He wants to show

---

[443]Nolland also suggests that Luke 16:19-31 is "on the use and abuse of riches." Nolland, *Luke 9:21-18:34*, 831.

[444]Fitzmyer, *Luke X-XXIV*, 1116.

how things happened in order, and that God fulfilled His promises to His people Israel and also extended His blessing to the Gentiles. Moreover, it is apparent that Luke has a theological motive in writing his account of Jesus' story.

The general theme of Luke-Acts is "the plan of God." This general theme braces the whole of Luke-Acts. It also braces a variety of thematic strands which are woven together to emphasize the certainty and consistency of the plan of God. The plan of God is that "all flesh will see the salvation of God" (Luke 3:6). This divine activity was carried out through history. This is called salvation history. This plan of God begins with the Jews in Jerusalem but extends to all nations, kindred, and people.

The structural-thematic analysis of Luke-Acts, Luke's travel narrative, and Luke 16 support the plausibility of the general theme. Furthermore, some sub-themes which are related to the general theme crop up. The structural-thematic analysis of Luke-Acts shows that both books are structurally and thematically parallel. In the analysis of Luke's structure, it was found out that there are promise-fulfillment-praise response literary patterns. It is also evident, in the structural analysis, that Jerusalem is very central in Luke's Gospel. It is the central point of its geographical and narrative structures. Luke's narrative begins and ends in Jerusalem. However, aside from the emphasis on Jerusalem, it is also very noticeable that the temple in Jerusalem takes the center stage in Luke. Luke's narrative begins at the temple and ends at the temple. However, there is a paradigm shift from Luke to Acts. The narrative of Acts begins at Jerusalem/ temple, but in chapter 7, it shifts its focus from the earthly temple to heaven/ heavenly temple. The gospel also shifts from the Jews to Gentiles. In Acts, the disciples start to evangelize Jerusalem but its narrative ends in Rome. In Luke, salvation proceeds from the temple where God dwells, as in the OT. Thus, while salvation starts with the Jews in Luke, it ends up with all nations in Acts.

The structure of Luke's travel narrative, as suggested by some scholars, shows a chiasm. Several themes are spelled out by this chiastic narrative structure. First, Jerusalem stands out as the focal point of the eschatological events. Second, the travel narrative, on the one hand, emphasizes the exaltation of the poor, the humble, and the marginalized of society. On the other hand, it debases the rich, the proud, and the socially and religiously prominent people of the Jewish society. The theme of humility is clearly spelled out not only in the travel narrative but also in the whole book. God's concern for the poor is also prominent here in both the travel narrative and in the whole book. The kingdom motif is also prominent in Luke's travel narrative. The kingdom already breaks into the world at the arrival of Jesus. In this travel narrative, Jesus taught His disciples the principles of His newly established spiritual kingdom. One of these principles is "prudent stewardship" that is apparent in Luke 16:1-31. The analysis of the structure of Luke 16:1-31 shows two parables in contrasting fashion. The first illustrates how to be a prudent steward, and the second exposes a foolish steward. Jesus addresses the first parable to His disciples, but the second is addressed to the Pharisees. In conclusion, the thematic-structural analysis of Luke-Acts indicates that the parable of the rich man and Lazarus is Jesus' illustration which He uses primarily to rebuke the Pharisees. Jesus stresses that they should listen to the Law and the Prophets, especially in their teachings on how to be prudent stewards of the unrighteous wealth they possess. It should be stressed, moreover, that nowhere in the parable (Luke 16:19-31) or in the Gospel of Luke including Luke's travel narrative is the theme of judgment and punishment in ᾅδης were emphasized. What is significantly stressed in Luke-Acts, the travel narrative, and Luke 16:1-31 is the exaltation of the oppressed poor, that is, the marginalized of society. In the larger perspective, the revelation of the truth——that salvation is for both Jews and Gentiles——receives emphasis.

THE EXEGETICAL ANALYSIS OF LUKE 16:19-31

T O FURTHER shed light on the interpretation of ἅδης in the parable of the rich man and Lazarus (16:19-31), this chapter exegetically analyzes Luke 16:19-31. First, it lexically analyzes some words.[445] Second, the structural-thematic analysis of the passage in the light of its immediate and wider contexts follows. Third, it examines the narrative in its immediate and wider literary-historical contexts. It considers the grammar and syntax. It also determines the main spiritual points or insights of the parable. Fourth, it considers the parable in the setting of Jesus' proclamation of the kingdom of God. Lastly, the theological implications of the story parable are drawn out.

Lexical Analysis

The word ἅδης was already analyzed in chapter 3 of this study especially in its occurrences in the OT–LXX version, and in other NT writings aside from the Synoptic Gospels and Acts.[446] This word occurs only ten times in the whole NT, but it appears six times in the Synoptics and Acts (Matt 11:23; 16:18; Luke 10:15; 16:23; Acts 2:27,31).

Bietenhard points out that in Greek literature ἅδης refers to the "underworld as the abode of the dead who lead a shadowy existence in it."[447] He also notes that

---

[445]The occurrences of ἅδης and γέεννα in the Synoptic Gospels and Acts will be lexically analyzed.

[446]In this lexical-contextual analysis, the Synoptic Gospels are joined together because the Synoptics have similar literary pattern. It includes Acts because Luke- and Acts have the same author. Therefore, ἅδης in Luke may have the same meaning as in Acts. Besides, the historical context of Acts is the continuation of the historical context of the gospel account. The link of Luke-Acts is further shown by Richard Sabuin through the growth patterns of Luke-Acts. See Richard Sabuin, "The Growth of Christ: Understanding Luke 2:40,56 in the Light of the Structural Pattern of Luke-Acts," *Journal of Asia Adventist Seminary* 10, no. 1 (2007): 15-25.

[447]Bietenhard, 2:206.

"it can mean the grave, death."[448] He adds,

> Only gradually did the Greeks also attach to the concept the ideas of reward and punishment. The good and the righteous were rewarded in *hadēs*, the wicked and the godless received a variety of punishments there.[449]

In the NT, Bauer notes that the word ᾅδης refers to the Greek god of the underworld; it also means the netherworld, the place of the dead.[450] Joachim Jeremias asserts that ᾅδης in the NT is closely linked with later Judaism. It refers to the abode of souls loosed from their bodies.[451] Furthermore, Wesley Perschbacher defines ᾅδης as "hell" the place of punishment, and the abode of the dead without citing any NT reference.[452] However, the NT seems to follow the OT concept of ᾅδης.[453]

As far as the lexical definitions of ᾅδης proposed by scholars are concerned, it seems that the idea of souls being punished in ᾅδης seems to originate with the Greeks. Significantly, this concept seems to be absent in the OT, but is present in later Judaism possibly because of Hellenistic influences as indicated in the background study in chapter 3. In this section the word ᾅδης and its synonym will be analyzed in the light of their immediate and wider contexts.[454] First, this section analyzes the word ᾅδης in Matthew. Second, it analyzes this word in Luke-Acts. Third, it analyzes the word ᾅδης in Luke 16:23.

---

[448] Bietenhard, 2:206.

[449] Ibid.

[450] Bauer, BAGD, s.v. "ᾅδης."

[451] Jeremias, "ᾅδης," 1:148.

[452] Perschbacher, *NAGL*, s.v. "ᾅδης."

[453] For the analysis of ᾅδης in NT except the Synoptic Gospels and Acts, see chapter 3. For the analysis of ᾅδης in the Synoptics and Acts, see below.

[454] The immediate literary context of the passage is Luke 16. The wider literary context includes the whole books of Luke and Acts. The historical context may include the rest of the Synoptic Gospels. The immediate literary context of the passage is Luke 16 because it seems reasonable to say that there is an unbroken literary link between the passage and the preceding narrative of Luke 16. The wider context includes Acts because Acts is the second volume of the two-volume series written by Luke to the same recipient, Theophilus.

The Usage of Ἅδης in Matthew

One occurrence of ᾅδης is in Matt 16:18. The foundation of the ἐκκλησι,a (ekklēsia) "Church" of Jesus is the context of this passage. According to the text, Jesus replies to Peter that His Church that is founded upon the rock could not be overcome κατισχύσουσιν (katischusousin) by the "πύλαι ᾅδου" (gates of *hadēs*). There are some issues in this text,[455] but the concern of this research is the usage of ᾅδης in the context of Matt 16:18.

In this text, ᾅδης is pictured as having gates. The imagery of ᾅδης having gates is well-known in Greek literature's description of ᾅδης[456] and also in Jewish inter-testamental writings.[457] However, this imagery is also found in the OT. It is found in Isa 38:10 (I said, "In the prime of my life must I go through the gates of death and be robbed of the rest of my years?" NIV).[458] It is set in the context of king Hezekiah's poem or song. This was his poem or song after his recovery from a terminal illness. This expression "שַׁעַר שְׁאוֹל"(ša' ar šᵉ'ol) or ""πύλαι ᾅδου" (pylai hadou, LXX) in Isaiah may be figurative. The literal gate—שַׁעַר—serves as a protection, especially from the attacks of the enemy. It serves also as a control to the city where people go in and out. When the gate of a city is toppled down, eventually, the whole city is captured (Isa 24:12). God uses this literal imagery in His covenant promise to Abraham after the latter showed an extreme faith in God by his willingness to offer his son Isaac (Gen 22). God's promise to Abraham is that, "Your seed shall possess the gates of his enemies" (Gen 22:17). This promise had been literally fulfilled to His covenant people Israel when they conquered the Land of Canaan. On the other hand, this promise may have a deeper meaning especially in the context of the NT. Apostle Paul, in his letter to the Galatians, speaks of Abraham and his seed—Jesus—to whom the promise

---

[455]One of the issues is the meaning and interpretation of the "rock" in Matt 16:18. See W. D. Davies and Dale C. Allison Jr., *The Gospel According to Saint Matthew VIII-XVIII*, ICC, 624; Craig Blomberg, *Matthew*, NAC, vol. 22, 252; Ulriz Luz, *Matthew 8-20*, Hermeneia, 373-77.

[456]For example, see Lucian *Menippus*, 6,8, (LCL, 4:82-87).

[457]For example, see 1QH XI:17; 4Q418 [Instructions], Frag. 127:2). Cf. Bauckham, "Hades," 3:15. Davies and Allison, 630.

[458]For similar expression, see Job 38:17 (gates of death).

was made (3:16,17). However, the believers in Christ also became Abraham's seed through their union with Christ (Gal 3:29). Now, one of the contents of the promise given to Abraham is that his seed will possess the gates of their enemies.

How has this promise been fulfilled in the NT? Going back to Isa 38:10, Hezekiah does not speak of literal gates of שְׁאוֹל.. He may be speaking of the power or control of death or grave over a person who was dead (see also Job 38:17; Ps 9:14; 107:18). No human being could escape the power or dominion of death and the grave. In the OT, death and the grave are feared. Job even believes that a man who went down to the grave would rise up no more (Job 7:9). שְׁאוֹל is also figuratively pictured to have bars (Job 15:17), as in a fortress portraying a stronghold. The Psalmist (Ps 49:16) also acknowledges the power of the שְׁאוֹל (grave, or death, cf. Ps 89:49).[459] However, Hosea reveals that Yahweh is able to deliver Israel from the "hand of death or grave" (מִיַּד שְׁאוֹל) (13:14). It seems that in Matt 16:18, ᾅδης which is portrayed as having gates similar to Isa 38:10 carries the OT meaning.[460] This is plausible because ᾅδης, like in the OT שְׁאוֹל, is considered as a powerful enemy of Israel (Hosea 13). It was also portrayed as a very powerful enemy of Jesus (the seed of Abraham) and of His Church (also seed of Abraham by her union with Christ), the New Covenant people of God.[461] However, like in Hos 13:14, ᾅδης could not prevail against the people of God because Jesus, the Son of God who has power over death and ᾅδης (John 11:25; Rev 1:18), was the one who built the Church. After considering the OT background, once again, it is reasonable to suggest that ᾅδης here in Matt

---

[459]The phrase "מִיַּד־שְׁאוֹל" (from the hand of šhᵉʾol—grave or death) may be similar to the phrase "שַׁעַר שְׁאוֹל " (gates of šhᵉʾol or gates of death).

[460]Bauckham argues that the imagery in Matt 16:18 reflects more of the OT (Isa 38:10; cf. Job 38:17; Ps 9:14; 107:18). Bauckham, "Hades," 3:15. However, Davies and Allison insist that "although 'gates of Hades' is a fixed expression in the OT, one must beware of reading the OT meaning into Matthew's text, for conceptions about Hades and Sheol changed over time. By the first century there was a tendency to think of Hades or certain sections of it as an underworld peopled not by the dead in general but by the *ungodly* dead, as well as by demons and evil spirits." Davis and Allison, 633.

[461]Paul in his first letter to the Corinthians considers death as one of the enemies of Jesus Christ (1 Cor 15:25,26). It will be destroyed in the last day. In the book of Apocalypse, John also reveals how "ὁ θάνατος καὶ ὁ ᾅδης" (thanatos kai hadēs) will be destroyed in the last day (Rev 20:14).

16:18 carries the OT meaning of שְׁאוֹל, that is, grave and death. Jesus reveals to His disciples that the Church which is built upon the rock[462] is impregnable against the gates of ᾅδης.[463] It (ᾅδης) will not prevail "κατισχύω" (katischuô)[464] against it. This suggests that Jesus' victory over death (Rev 1:18), and eventually the Church' victory over death (1 Cor 15:51-57), may be the meaning of this clause—the gates of ᾅδης shall not prevail against it (Matt 16:18). If this is so, then God's promise to Abraham in Gen 22:17, "Your seed will possess the gates of his enemies" is fulfilled. Based on this biblical evidence, it seems plausible to suggest that ᾅδης in Matt 16:18 means death or grave.[465]

---

[462]Several scholars say that the rock here is Peter. Davies and Allison argue that Matt 16 is parallel with Gen 17. In Gen 17, the OT people was born; in Matt 16, the NT people was born. In Gen 17, the key figure was given a new name (Abraham) signifying that he would be the father of a multitude; in Matt 16, the key figure was also given a new name (Peter) which means 'rock' on which the Church is founded. Davies and Allison, 624. Blomberg also argues that "the play on words in the Greek between Peter's name "πέτρος" (petros) and the word "rock" (πέτρα—petra) makes sense only if Peter is the rock." Blomberg, *Matthew*, 252. For the history of interpretation of the "rock" of Matt 16:18, see Luz, 373-77. However, the rock (πέτρα) of Matt 16:18 could be Jesus. The imagery of a "rock" in the OT usually refers to God. For example, in Deut 32:4, God is called "the Rock" because He is perfect, the God of truth, and without iniquity. In Deut 32:13, He is called the Rock of salvation (cf. Ps 18:47; 62:3,6). The gods of the pagans were also called "rock" (Deut 32:37). In 1 Sam 2:2, there is no other Rock like our God who is holy. In Ps 18:3, the idea concerning God as rock stresses "fortification" (cf. Ps 31:3; 71:3), "refuge" (cf. Ps 27:5), and "strength" (Ps 62:8). In Ps 18:32, David portrays the Lord as the Rock who alone is God. However, in a negative sense, Isaiah prophesied that the Lord becomes a rock of stumbling, or a rock of offense for the people of Israel and Judah (Isa 8:14). In the NT, Paul reveals that the Rock of Exodus, from whom the Israelites drank water, is Jesus (1 Cor 10:4; cf. Exod 17:6). Interestingly, Peter, who was given prominence by some scholars, called Jesus as the Rock (1 Pet 2:8), the cornerstone of God's spiritual house (vv. 4-6). Significantly, Peter, when referring to Jesus as a Rock, quoted Isa 8:14. In the context of Isaiah, the Rock there is Yahweh. Furthermore, Peter in this figurative passage, also called the believers as living stones (λίθοι) in God's spiritual house (v. 5). Paul also pointed out that the foundation of God's spiritual house is Jesus (1 Cor 3:11). In the context of Matt 16, it is safe to suggest that Jesus is the Rock to which the Church is built because He Himself has conquered death and ᾅδης (ὁ θάνατος καὶ ὁ ᾅδης). Therefore, the gates of ᾅδης could not prevail against the Church which is built on Jesus.

[463]There are many interpretations with regards to this phrase. See Davies and Allison, 630-33. The top two contending interpretations are the following:

　　1. "The gates of *Hadēs*" refers to the strength and power of Satan and his cohorts.

　　2. It refers to the power of death. See also D. A. Carson, "Matthew," *EBC*, 370.

[464]It means "prevail against, overcome, win out." Bauer, BAGD, s.v. "κατισχύω."

[465]R. T. France also suggests that the phrase, "'The gates of *hades*' is a metaphor for death, which here contrasts strikingly with the phrase 'the living God' in v. 16." R. T. France, *The Gospel of Matthew*, NICNT, 624.

The Usages of' Ἄδης in Luke-Acts

At this juncture, the usages of ᾅδης in Luke and Acts will be analyzed first before analyzing the usage of ᾅδης in Luke 16:23. Its occurrence in Luke 10:15 (parallel with Matt 11:23),[466] ᾅδης is in the context of Jesus' pronouncement of doom against the town of Capernaum. Jesus indicates that ᾅδης is the opposite of heaven. Heaven refers to the place where God dwells,[467] while ᾅδης may mean the place below the earth.

In this passage, it seems that Jesus' pronouncement against the people of Capernaum is in the setting of the arrival of the kingdom of God (10:8,11) and judgment (v. 14). Jesus' pronouncement against the towns of Chorazin and Bethsaida that did not believe the gospel of the kingdom of God culminates to their doom at the judgment (v. 14). It naturally follows that Jesus' pronouncement of woe against the city of Capernaum also culminates at the judgment, in the context of the arrival of the kingdom of God. This judgment is its abasement to a[|dhj (v. 15). It seems reasonable to believe then that ᾅδης here was used in the context of judgment in the last day.[468]   Furthermore, the clause "ἕως τοῦ ᾅδου καταβήσῃ" (You will be brought down to *hadēs*) is verbally and thematically parallel with the clause in Isa 14:15 (LXX) "εἰς ᾅδου καταβήσῃ." (You are brought down to *hadēs*). The possibility is that Jesus alludes to this well-known passage. Both passages have a similar thematic overtone, that is, God humbles the proud who exalt themselves. In Isaiah, it is the king of Babylon who figuratively represents

---

[466]Papaioannou notes that, in Matthew, the "woes are pronounced within the context of eschatological punishment. Matt 11:20 does not appear in Luke and in Matthew functions as an introduction to woes. It is a prelude to the final judgment." Papaioannou, 114.

[467]The word οὐρανός (heaven) is usually associated with the kingdom of God, and the dwelling place of God where His throne is (Matt 5:16,34; 7:11,21; 10:32,33, Luke 2:15; 6:23; 10:20; 12:33; 15:7).

[468]Contra Papaioannou who argues that the abasement of Capernaum to ᾅδης refers to its temporal destruction during the great Jewish war A.D. 66-70. Papaioannou, 116. However, the immediate context seems to suggest that the abasement of Capernaum in ᾅδης will be in the eschatological judgment because of two reasons:
 1. The preceding pronouncements of woe against Chorazin and Bethsaida has something to do with the judgment (last—day judgment; cf. Matt 11:22).
 2. The phrase "ἐν τῇ ἡμέρᾳ" (on that day) in 10:12 also refers to the day of judgment (cf. Matt 10:15; 11:24), when the cities who did not believe the message of the kingdom of God preached by the seventy-two messengers (10:2,9) would be destroyed. The other occurrences of the similar phrase (Matt 7:22; Matt 26:29) refer to the coming of the Son of Man.

Satan who desires to exalt himself above God. Here, in Luke, it was Capernaum who was too arrogant to repent. Consequently, both the king of Babylon and Capernaum would be brought low into ᾅδης. It seems that ᾅδης in Luke 10:15 carries also the meaning of שְׁאוֹל in Isa 14:15. In the context of Isa 14:15, שְׁאוֹל may mean "the place below the earth," or "the grave, the place of the dead."[469] Nolland suggests that the point of Jesus' statement is not probably so much about the idea of punishment in ᾅδης as about the idea of humiliation of the proud as evident in Isa 14:15.[470] However, the contexts of Isaiah (14; cf. 13) and Luke 10 seem to suggest the punishment and humiliation of both the king of Babylon and Capernaum. The next occurrences are found in Acts 2:27,31. In its literary context, Peter was delivering a sermon to the Jewish pilgrims from different nations during the Passover feast in Jerusalem (2:5). Peter began with an OT prophecy, specifically from Joel 2:28-32, declaring that what is happening in their midst is already a fulfillment of a significant OT prophecy. Peter then directs the men of Israel to Jesus of Nazareth (v. 22) pointing out that this man whom they nailed to the cross was raised again by God (v. 24). It should be noted that Peter says that Jesus was under the power of death (v. 24). However, He would not be held there. Right at this point, in vv. 25-28, Peter quotes Ps 16:8-11 as the basis for his presentation that Jesus would not be held by the power of death.[471] Looking at Ps 16:8-11, it seems that this Psalm is David's. In this Psalm, he seems to be speaking of himself.[472] However, in Acts, Peter has Jesus as the subject of this Psalm of David (2:22-25). Ernst Haenchen asserts, "The Christians found something else in the Greek text (LXX): the psalmist foretells the resurrection of

---

[469]See chapter 3. Nolland insists that "Hades in the LXX [Isa 14:15] represents the Sheol of the Hebrew text. Sheol was the sphere of the lingering and shadowy continuation of existence of those who had died. It is a place of deprivation and of oblivion, but not specifically of judgment." Nolland, *Luke 9:21-18:34*, 557.

[470]Cf. ibid.

[471]Gerhard Krodel sees a chiastic structure of vv. 22-36 asserting that vv. 22-24 is the kerygma followed by the proof from Scripture (vv. 25-28). Gerhard A. Krodel, *Acts*, Augsburg Commentary on the New Testament, 83.

[472]John B. Polhill also pointed out that "originally the psalm seems to have been a plea of the psalmist that God would vindicate him and that he might escape death and sheol." John B. Polhill, *Acts*, NAC, vol. 26, 113.

the Messiah, in as much as he speaks in the person of the anointed."[473] In short, this Psalm is messianic.

In the original Hebrew text of this Psalm, the word for ᾅδης is שְׁאוֹל. In the original context, the usage seems to follow the usual OT meaning which is "grave" or "death."[474] This is the possible meaning because in the original literary context, when the Psalmist mentions שְׁאוֹל, he associates it with death (v. 11).[475] Furthermore, looking at the original Hebrew text, the first line is thematically parallel with the second line: כִּי לֹא־תַעֲזֹב נַפְשִׁי לִשְׁאוֹל (For you will not leave my soul in sheol) [first line], לֹא־תִתֵּן חֲסִידְךָ לִרְאוֹת שָׁחַת[476] (Nor will you abandon your holy one to see the pit or grave) [second line]. Here are the parallels:

1. The word "soul" of the first line is parallel with "the holy one" of the second line.

2. The word שְׁאוֹל of the first line is parallel with "שַׁחַת" (shachath) which means "pit," or "grave."

Based on these parallels, it is now reasonable to suggest that the word שְׁאוֹל in Ps 16:10 may mean "grave," or a "place below the earth" (a place of the dead). It seems that in Acts, Peter has also the idea of שְׁאוֹל (from Ps 16:10) in his usage of ᾅδης in Acts 2:27,31.

First, it is evident especially in the clause, "God raised him up, loosing the pangs of death" (2:24, ESV). In this clause Peter refers to the death of Jesus. When Jesus died, He was buried in the grave. But, just as His body has begun to decay, God raised Him. So the statement, "Neither wilt thou suffer thine Holy One, to see corruption "διαφθορα," (diaphthora)"[477] (v. 27b, KJV), was fulfilled.

---

[473]Ernst Haenchen, *The Acts of the Apostles: A Commentary* (Oxford: Basil Blackwell, 1971), 181.

[474]NIV translates שְׁאוֹל as "grave." TEV translates it "power of death."

[475]This is apparent in v. 11 when he says that the Lord will show him the path of life. This statement implies that David was threatened by death. Naturally, he refers שְׁאוֹל as "grave."

[476]See Elliger, and Rudolph, *BHS*, 1097.

[477]It means destruction, ruin, death, in moral sense, corruption. Bauer, BAGD, s.v. "διαφθορα."

Second, it is also evident in v. 27 where the first clause is parallel with the second:[478] (1)"ὅτι οὐκ ἐγκαταλείψεις τὴν ψυχήν μου εἰς ᾅδην" (You will not leave my soul in *Hadēs*), (2) "οὐδὲ δώσεις τὸν ὅσιόν σου ἰδεῖν διαφθορα," (Nor will you deliver   up your Holy One to see corruption).[479]

Evidently, in the original Hebrew text, as shown above, these clauses are parallel because the word שַׁחַת in the second clause means "pit, or grave" is synonymous with שְׁאוֹל in the first clause. In the Greek text of Ps 16:10 in Acts 2:27, the word ᾅδης is parallel with διαφθορα (death, destruction, corruption). This may imply that the ψυχη, (soul) and its parallel ὅσιός (hosios) which is subject to corruption and decay in ᾅδης do not refer to an immortal soul who suffers or enjoys in ᾅδης as in the Greek concept.

In v. 31, in Peter's exposition of v. 27, σὰρξ is mentioned as the substitute of ὅσιός in v. 27.[480] This means that there seems to be no dichotomy with Christ's being when He died.[481] When Jesus died, what was said was that His ψυχη,[482] was in ᾅδης (v. 27), whereas in its parallel in v. 31 the parallel of ψυχη, is σὰρξ

---

[478]This is the LXX text of Ps 16:10 that was quoted by Peter. It is already demonstrated above that in the original Hebrew text of Ps 16:10, the first clause is thematically and lexically parallel or synonymous with the second clause. It is natural then that, in Acts, the same is true.

[479]Here are the parallels:
1. The verb ἐγκαταλείψεις (egkataleipseis) is thematically parallel with δώσεις (dōseis).
2. The word ψυχή is also parallel with ὅσιός (holy one).
3. The word ᾅδης is parallel with διαφθορα (death, destruction, corruption).

[480]Here are the parallels between v. 27 and v. 31:
   v. 27—first clause: (1)"ὅτι οὐκ ἐγκαταλείψεις τὴν ψυχήν μου εἰς ᾅδην" (You will not leave my soul in *Hadēs*)
   v. 31—first clause: (1) ὅτι οὔτε ἐγκατελείφθη εἰς ᾅδην (He was neither abandoned to *hadēs*)
   v. 27—second clause: (2)"οὐδὲ δώσεις τὸν ὅσιόν σου ἰδεῖν διαφθορα," (Nor will you deliver up your Holy One to see corruption).
   v. 31—second clause: (2) οὔτε ἡ σὰρξ αὐτοῦ εἶδεν διαφθοράν (Nor His flesh did see corruption).
   The NT Greek texts in this study are taken from Bible Works software. For a hard copy, see Barbara Aland, Kurt Aland, Johannes Karavidopoulos, Carlo M. Martini, and Bruce M. Metzger, eds., *The Greek New Testament* (GNT-UBS4), 4th ed. (Corrected) (Stuttgart: United Bible Societies, 1993), 413.

[481]KJV translation indicates a dichotomy of soul and body. In the original text, there is no yuch, in v. 31 only in v. 27.

[482]The word yuch, here may not mean "disembodied souls" that is separated from the body when a man dies as what the Greeks believed. This word may have a Hebrew OT meaning found in Ps 16:10.

(v. 31), which was said by Peter not to see corruption. The ψυχη, and σὰρξ are also parallel with ὅσιός (pious one). This means that when ψυχη, and σὰρξ are mentioned these refer to Jesus' being as a whole not a disembodied soul separate from the body.

It is therefore reasonable to conclude that Jesus was not divided into "disembodied soul" and the "body" at death. Jesus' whole being was in ᾅδης as far as the context is concerned. It is not the disembodied soul of Christ which was in ᾅδης like Greek concept, but the whole person minus the breath of life as in the original Hebrew concept in the OT.[483]

Peter's argument that God would not suffer Christ to decay in a[|dhj indicates that the word ψυχη, here in Acts 2:27 has an OT meaning rather than Greek meaning. Consequently, ᾅδης in Acts may have an OT meaning of שְׁאוֹל too, that is, grave or pit[484] where the body decays at death, rather than the classical Greek concept of ᾅδης which is the netherworld, the place of the conscious disembodied souls of the dead. Unfortunately, as shown in chapter 3, the early Christians, probably influenced by the Greek concept, believed that when Jesus died, He journeyed into ᾅδης, broke its gates, and set free its righteous prisoners. This belief was absent in the writings of Jesus' apostles.

The Usage of ᾍδης in Luke 16:23

In the problem passage of this study, it should be noted that ᾅδης occurs in Jesus' parable of the rich man and Lazarus (vv. 19-31).[485] In the parable, ᾅδης has similar descriptions with those of the stories in Greek and later Judaism

---

[483]Marshall also suggests that "the word *flesh*, which has been taken over from Ps 16:9, refers to the person of Jesus as a whole, and does not suggest that a flesh/soul dualism is in mind." I. Howard Marshall, *Acts*, TNTC, vol. 5, 77. However, some scholars assume "dualism" in this passage like in Greek concept. Cf. F. F. Bruce, *The Book of Acts*, NICNT, 71. Hans Conzelmann also downplays the notion that Jesus' soul journeyed to ᾅδης by saying that the phrase "'εἰς ᾅδην' by itself means 'abandon to Hades' (cf. Pss. Sol. 2:7). But Luke means 'leave in Hades,' that is, in death. The text cannot be understood as referring to a journey to Hades." Hans Conzelmann, *Acts of the Apostles*, Hermeneia, 20.

[484]Polhill also accedes to the NIV translation saying that "the NIV has wisely translated the Greek word *Hades* as 'the grave.' The reference is to שְׁאוֹל, the realm of the dead, and thus to death; and this is the sense in which Peter applied it." Polhill, 113.

[485]See the discussion on genre in chapter 2.

literature already mentioned in chapter 3, that is, as noted by Bietenhard, the wicked received punishments in ᾅδης. However, there are also differences.[486] Greek and later Judaism literature speak of disembodied soul in ᾅδης, whereas in the parable of Jesus, what were in ᾅδης seem to be persons with bodies. It should also be pointed out that this concept could not be found in the OT, in other NT literature, and even in Luke except in this passage. This means that ᾅδης, only in this story parable, lexically seems to carry the meaning of Greek popular concept of ᾅδης as the place of the souls of both the wicked and the righteous dead.[487] However, they were separated from each other (the wicked and the righteous). The rich man who is presumably wicked is suffering in the flame of ᾅδης, but the righteous Lazarus was in the bosom of Abraham. Thus, in the whole NT, only here in this passage that the word ᾅδης may mean "the netherworld" as perceived by the Greeks and later Judaism. However, it is clear that its occurrence here is in the context of the parable of the rich man and Lazarus, and the parable seems to be fictitious.[488] It was already pointed out in chapter 4 above that the theme of Luke 16 is on the wise and unwise use of wealth in this life.

The Usage of Γέεννα in the Synoptic Gospels

The word γέεννα,[489] which literally refers to the valley of Hinnom, is figuratively used in the NT. In the OT background, it literally refers to the valley of Hinnom, a ravine south of Jerusalem where fires were kept burning to consume the dead body of criminals, refuse, and animals.[490] Figuratively, it refers to the

---

[486]For more discussion on these differences, see the narrative-literary analysis below.

[487]However, there is no one-to-one correspondence between the concepts present in Greco-Roman literature and that of Luke 16:19-31. For example, the god ᾅδης in Greco-Roman literature is not present in Luke 16:19-31. The concept that the righteous are in the bosom of Abraham is absent in Greco-Roman literature.

[488]See chapter 2, and the narrative-literary analysis below.

[489]This study includes the analysis of the usages of γέεννα because, in the background, later Judaism used γέεννα and ᾅδης synonymously.

[490]According to Donald A. Hagner, Gehenna is from the Aramaic word gê hinnām "for the 'valley of Hinnom,' a despised place to the southwest of Jerusalem where at one time human sacrifices were offered to the god Molech (cf. 2 Kgs 23:10; Jer 7:31) and where in later times the city's refuse was burned. The constant burning there made the valley a particular metaphor for eternal punishment (cf. 4 Ezra 7:36; Sib. Or. 1.103; 2.292; Str-B 4.2:1029-1118)." Donald A. Hagner, Matthew 1-13, WBC, vol. 33A, 117.

fiery place where the wicked will be punished.[491] This is a Grecized form of the

Hebrew word גֵּי־הִנֹּם (gēhinnôm) "Valley of Hinnom," (Josh 15:8b; Neh 11:30).

There, according to later Jewish popular belief, God's final judgment is to take

place.[492] Jeremias also notes,

> Threats of judgment uttered over this sinister valley in Jer 7:32; 19:6; cf. Isa
> 31:9; 66:24, are the reason why the Valley of Hinnom came to be equated
> with the hell of the last judgment in apocalyptic literature from 2nd century
> B.C. (Eth. En. 90:26; 27:1 ff.; 56:3f.). The name *gehinnom* thus came to be
> used for the eschatological fire of hell).[493]

He further adds that this concept was reflected in the NT. In the first

century A.D., γέεννα was further extended to cover the place where the ungodly

were punished in the so called "intermediate state," a state between death and

resurrection.[494] Bietenhard also suggests that γέεννα, in Jewish apocalyptic, came

to be applied to the eschatological hell fire. In time however, it became simply

the place of punishment. Γέεννα became a temporary place of punishment (until

the final judgment).[495]

At this juncture, it is also needful to analyze the usages of γέεννα[496] in the

Synoptic Gospels. The word γέεννα occurs eleven times in the Synoptic Gospels,

seven in

Matthew (5:22,29,30; 10:28; 18:9; 23:15,33), thrice in Mark (9:43,45,47),

and once in Luke (12:5). In Matthew, γέεννα is associated with fire (5:22; 18:9)

that would destroy "ἀπολέσαι" (apolesai),[497] both soul and body "ψυχὴν καὶ σῶ

μα" (psych1n kai sôma, 10:28).[498] Donald Hagner notes that "the expression

---

[491]Bauer, BAGD, s.v. "γέεννα." See Matt 5:22,29,30, 10:28; 18:9; 23:15,23; Mark 9:43,45,47; Luke 12:5.

[492]Bauer, BAGD, s.v. "γέεννα."

[493]Joachim Jeremias, "γέεννα," *TDNT*, 1:657.

[494]Ibid., 658.

[495]Hans Bietenhard, "γέεννα," *NIDNTT*, 2:208.

[496]For a more detailed and comprehensive analysis of the usages of γέεννα in the Synoptic Gospels, see Papaioannou, 44-99.

[497]It means "to ruin, bring to ruin, kill, cease to exist." Bauer, BAGD, s.v. "ἀπολέσαι."

[498]The phrase "ψυχὴν καὶ σῶμα" may not refer to the dichotomized view of human beings, as taught by Plato (see chapter 3). For sure, ψυχη, here does not mean a separate immortal entity of man that survives when man dies. Papioannou argues that the destruction of ψυχη, in γέεννα in 10:28b negates this idea, and

'Gehenna of fire' is used only by Matthew."[499] The punishment in γέεννα has
something to do with the judgment.[500] The unrepentant Jews, like the Pharisees,
cannot escape this judgment 'κρίσις'[501] (23:33). This judgment would be at the
last day, at the coming of the Son of Man (Matt 25:31). In this judgment, He will
separate the righteous from the wicked (25:32-33). The righteous will inherit the
kingdom of God (v. 34) and will enter into life (18:9). On the other hand, the
wicked will be cast into the eternal fire of γέεννα (Matt 25:41; cf. John 5:28-29).

Mark, like Matthew, states that the righteous will enter into life (similar to
"enter into the kingdom of God"), but the wicked will go into the fire of γέεννα
(9:43, 45,47).[502] He also describes the fire of γέεννα as ἄσβεστος (asbestos),
which means "unquenchable,"[503] similar to Matthew's expression "the eternal fire"
(τὸ πῦρ τὸ αἰώνιον).[504] Papaioannou makes several plausible observations in
his analysis of γέεννα in Mark. First, he insists that Mark 9:43-48 may allude

---

it is supported by 10:39 where ψυχή, means "life." Papaioannou, 70. He further points out that the phrase
means the whole person rather than a dichotomy of soul and body. The emphasis is on the totality of the final
destruction. Ibid.

[499]Hagner, 117.

[500]The word ἔνοχος (enochos) in 5:22 is a legal technical term, which pertains to being required to
give an account for something held against one—liable, answerable, guilty. Bauer, BAGD, s.v. "ἔνοχος."

[501]Here it may refer to the activity of God in the last day for judging all people (cf. John 5:30). Bauer,
BAGD, s.v. "κρίσις."

[502]Collins notes, "The name 'Gehenna' became the regular designation for the place of eternal
punishment of the wicked [2 Esdr 7:36; 2 Bar 59:10; 85:13; Sib. Or. 1.103; 4.186]. This is the usage in Mark
9:43,45, and 47, which thus refer to eternal punishment." Adela Yarbro Collins, Mark, Hermeneia, 453.

[503]Papaiouannou points out that "unquenchable fire" does mean eternal duration but rather stresses
the certainty and completeness of God's punishment. Papaioannou, 48-49. He cites Isa 34:10-11, where
after the statement of the "unquenchable fire in v. 10, wild animals immediately were seen roaming around
the destroyed land (v. 11)." Ibid., 49.

[504]Eternal fire here may not mean unending fire that eternally punishes the wicked because Matthew
already mentioned in 10:28 that both body and soul would be destroyed in γέεννα. How will they suffer for
eternity if they were already destroyed? It would be reasonable to believe that "eternal fire" refers to the nature
of the fire rather than the punishment of the wicked. This means that this fire could not be quenched (Mark
9:43) until all the wicked would be destroyed. Papaiouannou also ably analyzed the word "αἰώνιον" (aiōnion).
He points out that in some cases the word has a quantitative sense while in other cases it has a qualitative sense.
The second option however is to be preferred in several passages. With regards to "eternal fire," it is more
plausible, he adds, to take it as having a qualitative meaning, which means that it is "a fire that came directly
from God, a punishment characteristic in its thoroughness, of the quality of the age to come." He cites Jude
7 as an example where αἰώνιον does not mean unending duration. Papaioannou, 64. For more details see
Papaioannou, 59-66.

to an OT prophecy that portrays God's judgment in a form of eschatological warfare between Him and His enemies that surround Jerusalem.[505] Second, the temporal death-bodily resurrection-judgment sequence is very common in Mark's eschatological understanding.[506] Third, Mark 9:43-50 gives evidence to the final destruction or annihilation of the wicked. The OT background of Mark (Isa 66 and Jeremiah's Ge-Hinnom) attest to it.[507] The context of the sole occurrence in Luke (12:5) is Jesus' teaching His disciples to beware of the leaven or yeast of the Pharisees which is hypocrisy (12:1). Jesus declares that nothing concealed that will not be disclosed, or hidden that will not be made known (v. 2). The same thought is expressed in v. 3. This principle seems parallel with the principle in Eccl 12:13-14. Both passages are also in the context of God's judgment. In Luke 12:4,5, Jesus seems to refer to the last-day judgment (cf. Matt 10:28). It shows the power of God to destroy the whole person in γέεννα.[508] In the survey of the usages of the occurrences of γέεννα in the Synoptic Gospels, it is evident that γέεννα is always associated with fire which is described as unquenchable and eternal. These adjectives stress the quality of God's judgment—thorough and complete, rather than the quantity of the time of punishment. The word γέεννα is used here in the Synoptics to refer to the place of punishment of the wicked at the last day, when the Son of Man comes to judge all the people of the nations.[509] It is also clear that the wicked are not disembodied souls in γέεννα but living beings (Matt 10:28). They would be destroyed by the eternal fire. Unlike other Rabbinic concept that was probably held by the Jews at the time of Jesus (see

---

[505]Ibid., 57.

[506]Ibid.

[507]Ibid. James Brooks also argues that 9:48 is quoted "from Isa 66:24 (LXX), which was important in the development of the symbol of γέεννα. The worm and the fire are symbols of destruction. Verses 44 and 46 are not found in the earliest and best textual witnesses and are scribal repetitions based on v. 48, where the statement is unquestionably authentic." James A. Brooks, *Mark*, NAC, vol. 23, 153. Cf. William Lane, *The Gospel According to Mark*, NICNT, 348.

[508]The destruction of the whole person in γέεννα implies a bodily resurrection (cf. John 5:28,29; Rev 20).

[509]Papaioannou also concludes that "all Synoptic Gehenna share an eschatological expectation that places the punishment of the wicked after their resurrection." Papaioannou, 43.

the background), there is nothing in the Synoptics that indicates that γέεννα is a place of punishment in the intermediate state[510] prior to the resurrection of the last day. This concept of γέεννα in the Synoptic Gospels suggests that the punishment of the wicked will be in the last day after the resurrection. This implies that the punishment of the rich man in ᾅδης in the parable is not an actual event. This further suggests that the story is fictitious, at least in the context of the Synoptic Gospels and the NT.

Structural-Thematic Analysis of Luke 16:19-31

In this section, the literary structure of Luke 16:19-31 will be analyzed first. Then, the theme(s) of the parable will be drawn out from the literary structure. The relationship between the theme(s) of the parable, the themes of Luke's travel narrative, and the themes of the whole book of Luke will be considered. Lastly, the significance of the themes of the parable and the book of Luke in relation to the interpretation of ᾅδης in the parable will be discussed.

Literary Structure of Luke 16:19-31

As the structure of Luke 16:19-31 is analyzed, it, at the same time, contributes to the debate on the unity and authenticity of the passage apart from its significance to the theme/s of the parable. The structure of Luke 16:19-31 generates a lot of discussions among scholars. Aside from the problematic unity and authenticity of the parable itself,[511] its connection with the preceding and following sections is also questioned. But chapter 4 already discussed the connection of the parable with the parable of the unjust steward (16:1-8a). Nolland asserts that this parable is linguistically and thematically linked with the earlier units of Luke 16:1-31.[512] Fitzmyer adds that this parable "further illustrates the teaching of the Lucan Jesus about the prudent use of material possessions and gives new meaning to

---

[510]Kendrick Grobel notes that the rich man is not in Gehenna of final retribution, "For there the last judgment is still future." Kendrick Grobel, ". . . Whose name was Neves," *NTS* 10 (1963-64): 379.

[511]Marshall, *The Gospel of Luke*, 633.

[512]Nolland, *Luke 9:21-18:34*, 825.

the 'dwellings that are everlasting'" (v.9).[513] Green also insists that "vv. 14-18 and vv. 19-31 stand in the closest interpretive relationship with the one subsection interpreting and being interpreted by the other."[514]

However, Aecio Cairus could hardly see any connection between this parable and the preceding parable—the dishonest steward. Hence, he suggests that "in view of the accumulated evidence, . . . the story of the rich man and Lazarus is at best suspect."[515]

The problem with the unit (16:19-31) is that it seems to be two parts. The first one is vv. 19-26, the second part is vv. 27-31.[516] Marshall notes that some scholars insist that the first part of the parable (vv. 19-26) might be patterned after an Egyptian folktale or a Jewish legend.[517] Furthermore, Marshall seems to suggest that the second part (vv. 27-31) "may be seen as a post-Easter addition by the early church in the light of Jewish failure to respond to the message of the resurrection, whether Jesus or Lazarus."[518] However, some scholars argue for the unity and authenticity of the whole parable.[519] This view seems to be evident in the structure of the parable.

There are several possible literary structures of the pericope. The first is the spatial/geographical structure. Verses 19-22 describe a scene on earth. Verses

---

[513]Fitzmyer, *Luke X-XXIV*, 1127.

[514]Green, 604. Cf. L. T. Johnson, *Luke*, 254.

[515]He presents several arguments:
  1. Based on external evidence, the story of poor Lazarus fits perfectly the apocryphal source, but not the gospel of Luke. Cairus, 38.
  2. The lack of clarity of the supposed Lukan form of the story, contrasted with clearly made points in the apocryphal source, again indicating the true source of the story. Ibid., 41.
  3. Irenaeus made use of the story, but early Church Fathers did not. Ignatius (ca. 120 C.E.) quotes some verses both before Luke 17:10 and after 16:15. The nature of his context is such that a reference to the rich man and Lazarus is not necessarily expected. Ibid., 42.
  4. The parable interrupts the smooth flow of the narrative between 16:18 and 17:1-2. If the parable is taken, there is coherence in Luke's narrative. Ibid., 42-44.

[516]See Fitmyer, *Luke X-XXIV*, 1126-27.

[517]Marshall, *The Gospel of Luke*, 633-34.

[518]Ibid., 634. He adds that "the parable thus falls under some suspicion of being a Lucan composition along with the other parables peculiar to this Gospel." Ibid.

[519]F. Schnider und W. Stenger, 275-83.

23-31 portray a scene in ᾅδης . In this structure, there are several contrasting parallels between the rich man and Lazarus:

On Earth (vv. 19-22)

Rich Man	Lazarus
(a) dressed in purple and fine linen	(a) covered with sores
(b) lived in luxury every day	(b) longing to eat what fell from rich man's table
(c) the rich man died and was buried	(c) Lazarus also died and the angels carried him to Abraham's bosom.

Apparently, there is an ABBA pattern or a chiastic structure in the narrative section (vv. 19-22). The first is the rich man and his material situation. Then, it is followed by Lazarus with his physical and economic condition.

However, when Luke describes their death, he first mentions what happened to Lazarus when he died followed by the description of the death and burial of the rich man. Here is the geographical structure:

On Earth

A——The Rich Man: Dressed in purple and lived a luxurious life (v.19).

> B——Lazarus: Covered with sores and longing to eat what fell from the rich man's table (vv. 20-21).

> B'——Lazarus the beggar: Died and was carried by the angels to Abraham's bosom (v. 22a).

A'——The Rich Man: Died and was buried (v. 22b).

There are also contrasting parallels between the rich man and Lazarus in ᾅδης.

In ᾅδης (vv. 23-26)

(a) The rich man is down in ᾅδης—he lifted up his eyes (v. 23a).	(a) Lazarus is up in the bosom of Abraham (v. 23b).
(b) The rich man is in torment (v. 23a).	(b) Lazarus is in bliss (v. 23b).

(c) The rich man longs to   (c) Lazarus was comforted
    be cooled (v. 25).   (v. 26).

Here is also the chiastic structure of vv. 23-25:

A——The Rich Man: Lifted up his eyes, being in torment (v.23a).

    B——Lazarus: He in the bosom of Abraham (v. 23b).

    B'——Lazarus: He is requested by the rich man to be sent
       to him to cool his tongue (v. 24).

A'——The Rich Man: Reminded by Abraham of his luxurious life on earth
    (v. 25).

There is another structure which is apparent in Luke 16:19-31. This may
be called "Reversal"[520] structure:

In Life on Earth	Time of Death, and in ᾅδης
The rich man cares for himself, neglects Lazarus (vv. 19-20).	The rich man was just buried (neglected by angels), while Lazarus was carried by the angels to the bosom of Abraham——cared (v. 22).
The rich man enjoys (v. 19), Lazarus suffers (v. 20).	Lazarus was comforted, The rich man was tormented (v. 23-24).
The rich man was full, Lazarus was longing to be fed (vv. 19-21).	Lazarus was presumably filled, while the rich was longing to be cooled with Lazarus' finger dipped in water (v. 24).
The rich man received good things, Lazarus bad things (v. 25a)	Lazarus is comforted The rich man is in agony (v. 25b).
The rich man and Lazarus were separated by the gate of the former's house (v. 20).	The rich man and Lazarus are separated by a great chasm (v. 26).

Another structure that could be suggested is the narrative-dialogue
structure. The narrative section (vv. 19-23) depicts the lives of the rich man and

---

[520]Reversal in terms of situation, position, and status.

Lazarus until their death, whereas the dialogue section (vv. 24-31) portrays the dialogue between the rich man and Abraham. Here is the narrative-dialogue structure:

The Narrative Section (vv. 19-23)

(A) In life on earth (vv. 19-22)——First scene

    (a) The rich man: Dressed in purple and fine linen, and lives in luxury every day (v. 19).

    (b) The poor man Lazarus: Laid at the rich man's gate, and Is covered with sores as he longs to be fed with what falls from the rich man's table (v. 20-21).

(B) When both died (vv. 22-23)——Second scene

    (a) Lazarus died: Carried by the angels to Abraham's bosom (v. 22a).

    (b) The rich man died: Buried (no angels) (v. 22b).

(C) In ᾅδης (v. 24)——Third scene[521]

    (a) The rich man: Lifted up his eyes, he is in torment (v. 24a).

    (b) Lazarus: In the bosom of Abraham (v. 24b).

The Dialogue Section (vv. 24-27)

(A) Dialogue between the rich man and Abraham——First part

    (a) The rich man requests Abraham to send Lazarus to cool his tongue with his finger dipped in water (v. 24).

    (b) Request denied: The reasons are (1) the rich man had already received good things in life, (2) there is a chasm between them (vv. 25-26).

(B) Dialogue between the rich man and Abraham——Second part[522]

---

[521]Walter Vogels divides the passage into three sections: (1) Before Death (vv. 19-21), (2) At Moment of Death (v. 22), (3) After Death (vv. 23-31). Walter Vogels, "Having and Longing: A Semiotic Analysis of Luke 16:19-31," Église et Théologie 20 (1989): 29-32.

[522]Hans Kvalbein's Narrative/Dialogue Structure has only two sections with two parts each:
The narrative part—vv. 19-23
  (a) Their life on earth—vv. 19-21
  (b) Their fate after death—vv. 22-23
The dialogue part—vv. 24-31

(a) The rich man requests Abraham to send Lazarus to his father's house to warn his five brothers so that they will not suffer his fate (vv. 27-28).

(b) Request denied: The reason is that they have
    Moses and the Prophets to warn them (v. 29).

(C) Dialogue between the rich man and Abraham——Third part

(a) The rich man insists: Argues that if someone
    rose from the dead, they will repent (v. 30).

(b) Request denied for the second time: For the reason
    that if they will not listen to Moses and the Prophets
    they will not be persuaded even if someone rises from the dead
    (v. 31).

Kvalbein seems right in saying that

from the structure of the story we see that only the rich man takes part in the dialogue. He is the main person. The last appeal of the story is directed to the five still-living brothers of the rich man, those who live like him. The story is a warning to the rich man and his brothers.[523]

Based on the narrative-dialogue structure, it is apparent that the main focus of the parable is not Lazarus[524] but the rich man and his brothers. This is likely because, as far as the literary context is concerned, the parable is directed to the Pharisees.

The Themes of Luke 16:19-31

In this section, the themes of the parable will be drawn especially as a result of the literary-structural analysis of the pericope. Moreover, it will consider these themes in the light of the themes of the travel narrative, and the themes of Luke-Acts.

It seems that the key theme of the spatial/geographical structure is that man's use/abuse of wealth on earth determines his position in the afterlife. In the

---

(a) The request of the rich man for relief is   refused——vv. 24-26
(b) The prayer of the rich man for his brothers is   refused——vv. 27-31. Hans Kvalbein, "Jesus and the Poor: Two Texts and a Tentative Conclusion," *Themelios* 12 (1987): 84.

[523]Ibid.

[524]Lazarus did not even speak in the whole story. The parable did not give reasons why Lazarus was saved. This means that this is not the concern of the parable. Kvalbein is right in saying that the parable "concentrates on the question of why the rich man was lost." Ibid.

story, the rich man is just so concerned with himself. He wears expensive clothes and lavishly "λαμπρῶς" (lamprôs) feasts on much food with great merriment and rejoicing "εὐφραίνω" (euphrainô), neglecting or ignoring Lazarus at his gate. In short, the rich man misused his wealth, consequently, he suffered in ᾅδης. This theme is in congruence with one of the major themes of Luke's travel narrative especially with the immediate context. As discussed in the structural-thematic analysis, the theme of the preceding parable the shrewd manager (16:1-8a), is the wise use of wealth.

In the wider literary context—in Luke's travel narrative, Luke already accentuates this theme especially in the parable of the rich fool (12:16-21). Moreover, in the subsequent passages, it is likewise related to the story of the rich young ruler who, because he has much wealth, turned away from Jesus (18:18-30). It is also thematically related to the story of a rich Zacchaeus' conversion who, in spite of his riches, became a follower of Jesus and resolved to share his possessions with the poor (19:1-10). The theme of "reversal" is very conspicuous in the reversal structure. This is evident in the lives of the rich man and Lazarus. The selfish rich man, who is dressed with very expensive garments and feasted extravagantly on much food while neglecting or ignoring Lazarus at his gate, ends in torment in ᾅδης. The presumably righteous but poor Lazarus, who is covered with sores, and who is longing for food that falls from the rich man's table, ends up being comforted in the bosom of Abraham.

It should be pointed out that being rich per se in this life does not mean that automatically a person ends up in torment in the afterlife. Vice versa, being poor and in suffering in this life does not automatically qualify a person to have a place in the bosom of Abraham in the afterlife. This is contrary to the whole teaching of Luke-Acts, the rest of the Synoptic Gospels, the NT, and the whole Scripture. What is emphasized in the theme of reversal is the humiliation of the proud, but the exaltation of the Gentiles, tax collectors, sinners, women, children, poor, and the marginalized of society who become citizens of God's kingdom.

The theme of reversal is very prominent in Luke's travel narrative as well, and significantly in the book of Luke. In Luke's travel narrative, the theme of reversal is very apparent. In Luke 10:15, the city of Capernaum, which is exalted to heaven, will be brought low to ᾅδης. This is also the theme of the parable of the guests in 14:7-11. The key emphasis of Jesus is in v. 11 that states the eternal principle, "For everyone who exalts himself will be humbled, and he who humbles himself will be exalted" (NASB).

This theme has again been repeated in the parable of the Pharisee and the tax collector (Luke 18:9-17). Obviously, the theme of reversal is very prominent in Luke's travel narrative. In a wider context, in the book of Luke, the theme of reversal is also noticeable. At the outset of the book, Luke emphasizes the theme of reversal in the experiences of Elizabeth and Mary. Elizabeth who conceived John after many years of barrenness exclaims, "This is the way the Lord has dealt with me in the days when He looked with favor upon me, to take away my disgrace among men" (1:25). Mary likewise proclaims,

> For He had regard for the humble state of His bondslave; For behold, from this time on all generations will count me blessed. For the Mighty One has done great things for me; And holy is His name. And His MERCY IS UPON GENERATION AFTER GENERATION TOWARD THOSE WHO FEAR HIM. He has done mighty deeds with His arm; He has scattered those who were proud in the thoughts of their hearts. He has brought down rulers from their thrones, and has exalted those who were humble. HE HAS FILLED THE HUNGRY WITH GOOD THINGS; and sent away the rich empty-handed.[525]

The third theme in the parable can be deduced from the narrative-dialogue structure. It is apparent that the parable stresses the crucial role of the Scripture (The Law and the Prophets) in the life of men on earth. The Scripture is the ultimate standard or rule of faith and practice for the citizens of the kingdom of God (Luke 16:17; cf. Matt 5:17-19). Miracles and extraordinary acts of Jesus in several occasions lead men to believe the gospel; however, Jesus stresses the supremacy of the Scripture over miracles and other extraordinary acts. This is one of the main themes of the parable (16:29,31). This theme is also apparent in the immediate context. In Luke 16:16-17, Jesus strengthens the perpetuity of the Law even in the period of the reign of the kingdom of God. Even at the last portion of the book, Luke narrates that Jesus uses the Law and the Prophets to

---

[525]Luke 1:48-53 (NASB).

show to His disciples that the things that has happened to Him had already been prophesied in the Scripture (24:27,44).

In the structural-thematic analysis of Luke 16:19-31, in the light of its immediate and wider contexts, it is crystallized that there are at least three major themes: (1) the use and abuse of wealth; (2) the theme of reversal—the abjection of the proud people, and the exaltation of the marginalized citizens of the kingdom; (3) the Scripture as the standard of ethical and moral life. These three themes are also shown in the immediate and wider contexts of the passage. It should be emphatically stressed that Jesus, in the original historical setting, does not teach the doctrine of the afterlife in Luke 16:19-31. It should also be pointed out that Luke, in his arrangement of his account of the Gospel, neither emphasize the state of the dead in the afterlife nor the description of ᾅδης.

Literary-Narrative Analysis of Luke 16:19-31

This section analyzes the narrative in Luke 16:19-31. It includes the syntax and grammar of the passage as well. This section seeks to provide a plausible interpretation of ᾅδης in Luke 16:19-31, whether the description about ᾅδης in the intermediate state is true or not. It also determines the main points of the story parable.

The passage begins in v. 19 and ends in v. 31. Verse 19 definitely begins a new pericope because Jesus relates an illustration or parable with a literary device, common introductory clause, Ἄνθρωπος δέ τις ἦν πλούσιος (Now there was a certain rich man, v. 19a).[526] Furthermore, the conjunction de, (de) is probably used here with a sense of transition which means that the passage denotes a further thought development in relation to the previous passage. It serves as a marker that links narrative segments.[527]

In vv. 19,20 the main characters of the story are introduced using similar

---

[526]Cf. Luke 10:30; 12:16; 14:16; 15:11; 16:1; 19:12; 20:9. G. W. Knight points out that this introductory formula which is found in other Lukan parables is one of the strong evidences that this story is fictitious. G. W. Knight, 277. Furthermore, he argues that the "indefinite phrase 'a certain man' would be unnatural for a story about known persons." Ibid.

[527]Bauer, BAGD, s.v. "δέ."

phrases, Ἄνθρωπος δέ τις ἦν πλούσιος (And there was a certain rich man); πτωχὸς δέ τις (And a certain poor man). The rich man is not named (v. 19), whereas the poor man's name is mentioned (v. 20). Some scholars argue that the mention of the names of Lazarus and Abraham indicates that this is a true story.[528] In all the parables told by Jesus, this is the only parable in which Jesus gave names to its characters.[529]

Khoo argues that "it is impossible to prove that Jesus did rely"[530] on those fables that exist in the NT world. Moreover, he argues that "if the story is fictitious, then Jesus would be defeating His own purpose in His effort to present a powerful warning on human responsibility in the present life."[531] However, the argument that the story is true because the characters are named is a weak argument. The evidence seems to favor the theory that Jesus uses the concept of the afterlife from Greco-Roman and Jewish afterlife stories prevailing during His time.[532] Based on this evidence, it is then logical to accept that Jesus also follows their customary practice of giving names to the characters of their stories.[533]

Another strong evidence to support the theory that Jesus utilizes those existing popular stories concerning the afterlife is the absence of these concepts in the OT and the NT. In the OT, it was already pointed out that there was no such thing as conscious souls in lWav.. The OT explicitly states that the dead know nothing at death (Eccl 9:5,6). The NT authors, excluding this parable, also agree with the OT as far as the meaning of ᾅδης is concerned.[534] The NT does not

---

[528]C. I. Scofield, *The Scofield Reference Bible* (New York: Oxford University Press, 1909), 1098; quoted in Jeffrey Khoo, "The Reality and Eternality of Hell: Luke 16:19-31 as Proof" *Stulos* 6 (1998): 69; Herbert Lockyer, *All the Parables of Jesus* (Grand Rapids: Zondervan, 1963), 292; quoted in Jeffrey Khoo, "The Reality and Eternality of Hell: Luke 16:19-31 as Proof" *Stulos* 6 (1998): 69; Khoo, 70.

[529]Khoo, 70-71. At least two of its three characters (Lazarus, and Abraham) were named.

[530]Ibid., 68.

[531]Ibid.

[532]Chapter 3 of this study shows an overwhelming thematic and conceptual parallels between Greco-Roman, Jewish stories, and Jesus' story in Luke 16:19-31.

[533]Cf. the names of an Egyptian folktale–Setme and Si-Osiris were given. The names of the characters of the Greek stories like that of Homer, Lucian of Samosata, and the rest were also given.

[534]There are concepts in Jesus' parable which are absent in the OT. For example, the concept of a dishonest steward is absent in the OT. It may be also true with the concept of ᾅδης in Luke 16:19-31. It is also

teach that souls separate from the body at death, and suffer in ᾅδης or enjoy in heaven. What the NT teaches is that souls are destructible rather than immortal (Matt 10:28).

The argument that the fictitiousness of the story defeats Jesus' purpose of presenting a powerful warning on human responsibility is evidently clumsy. The fictitious-ness of the parable of the rich man and Lazarus does not weaken Jesus' argument. In the same way, Jesus' use of the parable of the dishonest steward does not lessen its impact upon His audience.[535] The OT people and prophets, as mentioned in chapter 2, sometimes use fables to press their messages, but this does not in any way weaken their messages.

Jesus' teaching concerning the punishment of the wicked is that this will take place in the last day, in γέεννα (Matt 5:22,29,30; 10:28; 25:31-46; Mark 9:43; John 5:28-29). Even an ordinary Jew knew this, as reflected in the answer of Martha to Jesus concerning the resurrection of Lazarus—that it will take place in the last day (John 11:24). Furthermore, it should be significantly stressed that Luke also shares this idea in Luke 12:4,5. The idea of resurrection is implied in his statement, "Fear him who, after the killing of the body, has the power to throw you into γέεννα." It should be noted that what will be thrown into γέεννα is a living person. Since the person was already killed, he could only be thrown to γέεννα alive if he is resurrected. It is shown that resurrection will take place at the last day. Luke therefore concurs with other NT authors that the punishment of the wicked takes place at the last day. If the Jews believe that the wicked will definitely suffer at the coming of the "Son of Man" in the last day (John 5:28-29; cf. Dan 12:2), then the contention that Jesus' use of a fictitious story lessens its effect on His hearers is also decrepit. If they knew this story is based on stories which were fictitious, it would not still weaken Jesus' message, because, regardless of time, the wicked will really be punished. Besides, Jesus' audience,

---

absent in the OT.

[535]Definitely, in the parable of the unjust steward, Jesus did not emphasize the dishonesty of the shrewd steward. It is also likely that Jesus did not emphasize the consciousness of the dead in a[|dhj in the intermediate state.

most likely, knew that the real intent of Jesus, as far as the literary context is concerned, is not to delineate or teach the doctrine on the state of the dead or eschatology. He rather emphasizes the consequences of unfaithful stewardship of riches to the Pharisees. He also stresses the authority of the Scripture as the guide for ethical and moral living (16:9-12,17-18,29,31).

As already noted in the structural-thematic analysis of the passage, the parable definitely emphasizes the principle of reversal. The syntax shows the principle of reversal in describing the contrast between the two characters with their lives on earth and when they were in ᾅδης. In v. 19, the sentence that depicts the rich man begins syntactically with de, (now). Similarly, the sentence in v. 20 that describes the poor Lazarus syntactically begins with de, (and) as well. The contrast is visibly accented by Jesus as shown in the syntax. The rich man (v. 19) is evnedidu,sketo porfu,ran kai. bu,sson (dressed in purple and fine linen), while the poor Lazarus who probably does not have an outer garment is covered "εἱλκωμένος" (eilkômenos) with sores. Presumably, the rich man was enjoying much food and drinks, while Lazarus was just longing to be fed "ἐπιθυμῶν χορτασθῆναι" (epithumôn chortasthēnai) with the "πιπτόντων" (piptontôn) the food that fall from the rich man's table.

Apparently, v. 22 introduces another plot in the story with the conjunction δέ (now). It reports the death of both the rich man and Lazarus. Again, Jesus shows a contrast between them. However, their situation is reversed. The angels carry Lazarus away into Abraham's bosom,[536] whereas the rich man is just buried by men.

---

[536]William Hendriksen argues that the bosom of Abraham where the angels carried the soul of Lazarus is the paradise or heaven. William Hendriksen, *The Gospel of Luke*, New Testament Commentary, vol. 3 (Grand Rapids: Baker, 1978), 784. Cf. Madeleine I. Boucher, *The Parables* (Wilmington, DE: Michael Glazier, 1981), 135. Simon J. Kistemaker, "Jesus as Story Teller: Literary Perspectives on the Parables," *The Master's Seminary Journal* 16 (2005): 50 [journal-online]; available from Academic Search Premier database; Internet; accessed 4 December 2007. However, if the parable was adapted from popular Greco-Roman and Later Judaism stories, it would then be reasonable to suggest that, as what these popular stories portray, Abraham and the rest of the righteous who died were also in ᾅδης, they were just separated from the wicked. In the OT, both the righteous and the wicked would just go down to lWav.. The idea that the righteous would go to heaven to be with God was not yet developed in the time of Jesus (see chapter 3). The idea that the souls of the righteous are in heaven in the intermediate state is also foreign in the OT and NT. One possibility here is that when Jesus mentions that Lazarus was in "Abraham's bosom," He may be referring to the Jewish concept of messianic banquet of the righteous with the patriarchs Abraham, Isaac, and Jacob in the kingdom of heaven (Matt 8:11). This will be in the last day. Probably, Jesus brings this imagery from the "last day" to the intermediate state in this parable. Since this is a parable, Jesus was not concerned with precise eschatology but with the main point of the

In v. 23, the conjunction kai. (and) indicates that the scene being described here is a continuation of the plot that begins in v. 22. In v. 23, the contrast continues. Although both of them are in ᾅδης, they have contrasting situations. While on earth, the rich man was enjoying himself, in ᾅδης he is in torment (ὑπάρχων ἐν βασάνοις). On earth, Lazarus was hungry and suffering, in a[|dhj he is in the bosom of Abraham.

In v. 24, the contrast is still there. On earth, the rich man was full and was filled with food and drinks, but in ᾅδης he languishes and longs to be cooled with the fingers of Lazarus dipped in water. In v. 25, the contrast is explicitly declared by Abraham, the third character in the story. Abraham reminds the rich man that in his life on earth, he received good things while Lazarus received bad things. The contrasting reversal is highlighted by the phrase "νῦν δὲ" (but now). In ᾅδης, Lazarus is comforted; on the other hand, the rich man is in agony (ovduna,w). This principle of reversal is obviously one of the emphases of Jesus in this Lukan parable. Now, should the description of ᾅδης in this passage be taken as a factual event?[537] There are many features in the passage that betray the factuality of ᾅδης. For example, the characters in the story (the rich man, Lazarus, and Abraham) appear to have bodies, contrary to the popular belief that only souls go to ᾅδης. The rich man has still eyes (v. 23). He still has a tongue and an intact voice which could be heard by Abraham (vv. 24,27,30). Lazarus is also portrayed as having fingers (v. 24). Abraham likewise has a body because he carries Lazarus in his bosom (v. 22). How can Abraham literally carry all the righteous in his bosom? How can a literal water cool the tongue of a spirit-soul (v. 24)? Furthermore, in this story, contrary to the popular afterlife stories, the

---

parable—the law and the Prophets as the absolute ethical guide in the kingdom of God. Dennis Smith seems to suggest that Lazarus in the bosom of Abraham refers to a "banquet scene in which the banqueters recline and thus rest on the bosom of the diner to their left. Lazarus is said to be on the bosom of Abraham in order to indicate that he is to the right of the host, Abraham, and therefore in a position of honor." Dennis E. Smith, "Table Fellowship as a Literary Motif in the Gospel of Luke," *JBL* 106 (1987): 625-26.

[537]R. C. Trench insists that "it is the place [*Hadēs*] of painful restraints, where the souls of the wicked are reserved to the judgment of the great day; it is 'the deep' mentioned in Luke 8:31 for as *that* other place has a foretaste of heaven, so has this place a foretaste of hell." R. C. Trench, *Notes on the Parables of Our Lord* (Grand Rapids: Baker, 1945), 166. Bock, on the other hand, argues that the passage is a parable; however it reflects a serious reality. Bock, *Luke 9:51-24:53*, 851. Furthermore, he sees the imagery of 'fire' in the afterlife as metaphorical of conscious suffering. Idem, *Luke*, 433.

word yuch, is not even mentioned. Lastly, how can souls which are spirits be burned in a literal flame of fire in ᾅδης? Second, the description of ᾅδης with flo,x (flame)[538] in v. 24 is contrary to the description of ᾅδης in other NT occurrences.[539] All of the occurrences of ᾅδης in the NT seem to carry an OT meaning[540] except in this passage which seems to carry a Greek or inter-testamental Judaism meaning. It should be noted again that the story of the rich man and Lazarus has parallels in Greek literature, OT apocryphal and pseudepigraphal writings, and Egyptian folktale, as discussed in the historical background of this study. In view of the parallels of the story of the rich man and Lazarus in its historical context, it seems plausible to suggest that Jesus, when telling His own version,[541] may have been aware of those parallel stories in His time. This is supported by the fact that the rest of the NT do not describe ᾅδης as such, but rather carries the OT meaning in all of its occurrences except in this passage.

Third, in telling this parable, Jesus did not intend to establish a doctrine or belief concerning the state of men at death in ᾅδης.[542] He wants to show to the Pharisees that the unfaithful use of wealth in this life and the undermining of the warning of the Scripture will lead to punishment (Luke 16:27-31).[543]

---

[538]The occurrences of φλόξ is often associated with πῦρ "fire" (Acts 7:30; 2 Thess 1:8; Heb 1:7; Rev 1:14; 2:18; 19:12).

[539]See the lexical analysis, 208-26.

[540]The ᾅδης described in those NT passages does not mention a flame or fire. They just meant death or grave or the place below the earth like in the OT.

[541]Only the first part, vv. 19-26, has a parallel with existing Jewish and Greek literature at the time of Jesus which are extant today. The second part, vv. 27-31, has no parallel in any existing Greek and Jewish literature extant today. It is therefore probable that Jesus created this story with these existing popular stories available during His time.

[542]Simon J. Kistemaker, however, asserts that "Jesus taught a doctrine of hell in undisguised terms is evident from many references to hell fire in the Gospel." Kistemaker, *The Parables*, 240. However, the Synoptic Gospels' references on hell fire usually are seen in the context of the judgment at the coming of the Son of Man (Matt 13:40,42,50; 25:31-46; 18:8,9; Mark 9:43,45,47; cf. John 5:28-29). J. Gwyn Griffiths also argues that "it is widely agreed that Jesus in this parable was not aiming principally to convey information about the afterworld. An emphasis on moral recompense is clearly present." Gwyn J. Griffiths, "Cross-Cultural Eschatology with Dives and Lazarus," *ET* 105 (1993): 10. Cf. George A. Buttrick, *The Parables of Jesus* (Grand Rapids: Baker, 1973), 140.

[543]J. Duncan M. Derrett also observes, "Failure to deal righteously with *mammon* leads to 'hell.' . . . He was a flagrant wrongdoer though passive in his wrongdoing. He may not have been a robber or a usurer; he may well have been both, since both methods of being and staying rich were easy in Jesus' time. In any case he neglected his duty toward the poor." J. Duncan M. Derrett, "Fresh Light on St. Luke XVI: Dive and Lazarus and

The punishment of the wicked does not take place right away in the intermediate state. The eschatology of Luke 16:19-31 is contrary to the eschatology of the Synoptic Gospels and the rest of the NT. The punishment will take place at the last day, at the coming of the Son of Man (Matt 25:31-46; John 5:28-29). Fourth, ᾅδης in this story should not be taken as a fact but rather as fiction. The story has been most likely adapted from several parallel stories existing in the Greco-Roman, and Jewish world (see chapter 3). Jesus borrows the concept of this story from those parallel stories which are often believed to be true.[544] However, He tells it in a way that breaks away from the usual pattern of those stories. For example, He pictures the characters in the story with bodies. In usual Greco-Roman tales, the characters are usually souls apart from the body (for example, Micyllus and Megapenthes).[545]

Another pattern, which Jesus breaks away from those stories in Greek literature, is the pattern of communication from the dead for those people living on earth. Sometimes a living person visits the realm of the dead, then comes back to the land of the living.[546] At other times, they communicate to the living as ghosts in a dream or in a vision.[547] Bodily resurrection is never mentioned as a form of communication from the dead.

In Jesus' parable, the request of the rich man to send Lazarus from the dead to his five living brothers is by means of rising from the dead or resurrection.[548] Abraham's denial of the requests of the rich man to send Lazarus, for the reason that the Law and the Prophets are enough as a guide for his living brothers, has been one of the strongest arguments to prove that someone who communicates from the dead is not credible. Papaioannou argues that Abraham's refusal of the

---

the Preceding Sayings," *NTS* 7 (1960-61): 373.

[544]Those stories, in the Greco-Roman, were believed to be true (see Papaioannou, 140) with usual supposed eyewitnesses in those tales.

[545]See Lucian of Samosata *Cataplous—The Downward Journey or the Tyrant* (LCL, 2:3-49).

[546]See Homer *Odyssey*, 10.495 (LCL, 1:381).

[547]Papaioannou, 138-39.

[548]Ibid., 139.

rich man's request is tantamount to God's refusal also to any communication from the dead.[549]

Now, Jesus' reconstruction of the story of the rich Man and Lazarus upheld the Law and the prophets as the sole source or warning is a deconstruction of the popular concept (communication from the dead). Aside from downplaying it to be the means of warning the living, He also seems to downplay their credibility and truthfulness.

Fifth, the eschatology of this story is contrary to the eschatology of the rest of the NT. In the story, the rich man and Lazarus already received their reward and punishment immediately after their death while people are still living on earth (16:27-31).[550] However, in other passages in Luke (12:5; cf. Matt 10:28; 21:25-36) and in other NT writings, the righteous and the wicked will receive their reward and punishment at the last day——when the Son of Man comes again (Matt 5:22,29,30; 10:28; 18:19; 23:33; 25:31-46; Mark 9:43,45,47; Luke 12:5; John 5:28-29; John 11:24; 14:1-3; 1 Cor 15:23; 1 Thess 4:16-17; Heb 9:27-28; 10:27; 2 Pet 3:7,10,12; Rev 19:11-20:15). In the intermediate state,[551] the righteous and the wicked are in their tombs (John 5:28). They are asleep (1 Cor 15:20,51; 1 Thess 4:13), or have fallen asleep in Jesus (vv. 14,15). At present, the earth and the inhabitants thereof "are set aside, or laid up (θησαυρίζω) for fire, kept or held in reserve (τηρέω) for the day of judgment and destruction of the ungodly" (2 Pet 3:7). The unbiblical eschatology of the story is one of the proofs that this eschatological concept was already very popular at the time of Jesus. This kind of eschatology is inherent in those popular Greco-Roman and Jewish

---

[549]He says, "If something unnecessary, God will not grant it, and if God will not grant it now, he has neither done so in the past, nor will he do so in the future. This last of Abraham's statements destroys with one stroke the credibility and reliability of all tales that purport to come from the dead. Whether from heathen or Jewish background, with which the reader may have been familiar. Whatever the popularity of such tales, they are not from God." Ibid., 152.

[550]This kind of eschatology is prevalent in extra-biblical literature which were already existing at the time of Jesus. See chapter 3 for more details.

[551]Intermediate state in this study means the period between death and resurrection. In this period, the dead are asleep in the dust waiting for the resurrection (1 Thess 4:13-16; John 5:28, 29). This intermediate state is different from the doctrine of purgatory and the modern concept of hell where the souls are already suffering in the fire.

stories about the afterlife. Jesus' adaptation of His story from those extra-biblical stories of course is not to affirm the eschatology of those popular stories, but rather to stress different points.

The concept in v. 26 that there is a great chasm fixed (χάσμα μέγα ἐστήρικται) that separates the rich man from Lazarus and Abraham is significant. The concept of separation between the righteous and the wicked in ᾅδης is also very popular in extra-biblical afterlife stories. In 1 En 22:1-14, the righteous is separated from the wicked. The righteous has a spring of water, while the wicked are set apart in a certain place where they suffer with great pain in the fire. This concept is very widespread. It is also found in the writings of Josephus (*Jewish War* 3.375), in Plato (Laws 10.904), and in Lucian of Samosata (*Cat.* 25,28).[552] Again, this is an evidence to show that the story of the rich man and Lazarus is most likely Jesus' creation based on existing popular stories concerning the afterlife.[553]

In the first part of the dialogue (vv. 24-26), the rich man requests Abraham to send Lazarus to cool his tongue with Lazarus' finger dipped in water (v. 24). The request is denied for two reasons:

1. The rich man had already received good things in his life on earth, so it is his turn to receive bad things in ᾅδης. Lazarus had already received bad things on earth, and it is his time to receive good things in ᾅδης (v. 25).

2. There is a great uncrossable chasm that separates the rich man from Lazarus and Abraham (v. 26).[554] In the syntax of the dialogue portion of the story, v. 26 is linked with v. 25 since the conjunction kai. (kai) at the beginning of v. 26 indicates that it is a continuation of the answer of Abraham which started in v. 25 to the request of the rich man in v. 24. The phrase "εἶπεν δέ" (and he said) in v.

---

[552]For more details, see chapter 3. Gilmour also notes that the concept of separation in ᾅδης is also present in Homer's Odyssey. Gilmour, 28. Other concepts like "thirst not satisfied," "wealth in life not satisfying in death," "concern for living loved ones," "the value of burial," and a "wise man in the afterlife" which are present in Homer, are also present in Luke 16:19-31. Ibid., 29-31.

[553]This study suggests that probably Luke includes this story-parable of Jesus in his gospel account because Luke's audience who were mostly Gentiles (like Theophilus) very well knew the popular Greek stories. By including this, Luke's audience could easily get his point.

[554]Thorwald Lorenzen stresses the importance of the "great chasm" which gives the fate of the rich man and Lazarus a sense of finality. Lorenzen, 40.

27, like the phrase "εἶπεν δὲ" in v. 25 signals a new theme in the dialogue between the rich man and Abraham.

In the second part of the dialogue (vv. 27-29), the rich man requests Abraham to send Lazarus to his father's house to warn his brothers that they may escape the place of torment he is in (vv. 27-28). The answer of Abraham in   v. 29 is introduced by the phrase "λέγει δὲ" (and he says) instead of "εἶπεν δέ." This probably shows that v. 29 is still a part of the second part of the dialogue that started in v. 27. The second request of the rich man was denied for the reason that "they [his brothers] have Moses and the

prophets" ("Εχουσι Μωϋσέα καὶ τοὺς προφήτας).[555] His brothers have to take heed (ἀκούω)[556] to the Law and the Prophets.

What specific OT message that the rich man's five brothers have to pay attention to so that they will not suffer the same punishment that the rich man now suffers? Definitely, the OT is not against wealth. What really was the cause of the rich man's suffering in the place of torment? Definitely, it is not because he is rich.

The whole Scripture is full of people who were rich who would definitely enter the kingdom of God. Abraham himself was rich (Gen 13:6). Other OT rich people were Job (1:3; 42:10-12), Solomon (1 Kgs 3:13; 4:20-34; 10:14-29), and a non-Israelite King Nebuchadnezzar (Dan 4:28-37). The NT rich people of God who would most likely enter His kingdom were Nicodemus (John 3:1; 19:39), Zacchaeus (Luke 19:2), Joseph of Arimathaea (Matt 27:57; Mark 15:43; Luke 23:50; John 19:38), and probably Theophilus (Luke 1:3). The problem probably with the rich man, as evident in the story itself, was his neglect to care

---

[555]This phrase means that they have the OT Scripture (Luke 24:27,44-46) to listen to, especially during Sabbath in their synagogues (Luke 4:16-21).

[556]This word has nuances such as the following: (1) literally, to have or exercise the faculty of hearing—*hear*; (2) legally, to hear legal case–*grant a hearing*; (3) to receive news or information about something, (4) to give careful attention to—*listen to, heed*; (5) to pay attention to—*listen to*, (6) to be given a nickname or other identifying label—*be called*, and (7) to hear and understand a message—*understand*. Bauer, BAGD, s.v. "avkou,w." The possible meaning in this context is "to heed or listen to" because the OT injunctions are too clear to be misunderstood. The meaning to *heed* may carry the sense of "obedience." In this sense, the rich man failed to obey the OT laws dealing with the poor.

for the poor Lazarus[557] who was thrown or laid down (βάλλω) at (πρός)[558] his gate (Luke 16:20). Since the rich man in the story is a Jew (calling Abraham as father, v. 24),[559] he is under obligation, according to OT Laws, to care for the poor Lazarus by feeding him. He is even duty bound to bring him into his house (Exod 22:21-25; Deut 14:28,29; 15:1-4,7-11; 24:10-15; Isa 58:7; Amos 2:6,7; 4:1; 5:11; 6:1-7), which he deliberately[560] never did.[561] In this parable, Jesus is implying that being a son of Abraham by virtue of blood relationship is not the means to escape the punishment in the afterlife.[562] The rich man realizes that what he lacks is "μετανοέω"[563] (to repent). This is what his brothers need (v. 30). The phrase "εἶπεν δε" (but he said) in v. 30 conspicuously introduces another theme in the dialogue between the rich man and Abraham. This time, he presses on the issue that someone from the dead should warn his brothers. He is therefore implying that the Scripture is not enough to convince his brothers. He suggests that a miraculous event like someone rising from the dead would really be a powerful witness to convict his siblings. However, Abraham once again denies his request, sticking to his argument that the Scripture is enough to warn them. Abraham argues that if they will not listen to the Scripture which is an absolute guide in Jewish faith and practice, neither will they be persuaded if someone rises

---

[557]Based on the theme of Luke's narrative of Jesus' social life—invite the poor, blind, and needy into table fellowship (Luke 14)—the rich man failed to invite poor Lazarus into table fellowship with him. Consequently, he is also excluded in the messianic banquet with Abraham (cf. Matt 8:11). D. Smith notes that Luke may have probably used the theme of messianic banquet popular in apocalyptic Jewish literature in Luke 16:19-31 and Luke 14. D. Smith, "Table Fellowship," 627.

[558]"Near" (Jerusalem Bible).

[559]The Jews were used to call Abraham their father (cf. John 8:39).

[560]The rich man's neglect of Lazarus was deliberate because he knew Lazarus very well (vv. 23,24).

[561]Wade P. Huie Jr. also notes that "Dives was punished, not because of his wealth, but because he did not use his wealth as a trust; not because he enjoyed his wealth, but because he neglected the needy at his doorstep." Wade P. Huie Jr., "The Poverty of Abundance: From Text to Sermon on Luke 16:19-31," *Interpretation* 22 (1968): 407.

[562]The Jews, like the Pharisees in this context, need to "ποιήσατε οὖν καρποὺς ἀξίους τῆς μετανοίας" (bring forth fruits worthy of repentance, Luke 3:8; cf. Matt 3:7-10).

[563]This word means (1) change one's mind, (2) feel remorse, repent, be converted. Bauer, BAGD, s.v. "μετανοέω"

"ἀναστῆ"[564] from the dead (v. 31). The argument of Abraham really sets forth the Scripture as a rule over miraculous events in matters of faith and practice.

The dialogue between the rich man and Abraham in vv. 27-31 that speaks about the role of the Scripture does not have any parallel in any extra-biblical literature. Some scholars suggest that this part may be Jesus' addition to the first part of the story (vv. 19-26).[565] However, as far as the immediate context is concerned, vv. 27-31 may still be Jesus' utterances (cf. vv. 16-18).

Furthermore, the structural analysis shows that there is a unity. Vincent Tanghe also suggests, "Que la parabole contient une suite logique d'idées et une argumentation qui lui assurent son unité."[566] This study proposes that the whole story is Jesus' creation[567] possibly with the awareness of the extra-biblical stories about the afterlife which are very popular during His time.

What are then the main points of this parable? To answer this question, it is important to answer the question, What is really the purpose of Jesus in telling this parable? Why did He tell this parable? In addition, what was Luke's purpose in including this parable in this literary context?

The preceding parables of Jesus may give hints in answering these questions. What prompted Jesus to tell the parables of the lost sheep (15:4-7), the lost coin (15:8-10), and the prodigal son (15:11-32) is that the Pharisees and Scribes grumble or express dissatisfaction "διαγογγύζω" (diagonguzô) when

---

[564]The word ἀνίστημι (anistēmi) has several nuances. In this context, it means, bringing a dead person to life. Bauer, BAGD, s.v. "ἀνίστημι."

[565]See Lorenzen, 40; Jeremias, *The Parables*, 186. Crossan insists that vv. 19-26 is the original parable of Jesus, and vv. 27-31 is an interpretation, in the light of the resurrection of Jesus. This interpretation originates from the early church. Crossan, *In Parables*, 66-68.

[566]An English translation may be like this, "That the parable contains a logical flow of thought and an argumentation which assures its unity." Vincent Tanghe, "Abraham, son Fils et son Envoyé (Luke 16:19-31)" *Revue Biblique* XCI (1984): 565. Wehrli also insists that "any separation of the two parts of the story because they seem contradictory or unrelated is a misunderstanding. The story is an urgent call to life on both its levels. (1) In the concluding dialogue life comes from hearing the gospel as it is uttered through the words of Moses, the prophets and above all, Jesus. . . . (2) In the initial narrative life comes from hearing the invitation to the table. . . ." Wehrli, 279.

[567]Although there are similarities in themes and concepts—reversal, punishment, and reward—there are several differences between this story and the popular extra-biblical story about the afterlife: (1) judgment—they were judged already in extra-biblical literature, (2) righteousness by works is explicit, (3) reincarnation, (4) return of the dead, and (5) Jewish concepts in this biblical story.

they saw the tax gatherers "τελῶναι" (telônai)[568] and sinners coming near to Jesus (15:1). Hence, in these three parables Jesus wants to stress a very important truth to the Pharisees and the Scribes (15:3) that there is joy in heaven for one sinner who repents (15:7,10,32). Jesus' purpose is clear. He told the three parables primarily for the Pharisees and Scribes who grumbled over His attitude toward what they consider "sinners."

The next parable, the unjust steward (16:1-13) is directed to His disciples (16:1). In this parable, Jesus seems to teach His disciples several spiritual truths. One of these truths is stated in 16:8b, "For the sons of this age are more shrewd in relation to their own kind than the sons of light" (NASB).[569] Then in v. 14 Luke comments that the Pharisees are lovers of money "φιλάργυροι" (philarguroi).[570] For this reason, they reacted to Jesus' teaching concerning the use of wealth. Luke describes that they are scoffing "ἐξεμυκτήριζον" (exemuktērizon)[571] Him. They were probably scoffing at Jesus' teaching concerning wealth because for them being rich already attests that a person is righteous. For them, "wealth is a reward for righteousness."[572] The conjunction "de" in v. 14 signals a new pericope in this narrative, and the conjunction "kai." in v. 15 connects it to v. 14. In addition, the antecedent of "αὐτοῖς" (them) are the Pharisees in v. 14. Thus, the primary target of Jesus' teaching or rebuke shifts from the disciples in 16:1 to

---

[568]From the word telw/nhj which means, tax collector, or revenue officer. These men are not the Publicans (Latin, *Publicani*) or the holders of 'taxfarming' contracts but their subordinates (Latin, *Portitores*). They were hired by the Publicans which were usually foreigners. Bauer, BAGD, s.v. "τελώνης."

[569]In v. 9, Jesus points out to His disciples how to be shrewd like what the unjust steward did (v. 4), that is, they should make friends for themselves by means of the mammon of unrighteousness that when it fails, they may be received into the eternal dwellings. In vv. 10-13, Jesus stresses another spiritual truth, that is, faithfulness: faithfulness in small things (v. 10), faithfulness in the use of unrighteous mammon (v. 11), faithfulness of that which is another's (v. 12), and faithfulness in serving God above mammon (v. 13). Francis E. Williams argues that the point of the parable of the unjust steward is almsgiving. Francis E. Williams, "Is Almsgiving the Point of the 'Unjust Steward'?" *JBL* 83 (1964): 297. He concludes in this way because he insists that vv. 10-13 were just added later to the original parable (vv. 1-9). Ibid., 296-97. David Landry suggests that one of the emphases of this parable is restoration of the master's honor by the prudent action of the steward. David Landry, "Honor Restored: New Light on the Parable of the Prudent Steward (Luke 16:1-8a)," *JBL* 119 (2000): 309.

[570]The word φιλάργυρια means "love of money, avarice, miserliness." Bauer, BAGD, s.v. "φιλάργυρια."

[571]The word ἐξεμυκτήριζον is imperfect tense; the present tense μυκτηρίζω (from μυκτηρ "nostril") refers to using the nose as a means to ridicule. Bauer, BAGD, s.v. "ἐξεμυκτήριζω."

[572]"Justify Yourselves" (Luke 16:15), *SDABC*, 5:828.

the Pharisees in vv. 14,15.

In v. 15, Jesus rebukes the Pharisees, telling them that they justify themselves among men.[573] Probably, Jesus wants to tell them that their teaching concerning wealth is just to justify their own hidden greed for wealth.[574] Hence Jesus said, "God knows your hearts" (16:15b). The Pharisees are highly esteemed among the Jews because of their rigid religiosity (16:15c),[575] but their religiosity concerns only with the letter of the Law. They neglected the spirit of the Law which is the weightier matter in the Law (Matt 23:23). They were called by Jesus as hypocrites (ὑποκριτής)[576] (Matt 23:23,25,27,29,) because they appeared righteous outwardly, but inwardly they are full of "ἁρπαγῆς καὶ ἀκρασίας" (plunder and self-indulgence) (23:28).

The question that arises is, What is the connection of v. 16 with Jesus' strong words against the Pharisees in v. 15? Jesus says in v. 16, "Ὁ νόμος καὶ οἱ προφῆ ται μέχρι 'ιωάννου· ἀπὸ τότε ἡ βασιλεία τοῦ θεοῦ εὐαγγελίζεται" (The Law and the Prophets [were proclaimed] until John. Since then the gospel of the kingdom of God is preached, and everyone is forcing his way into it, NASB). The word "μέχρι"[577] and "τότε,"[578] may both carry a temporal sense, which may mean that the period before the preaching of the kingdom of God was the period or era when the sole guide of Israel is the OT Scripture or the Law and the Prophets. This period was until the time of John. But when John arrived, the era of the

---

[573]S. Aalen points out that "the topic of man justifying himself is characteristic of the peculiar material of Luke; see besides 10:29; 16:15; 20:20, the parable of the *Pharisee and the Publican*, Luke 18:10ff." S. Aalen, "St Luke's Gospel and the Last Chapter of 1 Enoch," *NTS* 13 (1966): 2.

[574]The Rabbis taught that riches or wealth are evidence that a person is righteous before God.

[575]However, Jesus exposes their rapaciousness and avarice (11;39. They are self-righteous, proud, they love to exalt themselves over others (11:43). In Luke 14:1-14, Jesus rebukes them for seeking after honor. David B. Gowler, "At His Gate Lay a Poor Man": A Dialogic Reading of Luke 16:19-31," *Perspective in Religious studies* 32 (2005): 253 [journal on-line]; available from Academic Search Premier database; Internet; accessed 4 December 2007.

[576]The word ὑποκριτής means "play-actor" or role-player, actor, in the sense "pretender," or "dissembler." Bauer, BAGD, s.v. "ὑποκριτής."

[577]It is an adverb of place (Rom 15:19); and of time (Matt 11:23; 13:30). Perschbacher, *NAGL*, s.v. "μέχρι."

[578]It is an adverb of time—then, at that time (Matt 2:17; 3:5; 11:20, *thereupon, from that time* (Matt 12:29; 13:26; 25:31). Ibid., s.v. "τότε."

preaching of the gospel of the kingdom of God has begun. However, the arrival

of the kingdom of God, did not, in any way, abolish the Law and the Prophets

(v. 17),[579] which authority the Pharisees already undermined by not following its

injunctions regarding the proper use of wealth because of their greediness. This

seems to be the connection of v. 16 to the previous preceding discussions in

the narrative of Luke 16. Jesus' statement in v. 18 "serves as an example of the

permanent force of the Law."[580]

Jesus' primary purpose in telling the parable of the rich man and Lazarus is

now apparent if we can see its connection to vv. 14-18. The only connection of

vv. 19-31 with vv. 14-18 is the theme on the Law and the Prophets. In vv. 14-18,

Jesus confirms the validity and permanence of the Law and the Prophets even in

the era of the kingdom of God, which the Pharisees undermined. In vv. 19-31,

Jesus still stresses the importance of the Law and the Prophets as the absolute[581]

rule of faith and practice. In the immediate context, Jesus urges the Pharisees[582]

to take heed to it, specifically in matters of handling their wealth.[583] This is Jesus'

primary purpose in telling the parable. It seems that this is the main spiritual

---

[579]Marshall also notes that the Law and the Prophets continues to be valid. Marshall, *The Gospel of Luke*, 626. Bock also insists that "the change of era does not mean a change in moral standards in terms of commitments made to God and others." Bock, *Luke 9:51-24:53*, 1344. He adds, "The Law has a lasting role, however, despite the kingdom's coming." Ibid., 1348.

[580]Marshall, *The Gospel of Luke*, 627.

[581]Lorenzen suggests that "ultimately, man's destiny and fulfillment is determined by his relation and encounter with the word of God. Had the rich man listened Lev 19:18 '. . . thou shalt love thy neighbor as thyself . . .' then he could not have overlooked Lazarus and left him outside his gate." Lorenzen, 40.

[582]The parable is directed to the Pharisees, if vv. 19-31 is connected to vv. 14-18. Fred B. Craddock sees the connection in saying that the second parable in Luke 16 "is preceded by comments that bear upon the parable (vv. 14-18), although in ways not explicit or clear to the reader." Fred B. Craddock, *Luke*, Interpretation, 192. The audience is no longer the disciples but the Pharisees. Ibid. Gowler also argues, "The change of audience for particular teachings of Jesus are quite specific (for example, 15:2-3; 16:1,15). Therefore, to a considerable degree, the content of Jesus' sayings are appropriate to the nature of the group addressed. Jesus often speaks to His disciples, not surprisingly, about the nature of discipleship (for example, 12:22-53). The crowds are often given warnings and calls to repentance (for example, 12:54-13:9). Jesus often condemns the Lukan Pharisees (for example, Luke 11:37-54). So it is clear from this pattern that the parable of the rich man and Lazarus should be read in the light of the narrative's characterization of the Pharisees, because no change of audience is mentioned until 17:1. The parable is merely directed to the Lukan Pharisees—and people like them—who are 'lovers of money' (16:14)." Gowler, "At His Gate," 252.

[583]Papaioannou may be right in his observation that the true parallel to the Pharisees in the parable "is not the rich man but his five brothers." Papaioannou, 147-48.

point of this parable as far as the immediate literary context of the narrative is concerned.[584] This conclusion is based on several reasons:

1. This is the main theme of the dialogue part of the parable (vv. 29,31).

2. The story of vv. 19-26 is primarily used by Jesus to stress the importance of heeding the Law and the Prophets during man's life on earth. This is the significant point that Abraham brought up especially for the rich man's five brothers[585] who are still living on earth (vv. 28-29).

3. The immediate context also stresses the permanence of the Law and the Prophets even in the era of the kingdom of God (vv. 16-18).

However, in Luke's structural-thematic arrangement of his gospel account, with his own theological motive in mind, it is apparent that in Luke 16 he shows that Jesus has another purpose; that is, being faithful stewards of the temporary evil wealth on earth.[586] The rich man in the parable has failed to do it in contrast to the shrewd manager in 16:1-13.[587] The other purpose of the parable is now probably more of the Lukan emphasis in his arrangement of the gospel. Luke shows that Jesus, as seen in the wider context, emphasizes the theme of reversal in the parable. This is shown in the structural-thematic analysis of the passage, of Luke's travel narrative, and the whole book of Luke.

---

[584]Jeremias argues that Jesus in telling this parable "does not want to comment on social problem, nor does He intend to give teaching about the afterlife, but He relates the parable to warn men who resemble the brothers of the rich man of the impending danger. Hence the poor Lazarus is only a secondary figure, introduced by way of contrast. The parable is about the five brothers, and it should not be styled the parable of the rich man and Lazarus, but the parable of the Six Brothers." Jeremias, *The Parables*, 186. However, Christopher F. Evans argues that "the second part which is launched on the basis of the first has very little connection with it. It involves not a further extension of the a theme, but somewhat violent change of direction and of the subject matter." C. F. Evans, "Uncomfortable Words–V," 229.

[585]Why did Jesus use five brothers in the parable instead of just two or three? Probably He just wants to make a parallel with the Pentateuch, the Law of Moses that contains the rules which concerns the care for the poor.

[586]Crossan suggests, "Whatever may be the redactional activity of Luke himself in all this it is clear that the positioning of 16:19-31 within this larger literary complex places the emphasis on the proper use of worldly goods and the failure of the rich man to do so." Crossan, *In Parables*, 66.

[587]Michael Ball suggests that "a 'rule of two' also operates in Luke 16, so that the two parables of the Unjust Steward and the Rich Man and Lazarus, separated by various sayings mostly about wealth, should be interpreted in parallel, comparing and contrasting them, so that they illuminate each other." Michael Ball, "The Parables of the Unjust Steward and the Rich Man and Lazarus," *Expository Times* 106 (1995): 329.

Luke 16:19-31: In the Setting of the Proclamation
of the Kingdom of God

Jesus Himself declares that the gospel of the kingdom of God is being proclaimed since the time of John the Baptist,[344] and many people are forcing their way into it (16:16).[349] Jesus hinted that at the arrival of the kingdom of God, the Law and the Prophets continue to be valid and authoritative (vv. 16-18,29,31). This means that the Law and the Prophets are still the source of ethical norms for the people of the kingdom of God.

The rich man's neglect in feeding the poor Lazarus was a disobedience to the Law and the Prophets' rules which are also the rules of the kingdom of God.[391] The banquet or a meal is one of the themes of Luke 14.[392] In the three parables, Jesus gives importance for the humble, the poor, the maimed, and the blind (vv. 11,13,21). The rich are oftentimes doomed to miss the kingdom of God, not for the reason that they are rich but because of their refusal to share their riches to the poor (Luke 18:18-25; cf. Matt 19:16-24).

The kingdom is usually for the marginalized of society, like the poor disciples (Luke 6:20) who had left their houses, parents, wives, children, and brethren for the sake of the kingdom of God (Luke 18:29; cf. Matt 19:27-29). It is also for children who want to come to Jesus (Luke 18:16). The kingdom of God should be received as the little children (18:17; cf. Matt 18:3,4) in order to enter therein. The proclamation of the kingdom of God also involved healing all manners of sickness and disease of the people (Matt 4:23; 9:35; Luke 9:2,11). The rich man in the parable not only neglected to feed Lazarus, he also neglected to care for Lazarus' physical malady——body full of sores (Luke 16:20c). John

---

[588]Cf. Matt 3:2; Mark 1:15.

[589]Cf. Matt 11:12.

[590]Eating bread and drinking of wine in the kingdom of God is one of the central motif in the gospel (Luke 14:15; 22:16; 22:30). The rich man, in the parable, denied Lazarus of the bread. Consequently, he is not fit to enter the kingdom because he did not manifest in his life its ethics. One of the ethical norms of the kingdom of God is to invite the poor, the crippled, the lame, and the blind in a fellowship dinner (Luke 14:13).

[591]James L. Resseguie notes that the last parable in Luke 14 has a clear reference to the messianic banquet. James L. Resseguie, "Point of View in the Central Section of Luke," *Journal of Evangelical & Theological Society* 25 (1982): 45.

the Baptist's proclamation of the kingdom of God urges the Jews to repent (Matt 3:2). This is one of the prerequisites in order to enter the kingdom of God. This is also the center of Jesus' preaching (Matt 4:17), with addition of being converted (Matt 18:3). Those who do the Law and the Prophets and teach them will be called great in the kingdom of heaven (Matt 5:19). Our righteousness should surpass the righteousness of the Scribes and Pharisees in order to enter the kingdom (Matt 5:20). The righteousness that could surpass the righteousness of the Scribes and Pharisees is the righteousness of God. We should seek it first and foremost (Matt 6:33). Doing the will of God is also important in the kingdom of God (Matt 6:21). Clearly, the rich man did not repent in his life as indicated in the parable (Luke 16:30). He did not as well keep the commandments by neglecting the OT rules on proper use of wealth. Consequently, he failed also to teach it to his five brothers while living on earth (Luke 16:27,28). He has only the righteousness of the Scribes and Pharisees who professed to be children of Abraham but their deeds are fell short to measure up to God's standard (Luke 16:24,30; cf. John 8:39,40).

In the setting of the proclamation of the kingdom of God, those who do not live according to the ethics of the kingdom of God will be damned in γέεννα in the last day (Matt 23:23; Mark 9:45,47; John 5:28,29; 11:24). In the parable of the harvest in Matt 13, the harvest is the last day   (vv. 39). The Son of Man comes to "gather out of His kingdom all stumbling blocks, and those who commit lawlessness" (v. 41). They will be cast into the fire where there will be weeping and gnashing of teeth (v. 42).[592] If we view the punishment of the rich man in ᾅδης, in light of the eschatology of the Synoptic Gospels, and in relation to the proclamation of the kingdom of God, it is clear that the eschatology of the parable is contrary to the whole Synoptic Gospel. Then, it is plausible to say that Jesus' intention in telling the parable is not to teach His disciples His view concerning the afterlife,[593]

---

[592]Cf. Matt 13:47-52.

[593]Aalen argues that the wicked in Luke 16:19-31 suffers a preliminary punishment in ᾅδης, and then has to appear before God's judgment at the beginning of the New Age (20:35). Aalen, 8. However, the absence

but to rebuke the Pharisees for neglecting the OT rules on the proper use of wealth.

The Theological Implication of Luke 16:19-31

There are three theological implications of the parable of the rich man and Lazarus. First, in the light of the whole book of Luke, Luke stresses the theology of reversal[594] in his account of the life of Jesus. He sees Jesus as the champion of the marginalized of society such as the poor, the tax collectors, the Gentiles, women, and children. At the outset of the book, Luke right away stresses the principle of reversal. God would act in behalf of the lowly. He hath scattered the proud (v. 51, KJV), He has brought down the mighty from their thrones (v. 52a, ESV), He has exalted those of humble estate (v. 52b, ESV), and He has filled the hungry with good things and the rich He has sent them empty (v.53). In his description of the Jubilee mission of Jesus (4:18-19), he pointed out that Jesus' mission was first directed to the poor, captives, blind, and the oppressed. In his version of the beatitudes, he also specifically mentions that the kingdom of God is for the materially poor in the context of Luke 6:20. Furthermore, the theme of reversal is very obvious in his version of the beatitudes: (1) in v. 21a—Blessed are those who are hungry now, for they will be satisfied, (2) v. 21b—Blessed are those who weep now, for they will laugh, and (3) v. 23—Blessed are those who are hated now for they will rejoice in that day. Interestingly, the next discourse is concerning the woes which are opposite to the blessedness in the previous discourse. The first woe significantly is for the rich (v. 24). The second woe is for those who are full now for they will be hungry (v. 25a). The third woe is for those who laugh now for they will mourn and weep (v. 25b).

The theme of reversal, is also stressed in Luke 14:8-11. In v. 11, "Everyone

---

of this preliminary punishment in ᾅδης in the whole NT except this one in Luke 16:19-31 would invalidate this argument. The popularity of this Greco-Roman, and Jewish concept in the time of Christ does not mean that this is also the concept of the biblical authors.

[594]Douglas Parrot observes, "The theme of the parable collection, as edited, is the humbling of the proud and the raising up of the humble—here, in relation to repentance. This theme is characteristic of Luke." Douglas M. Parrot, "The Dishonest Steward (Luke 16:1-8a) and Luke's Special Parable Collection," *NTS* 37 (1991): 508.

who exalts himself will be humbled, and he who humbles himself will be exalted." This is repeated in Luke 18:14, where the Pharisee who exalts himself is not justified, but the tax collector who humbles himself.

It is clear that Luke 16:19-31 reiterates and emphasizes the principle of reversal. The rich man who neglected the poor found himself in ᾅδης. On the contrary, Lazarus ended up in the bosom of Abraham. Indeed, one of Luke's theology in this parable, in the light of the whole book, is that when a person exalts himself now, enjoys now, laughs now, lives an extravagant life now, without caring for those who are in need, he or she will be abased and will suffer the punishment for such neglect.

The second theological implication of the parable is that those who profess to be children of Abraham should be wise and faithful stewards of temporary riches. Those who take heed of the message of the parables (16:1-13; vv. 19-31) will dwell in eternal dwellings or in the bosom of Abraham. Those who are unfaithful will end up in torment. Faithful stewardship is also emphasized in the wider context of Luke (12:13-21; 19:1-10; 11-27).

The third theological implication of the parable is that the Law and the Prophets remain as the ethical guide for those who are living in the era of the kingdom of God. It should be the ultimate basis for man's conversion and repentance over extraordinary phenomena like the resurrection from the dead. The permanence and validity of the Law and the Prophets were emphasized by Jesus (16:16, 17,29,31; cf. Matt 5:17-20). He also uses it to show to His disciples that He would suffer but would rise again on the third day.

Many scholars agree, as shown above, that the parable does not teach about the doctrine of the afterlife. In telling the parable, it is not the purpose of Jesus to describe the condition of man after death nor the intention of Luke in his account of the gospel of Jesus. Therefore, the parable should not be taken as a basis for the theology of the state of the dead in the intermediate state. The eschatology of the parable is not in harmony with the eschatology of the Synoptic Gospels and John, and the whole NT.

Summary

This section summarizes the lexical, structural-thematic, literary-narrative, kingdom of God setting, and theological implications. In the lexical analysis, the usage of the word ᾅδης in Luke 10:15 is used in the context of the eschatological judgment, when the city of Capernaum would be humbled. The meaning of ᾅδης may carry the OT meaning, that is, "grave," "the place below the earth," "death," or the "place of the dead." In Acts 2:27,31, ᾅδης, once again, carries its OT equivalent word שְׁאוֹל. The reason is that Peter quotes Ps 16:8-11 which was originally applied to David in its original context.

In Acts, it is given messianic significance. However, the meaning of שְׁאוֹל in Ps 16:10 is still carried, that is, "grave" or "death." In Matt 16:18, the phrase "πύλαι ᾅδου" is seen to have an OT parallel expression "שַׁעַר שְׁאוֹל" (ša'ar šhe'ol, πύλαι ᾅδου, LXX). Jesus' pronouncement that the πύλαι ᾅδου (gates of *hadēs*) will not prevail against the Church seems to be the fulfillment of Yahweh's covenant promise to Abraham, that is, "Your seed will possess the gates of his enemies" (Gen 22:17). Paul says that the seed of Abraham is Jesus and those who believe in Him. One of the enemies of Jesus and the Church is death. The OT lAav. r[;v; (Isa 38:10) which is translated "gates of death" (NIV), "grave" (KJV, LXE) is parallel to πύλαι ᾅδου (gates of *hadēs*) in Matt 16:18. Death did not prevail against Jesus, it will not also prevail against the Church either. Thus, the meaning of ᾅδης in Matt 16:18 may be "death" or "grave."

The meaning of ᾅδης in Luke 16:23 diverts from the meaning of the rest of the NT. If the story in Luke 16:19-31 reflects popular Greco-Roman and inter-testamental Judaism afterlife stories, then ᾅδης in v. 23 may carry its Greek and Hellenistic Judaism meaning, that is, "the netherworld" the place of the disembodied souls in the intermediate state. However, Jesus' use here has a slight difference with that of the Greeks and the Jewish literature. He pictures the characters in the story as living persons with bodies. The imagery that a god is ruling in the underworld is absent in Luke 16:19-31. This indicates that the story is not really a true description of ᾅδης.

In the survey of the usages of the occurrences of γέεννα in the Synoptic Gospel, it is apparent that γέεννα is always associated with fire which is described as unquenchable and eternal.   These adjectives stress the quality of God's judgment—thorough and complete—rather than the quantity of the time of punishment.   The word γέεννα is used here in the Synoptics to refer to the place of punishment of the wicked at the last day, when the Son of Man comes to judge all the people of the nations.   It is also clear that the wicked are not disembodied souls in γέεννα but living beings (Matt 10:28).   They would be destroyed by the eternal fire.   Unlike other Rabbinic concept which was probably held by the Jews at the time of Jesus, there is nothing in the Synoptics that indicates that γέεννα is a place of punishment even in the intermediate state prior to the resurrection of the last day.

In the structural-thematic analysis, Luke 16:19-31 displays unity.   There are three possible structures of the passage.   The first one is the spatial/geographical structure which also shows a chiasm, the second is the reversal structure, and the third is the narrative/dialogue structure.   The structural analysis displays several themes of the passage.   The first theme is man's use/abuse of wealth.   The second is the reversal theme which is not only seen here but even in the whole book of Luke.   The third theme in the parable is the supremacy and permanence of the Scripture over miracles and extraordinary events.   This theme is also apparent in the immediate literary context.   The passage does not emphasize the theme of the afterlife.   It is not supported by the immediate and wider literary context.   In the literary-narrative analysis, the use of the introductory formula ""Ανθρωπος τις" (a certain man) that is common in an introduction of a parable in Luke is one of the evidences that the story is a fictitious one.   Jesus' use of names for the two of the characters of the story does not mean that the story is true.   Since Jesus adapts the story from the popular afterlife stories, it is natural for Him to use names since those stories usually use names to make them appear to be true stories. There are evidences to show that Jesus borrows the concepts of His story from those popular stories.   One of the evidences is the absence of this concept in the

OT. The fictitiousness of the story of the rich man and Lazarus does not affect the impact of the message Jesus wants to convey, just as His use of the parable of a dishonest steward does not weaken its message to His disciples. Furthermore, the Jews believe that the wicked will really be punished in the last day. Besides, the audience might have understood that Jesus' emphasis is not on the doctrine of the afterlife but on stewardship.

The description of ᾅδης in 16:19-31 should not be taken as an actual event. Here are several reasons:

1. The characters in the story are portrayed as living persons with bodies, unlike Greek afterlife stories.

. All of the occurrences of ᾅδης in the NT except here carry an OT meaning—grave or death.

3. Jesus' purpose is not to teach the doctrine of the afterlife but to emphasize that the unwise use of wealth and the neglect of the warning of the Scripture will end in punishment.

4. The story is fiction. This is seen in Abraham's refusal to send Lazarus to warn the five living brothers of the rich man. This means that there was no one who has done it before. This weakens the credibility of the truthfulness of the popular stories. Jesus also de-constructs those stories by breaking away from their usual patterns.

5. The eschatology of the parable is contrary to the eschatology of the Synoptics and the rest of the NT.

The main point of the parable is that Jesus stresses to the Pharisees the permanence and validity of the Scripture, especially in rules regarding stewardship of wealth. However, it is also evident that Jesus stresses faithfulness in handling evil wealth as seen in the immediate and wider context. It is also evident that Jesus emphasizes the theme of reversal. Hence, this is also one of the points of the parable.

In the setting of the proclamation of the kingdom of God, the rich man's neglect of the poor which is contrary to the ethics of the kingdom of God is the reason why they are doomed. Jesus' emphasis in caring for the poor is very prominent in His kingdom proclamation.

In the theological implications of Luke 16:19-31, it is clear that the principle of reversal is being stressed by the Lukan Jesus. Another theological implication is that the faithful or unfaithful use of wealth leads to reward or punishment. Lastly, the permanence of the Scripture even in the era of the kingdom of God is also emphasized.

It is therefore suggested that the story does not teach the doctrine of the afterlife. Its emphasis is on faithful stewardship and the permanence of the Scripture. The status of those who will not take heed like the Pharisees as the primary object of the parable will be reversed. The story is fictitious, which means that the description of ᾅδης in the story should not be taken as an actual event.

SUMMARY AND CONCLUSION

T HE INTERPRETATION of the concept of ᾅδης as described in Luke 16:19-31 has been the subject of this research. The historical-grammatical method has been used to analyze the passage in its immediate and wider contexts. It considers the genre, background, structure, themes, lexical-syntactical, literary-narrative aspects of exegesis. Now, this chapter summarizes the study which will then be followed by a concise conclusion.

Summary

At the outset of this study, it has been brought out that there are several issues in Luke 16:19-31. However, this study focuses on the interpretation of concept of ᾅδης. Scholars are divided in their interpretation of this concept. There are at least four views:

1. The concept of ᾅδης in Luke 16:19-31 is a factual event. The souls of the wicked are tormented, while the souls of the righteous are in bliss. This happens between death and resurrection of the body.

2. The concept of ᾅδης in Luke 16:19-31 is factual, like the first view, but the situation is after the last day judgment.

3. The concept of ᾅδης in Luke 16:19-31 is not factual. It is symbolical, it only reflects the reality of torments or blissfulness of souls in the intermediate state.

4. The concept of ᾅδης in Luke 16:19-31 is not factual. It functions as a parable in the Lukan narrative to give moral lessons. In reality, there are no souls in torment or in bliss in the intermediate. All the dead just sleep in the dust waiting for the resurrection.

In providing an extensive exegetical analysis of the concept of ᾅδης in Luke, this study considers the genre of Luke 16:19-31 in chapter 2. Chapter 3 deals with the backgrounds. Chapter 4 tackles the structural-thematic analysis. Chapter 5 undertakes the analysis of the passage considering the structure and themes of the passage, the lexical analysis of ᾅδης and its synonym, the literary-narrative analysis, its kingdom setting, and theological implications.

In chapter 2, this study analyzes the genre of OT מָשָׁל. The result suggests that מָשָׁל has a wide range of meanings and as a genre it has several subgenres. Its subgenres could be also its lexical meanings: (1) proverbial saying, (2) by-word, (3) prophetic figurative discourse, (4) similitude and parable, (5) poem, and (6) sentences of ethical wisdom. Its essence is comparison.

After the word מָשָׁל has been analyzed, several patterns are suggested. It shows that one of the significant patterns that came out is that there is usually an idea of comparison in almost all subgenres of מָשָׁל.

One subgenre of OT מָשָׁל which became significant for this study is the Narrative Parable. This is classified into several types: (1) Fable Parable, (2) Juridical Parable, (3) Allegorical Parable, and (4) Fable Allegory or Parabolic Allegory.

There are five OT narrative parables which were analyzed in chapter 2. Several significant points came out. There are parables which could be labeled as "Fable-Parables." It has been found out that there are some items in the parables which do not have correspondences in the application. There is at least one narrative which could be labeled as an allegory. In some instances, the applications given by the prophets go beyond what was apparent in the parables. it is also established that these narrative parables are fictitious stories used only as an instrument in order to convey a rebuke or a divine judgment. Some of these narrative parables are called "Juridical Parables." Usually, there are preceding events in the literary contexts of these narrative parables that become the bases why these parables were uttered. There is also usually an intended audience to whom the messages of the parables are directed.

In the analysis of NT παραβολή, it shows that it has some similarity with OT מָשָׁל. It has also a range of meanings and subgenres. One subgenre is what we technically labeled as "parable."

It has been shown that Luke's narrative parables have similar characteristics to the OT narrative parables. For example, Nathan's parable and the rich fool have identical characteristics. Both parables are intended to give a rebuke to the audience. Isa 5:1-7 is similar to the parable of the sower (Luke 8:4-15). Both have several one-to-one correspondences pointed out by both Isaiah and Jesus. However, not everything in both parables has correspondences.

Furthermore, some significantly similar characteristics between OT and NT narrative parables should be pointed out. There is an idea of comparison in both. Their messages are specifically intended to their audience in the literary contexts. These messages were given because of certain problems or situations that confront the audience. There are apparently allegorical elements in some parables. Not all items in both have correspondences in real life, application, and interpretation. Usually, both have ethical and behavioral focus.

There are differences between OT מָשָׁל and NT παραβολή. The one that is helpful for this study is that some OT narrative parables are used to convey divine judgments against the apostasies of its intended audience.[595] NT narrative parables are used to teach spiritual truths and principles pertaining to the kingdom of God which Jesus proclaimed and taught to His audience.

The narrative of the rich man and Lazarus in Luke 16:19-31, like the parable of the rich fool in Luke 12:16-21 and Nathan's parable in 2 Sam 12:1-7, is a

---

[595]The parable of the rich fool (Luke 12:16-21) has a theme of judgment. God pronounced judgment against the rich fool. The judgment is in the story, but not in the application. The intended audience was not judged like the rich fool in the story.

parable. Its type is a story parable or parabolic story as its subgenre. There are several reasons to prove it. First, the rich fool is explicitly called a parabolh,. If it is true to one, it may be true to the other two. Second, both parables of the rich fool and the rich man and Lazarus have identical introductions usually common to parables. Third, these three narratives are prompted with moral issues among their audience. Fourth, their specific messages are intended to an individual or group of individuals. Fifth, there are at least one or two characters in these stories that correspond to one of the audience.

On the issue on factuality or fictionality, it is also suggested that Luke 16:16-31 is a fictitious story like the rich fool and Nathan's parable. The imagery of the parable itself betrays some scholars' claim to its factuality.

In the analysis of the background in chapter 3, it shows that there are commonalities and differences among extra-biblical literature on the concept of ᾅδης and its synonym. There are several commonalities among these bodies of literature which ranges from second millennium B.C. up to the third or fourth centuries of the Christian era.

Several commonalities have shown up. First, almost all of these literature agree that ᾅδης or מְשׁל is located below the earth. It is also called "grave," "pit," or "deep pit." The OT, NT, and some Jewish extra-biblical literature express the same idea that ᾅδης or שְׁאוֹל is parallel to death. Second, it is portrayed as dark and gloomy. It has gatekeepers who hold the souls of the dead as prisoners. Third, these bodies of literature agree, except for the OT–LXX and NT, that some gods are in charge of the underworld. Fourth, many of these literature, except OT and NT (excluding Luke 16:19-31), say that the dead are conscious in ᾅδης.

Fifth, majority of the extra-biblical literature shows that the souls of the dead will face the judge in the underworld immediately after their death. After their judgment, the souls will be separated spatially in ᾅδης. The wicked will suffer some sort of punishment, while the righteous will enjoy the afterlife in a place of blissfulness. The most common agent of punishment in ᾅδης is fire. The idea of a burning ᾅδης is the most common concept among these literature, except for the OT and NT. Sixth, in majority of these extra-biblical literature, there is always a story about a human being or a goddess (in *ANET*) who was able to enter ᾅδης but was able to escape it and return to the land of the living. In NT Apocrypha, it tells the story of Jesus Christ who entered ᾅδης at His death and delivered some righteous individuals from it and brought them to life with Him.

However, some differences are noteworthy. The differences between these biblical and extra-biblical literature are also noteworthy. First, in all Jewish and Christian literature, including the OT and NT, there is a uniform belief that ᾅδης or שְׁאוֹל is just a temporary place for the righteous. It is reflected in the contexts of its occurrences. There is an overwhelming idea that God would deliver them from ᾅδης or שְׁאוֹל. They will be resurrected in the last day and will receive eternal life. They will live in the new heaven and new earth with a glorified body; whereas, in all Greco-Roman literature, ᾅδης is a permanent place for the good souls and for the bad souls. They are immediately judged and are right away separated from each other. The good souls would reside in a blissful and peaceful place, whereas the bad souls would be punished in the fiery place.

Second, in several extra-biblical Jewish literature, the wicked would also suffer in a fire before the day of judgment. After the judgment in the last day, they would suffer for eternity in ᾅδης, whereas in the OT and NT (except Luke 16:19-31), the righteous and the wicked are just asleep in ᾅδης in the intermediate state. They are unconscious. There are no souls suffering in torment in the OT and NT (except in the parable). After the judgment, the wicked would suffer in the fire of γέεννα not in ᾅδης because it was even described as being burned in the lake of fire. The wicked would not suffer in the fire for eternity.

Third, in the OT and NT, and some extra-biblical Jewish and Christian literature, the judgment would be at the last day. In Greco-Roman literature, the souls of the dead are judged right away as soon as they arrive in ᾅδης. Fourth, in the OT and NT (except Luke 16:19-31), there is no burning fire in ᾅδης or שְׁאוֹל. that tortures the souls of the wicked unlike Greco-Roman, Jewish, and Christian extra-biblical literature. Fifth, ᾅδης is also parallel to grave and death in the OT and NT and in some Jewish extra-biblical literature, unlike the Greco-Roman literature. The idea of the separation of the wicked and the righteous is found in Greco-Roman, Jewish-Christian extra-biblical literature, unlike in the OT and NT (except Luke 16:19-31).

Sixth, many Greco-Roman and Jewish-Christian literature describe the place of punishment and the place of bliss as just near each other in ᾅδης, whereas in the OT and NT (except Luke 16:19-31) there are no such places. The dead are just sleeping in the dust or in the grave and they are not conscious. Seventh, unlike Greco-Roman literature, the OT and other Jewish literature often describe ᾅδης or שְׁאוֹל. in a figurative way. They describe the spiritual separation of a righteous man from his God as a שְׁאוֹל-like experience.

Eighth, in some Jewish extra-biblical literature in the first century C.E., there was already a belief that the souls of the righteous would go to heaven the moment they die. This belief is absent from the OT, inter-testamental Jewish literature, and from NT biblical literature.

Ninth, the OT, and NT speak of the whole person going down to שְׁאוֹל. at death. When the OT speaks of a man who had died and is already in שְׁאוֹל it does not speak of him as soul but dead. In the NT biblical literature, there are no explicit statements or teachings from Jesus and from the apostles that souls are conscious in ᾅδης. The rest of the NT is clear that the punishment and reward of the wicked and righteous will be at the last day.

In the analysis of the general background of Luke-Acts, and its structure and themes in chapter 4, there are several insights drawn. If Luke, a Gentile convert was the author, and the recipients were also Gentiles, it helps us understand why he included the parable of the rich man and Lazarus in his gospel account. The genre of the gospel of Luke may be "narrative" or "story." Some portions in Luke belong to an ancient literary tradition called "historiography." The purpose of Luke-Acts is to write a chronological account to Theophilus. He wants to show how things happened in order, and that God fulfilled His promises to His people of Israel and also extended His blessing to the Gentiles. However, it seems obvious that Luke has theological emphases in writing Jesus' story. His theological focus is very evident in the thematic analysis. The general theme of Luke-Acts is "the plan of God." The plan of God is that all flesh will see His salvation. This divine activity was carried on throughout history. This plan of God begins with the Jews in Jerusalem but ends with the whole nations, kindred, and people.

The structural-thematic analysis of Luke-Acts, Luke' travel narrative, and Luke 16 support the plausibility of the general theme. Furthermore, some sub-themes which are related to the general theme cropped up. It is also evident in the structural analysis that Jerusalem/temple is very central in Luke's gospel. It is the central point of its geographical and narrative structure. Luke's narrative begins and ends in Jerusalem/temple. However, there is a paradigm shift from Luke to Acts. The narrative of Acts begins at Jerusalem/temple, but in chapter 7, it shifts its focus, from earthly Jerusalem/ temple to heavenly Jerusalem/temple. The preaching of the gospel also shifts from local or nationalistic to international or empire-wide. In Acts, the disciples started to evangelize Jerusalem but its narrative ends in Rome. In Luke, salvation proceeds from the temple where God dwells, as in the OT. However, in Acts, the locus of the geographical structure shifts from an earthly temple to a heavenly temple. Salvation also starts from the Jews in Luke, and ends up to all nations in Acts. These pieces of insights on general structure and theme enlighten our understanding of the passage. Luke wants his readers to understand that the gospel is for everyone even to the very least. It also fosters a sense of mission—reaching out to all kinds of people in the society especially the poor, outcast, and a marginalized sector of society.

The themes which are spelled out by the chiastic narrative structure include Jerusalem as the focal point of the eschatological events. One of the themes emphasized by Luke's travel narrative is the theme of exaltation of the poor and the abasement of the rich, the proud, and the socially and religiously prominent of Jewish society. God's concern for the poor is very well emphasized. The kingdom motif is also prominent in Luke's travel narrative. The kingdom was already present at the arrival of Jesus. In this travel narrative, Jesus taught His disciples the principles of His newly established spiritual kingdom. One of these principles is prudent stewardship that is apparent in Luke 16:1-31. The analysis of the structure of Luke 16:1-31 shows two parables in contrasting fashion. The first illustrates how to be a prudent steward; the second shows the destiny of a foolish steward. Jesus addressed the first one to His disciples, and the second one was addressed to the Pharisees.

The exegetical analysis of the passage in chapter 5 yields some solutions to the problem of the study. In the lexical analysis, the usage of the word a[|dhj in Luke 10:15 was used in the context of the eschatological judgment. The meaning of ἅδης in Luke-Acts may carry the OT meaning, that is, "grave," "the place below the earth," "death," or the "place of the dead." One reason is that Peter quotes Ps 16:8-11 which shows that the meaning of lAav. in Ps 16:10——— grave, or death, is still carried in Acts 2:27,31.

In Matt 16:18, the phrase "πύλαι ᾅδου" is seen to have an OT parallel expression "שַׁעֲרֵי שְׁאוֹל" (πύλαι ᾅδου, LXX). Jesus' pronouncement that the πύλαι ᾅδου will not prevail against the Church seems to be the fulfillment of Yahweh's covenant promise to Abraham, that is, "your seed will possess the gates of his enemies" (Gen 22:17). Paul said that the seed of Abraham is Jesus and those who believe in Him. One of the enemies of Jesus and the Church is death. Death did not prevail against Jesus. It will not prevail against the Church either. Thus, the meaning of ᾅδης in Matt 16:18 may be "death" or "grave."

The word ᾅδης in Luke 16:23 diverts from the meaning of the rest of the NT. If the story in Luke 16:19-31 reflects popular Greco-Roman, and inter-testamental Judaism afterlife stories, then ᾅδης in v. 23 may carry its Greek and Hellenistic Judaism meaning, that is, "the netherworld" the place of the disembodied souls in the intermediate state. However, Jesus' use here has a slight difference with that of the Greek and Jewish literature. He pictured the characters in the story as living persons with bodies. This indicates that Jesus' story is not really a true description of ᾅδης as what the Greeks believed. In the usages of γέεννα in the Synoptic Gospels, it is obvious that it is always associated with fire that is described as unquenchable and eternal. These adjectives stress the quality of God's judgment—thorough and complete—rather than the quantity of the time of punishment. The word γέεννα is used here in the Synoptics to refer to the place of punishment of the wicked at the last day, when the Son of Man comes to judge all the people of the nations. It is also clear that the wicked are not disembodied souls in γέεννα but living beings (Matt 10:28). They would be destroyed by the eternal fire. Unlike other Rabbinic concept which was probably held by the Jews at the time of Jesus, there is nothing in the Synoptics that indicates that γέεννα is a place of punishment even in the intermediate state prior to the resurrection of the last day.

In the structural-thematic analysis, Luke 16:19-31 displays unity. The three possible structures of the passage are the following: (1) spatial-geographical structure which also shows a chiasm, (2) reversal structure, and (3) narrative/ dialogue structure. The several themes of the passage are the following: (1) the man's use/abuse of wealth, (2) the reversal theme which is not only seen here but even in the whole book of Luke, and (3) the supremacy and permanence of the Scripture over a miracle and extraordinary event.[596]

In the literary-narrative analysis, the use of the introductory formula " ̈Ανθρωπος τις" (a certain man), which is common in an introduction of a parable in Luke, is one of the evidences that the story is a fictitious one. Jesus' use of names in the parable is just one way of adapting to His source. There are evidences to show that Jesus borrowed the concepts of His story from those popular stories. One evidence is the absence of this concept in the OT. The fictitiousness of the story does not affect the impact of the message Jesus wants to convey, just as Jesus' use of the parable of a dishonest steward does not weaken its message to His disciples.

The description ἅδης in Luke 16:19-31 should not be taken as an actual event. There are several reasons to prove it. First, the characters in the story are portrayed as living persons with bodies, unlike Greek afterlife stories. Second,

---

[596]This theme is also apparent in the immediate literary context. The passage does not emphasize the theme of the afterlife. It is not supported by the immediate and wider literary context.

ᾅδης in the NT (except in Luke 16:19-31) carries an OT meaning—grave, or death. Third, Jesus' purpose is not to teach the doctrine of the afterlife but to emphasize that the unwise use of wealth and neglecting the warning of the Scripture will end in punishment. Fourth, Abraham's refusal to send Lazarus to warn the five living brothers of the rich man may imply, at least in the light of the Scripture, that no one has done it before—a dead person who came back to life to warn the living in order to avoid suffering in ᾅδης. This may weaken the credibility and truthfulness of the popular stories. Jesus also de-constructs those stories by breaking away from their usual patterns. Fourth, the eschatology of the parable is contrary to the eschatology of the Synoptics and the rest of the NT.

Fifth, Jesus' main emphasis is the permanence and validity of the Scripture, especially in rules regarding stewardship of wealth. On the other hand, Jesus also stressed faithfulness in handling evil wealth as seen in the immediate and wider context. Furthermore, Jesus also emphasizes the theme of reversal.

In the setting of the proclamation of the kingdom of God, the reason why the rich man was doomed because he ignored the OT laws on how to deal with the poor. Caring for the poor became one of the ethics of the kingdom of God inaugurated at the arrival of Jesus. Jesus' emphasis in caring for the poor is very prominent in His kingdom proclamation.

In the theological implications of Luke 16:19-31, it is obvious that the principle of reversal is being stressed by the Lukan Jesus. Another theological implication is that the faithful or unfaithful use of wealth leads to reward or punishment. Lastly, the permanence of the Scripture even in the era of the kingdom of God is also emphasized.

It is therefore suggested that the story does not teach the doctrine of the afterlife. Its emphasis is the permanence of the Scripture even at the era of Jesus' messianic kingdom. The status of those who will not take heed like the Pharisees as the primary object of the parable will be reversed. The story is fictitious. The description of ᾅδης in the story should not be taken as an actual event.

Conclusion

This study, after exegetically analyzing the concept of ἅδης in Luke 16:19-31 in its immediate and wider literary and historical contexts, would like to suggest that the concept of ἅδης in Luke 16:19-31, in line with the fourth view, is not a factual event but rather a fictitious one. Several evidences and arguments which lead to this suggestion are the following:

1. The genre analysis in chapter 2 shows that OT and NT narrative parables are usually fictitious stories created for a specific purpose for a specific person or audience in its literary context. Furthermore, the comparison of Luke 16:19-31 with OT and other Lukan parables shows that 16:19-31 is similar to those parables. Hence, it is also accepted as a parable, and that it is fictitious.

2. The analysis of the extra-biblical and biblical backgrounds of the concept of ἅδης in Luke 16:19-31 demonstrates that this concept was very popular in Ancient Near Eastern, Greek, later Jewish, and even in early Christian literature. The thematic parallels between the stories about ἅδης in extra-biblical literature and in 16:19-31 lead us to suggest that Jesus may have adapted His story in 16:19-31 from those stories. However, while reconstructing His own story, He made a deconstruction of some themes in those stories. One of the significant themes de-constructed by Jesus is the communication from the dead. The other one is the soul being separated from the body. In Jesus' story it is not a soul that separates from the body anymore, but it is the whole person that is portrayed as suffering in ἅδης.

Furthermore, the OT and NT concept of ἅδης is different from Greek and later Jewish concepts. It portrays ἅδης as the grave, deep pit, or even death. It also shows that the dead know nothing in death. They are asleep in the dust waiting for resurrection in the last day.

3. The structures and themes of Luke-Acts, Luke's travel narrative, Luke 16, and 16:19-31 show that the concept of ἅδης is not one of the themes of Luke.

The most obvious theme is the Law and the Prophets which serves as guide for those who live in the era of the kingdom of God, especially in their teachings on how to be prudent stewards of the unrighteous wealth they possess. The bigger theme is that God's plan of salvation is for all people, even for the poor and the marginalized of society.

4. The exegetical analysis of Luke 16:19-31 also shows that ᾅδης in the Synoptic Gospels may mean death or grave. In the occurrences of ᾅδης, except in the parable, there is nothing that speaks concerning disembodied souls suffering in ᾅδης. It also shows that the punishment of the wicked and the reward of the righteous will take place after the last day judgment. It also shows that the description of the situation in ᾅδης indicates that it is not a true event. To be highlighted is the description that the characters in the story are not souls but seem to be persons with bodies. It also shows that, in the immediate context, Jesus' main purpose is to rebuke the Pharisees because they are lovers of money and by doing so neglect the need of the poor among them, ignoring the Law and the Prophets. It also shows that Jesus' emphasis is on use/abuse of wealth. He is not endorsing the concept ᾅδης in the parable, as He is not endorsing the dishonesty of the shrewd steward in 16:1-8a.

In view of these very convincing evidences and arguments this study wants to suggest that the concept ᾅδης in Luke 16:19-31 should not be taken as a factual event similar to the fourth view. This means that there is no such thing as conscious souls that separate from the body at death in the intermediate state. There are no souls that suffer in ᾅδης or enjoy a blissful rest in paradise in the intermediate state. In the light of the OT and NT, it is clear that the wicked and the righteous are asleep in the dust or grave at death. However, the authoritative word of God also emphasizes that both the righteous and the wicked will be resurrected and will be judged at the last day when the Son of Man comes. At that time, the wicked will be punished in the fire, while the righteous will live in the home of the bliss forevermore. The story is a parable. As a parable, it has a specific spiritual point or message intended primarily for the Pharisees. It does not teach about the state of the dead in the intermediate state. Its main message is that the Scripture is enough to guide men on how to be faithful stewards of the things that they possess in this life.

This study, unlike the previous biblical scholars and theologians who wrote on this topic, has made an extensive exegetical analysis of the passage. It also provides a methodological insight especially in dealing with the interpretation of an NT parable—the genre and structural-thematic analyses.

To further strengthen the conclusions of this study, the following possible studies are recommended: (1) the meaning of the OT word נֶפֶשׁ (nepheš) or its Greek equivalent—הַיָּצִיר, (2) the interpretation of 1 Pet 3:18-22—the spirits in prison, and (3) the meaning of the phrase, "away from the body, at home with the LORD" (2 Cor 5:6).

APPENDIX

TABLE A1

FOUR MAJOR INTERPRETATIONS OF THE CONCEPT OF
ʿ Ἀδης IN LUKE 16:19-31

First View	The Description of the concept of ʿ Ἀδης Luke 16:19-31 is factual and literal torment or blissfulness of souls in the intermediate state (between death and resurrection).
Second View	The description of the concept of ʿ Ἀδης Luke 16:19-31 is factual and literal torment or enjoyment of souls after the judgment at the last day.
Third View	The description of ʿ Ἀδης Luke 16:19-31 is not factual or literal but symbolical. It is a parable that only reflects the reality of the torment or blissfulness of souls in the intermediate state or final judgment.
Fourth View	The description of ʿ Ἀδης Luke 16:19-31 is not a factual event. It is a parable that gives a moral lesson. In reality, there are no souls who are tormented or already in bliss in the intermediate state.

TABLE A2

FOUR MAJOR INTERPRETATIONS, AND THIS STUDY:
METHODOLOGY, AND EXTENT OF THEIR
WORK ON THE TOPIC

Four Major Interpretations, and this study	Genre of Luke 16:19-31	Historical Religious Background of Ἀδης	Structural Thematic	Literary Narrative Analysis
First View	Parablefactual story	No discussion	No discussion	Not enough discussion
Second View	parablefactual story	No discussion	No discussion	Not enough discussion
Third View	ParableFictitious story	Little discussion	Little discussion	Enough discussion
Fourth View	ParableFictitious story	Little discussion	Little discussion	Enough discussion
This Study	ParableFictitious	Extensive discussion	Extensive discussion	More discussion

Four major Interpretations, and this study	Lexical-Syntactical, and Grammatical	Theological Analysis
First View	Less discussion	More discussion on doctrinal aspects
Second View	Less discussion	More discussion on doctrinal aspects
Third View	less discussion	More discussion on biblical theology
Fourth View	More discussion	More discussion on biblical theology
This Study	More discussion	More discussion on biblical theology

TABLE A3

THE DESCRIPTION OF ῎Αδης IN JEWISH BIBLICAL AND
EXTRA-BIBLICAL LITERATURE IN THE
INTERMEDIATE STATE

Literature	Description and Meaning
OT-LXX	1. ῎Αδης is the word used in LXX for שְׁאוֹל. It means "grave," "death," "a place beneath the earth," "pit," "the place of the dead." 2. The dead knows nothing anymore in שְׁאוֹל. 3. The dead sleep in the dust. 4. No conscious souls in ῎Αδης. 5. Temporary place for both the wicked and the righteous.
OT Apocrypha and Pseudepigrapha	The same with OT-LXX (numbers 1 and 5), except numbers 2, 3, and 4. The wicked and the righteous are separated from each other.
The DSS	The same with OT-LXX except numbers 2, 3, and 4.
Philo	The same with OT-LXX except numbers 2, 3, and 4.
Josephus	The same with OT-LXX except numbers 2, 3, and 4.
Talmud	The same with OT-LXX except numbers 2, 3, 4. On the other hand it prefers the word Gehenna than ῎Αδης.

TABLE A4

THE DESCRIPTION OF ῾Αδης IN *ANET* AND GRECO-ROMAN
LITERATURE

Literature	Description ans Meaning
Ancient Near Eastern Text	1. It is called, "the Nether World." 2. The place of the conscious souls of the dead. 3. The good and bad souls are separated from each other especially in Egyptian tale. 4. A god is in-charge of the the Nether World. 5. The souls are judged and punished by the gods of the Nether World. 6. It is the final destination of the dead.
Homer	The same with ANET but the gods have different names. The bad are separated from the good souls.
Plato	The same with the ANET and Homer, the names of the gods are the same with Homer.
Other Greco-Roman Writers	The same with ANET, Plato, and Homer; the names of the gods are the same with Plato and Homer.

TABLE A5

THE DESCRIPTION OF Ἅδης IN CHRISTIAN BIBLICAL
AND EXTRA-BIBLICAL LITERATURE
THE INTERMEDIATE STATE

Literature	Description and Meaning
Synoptic Gospels	1. Like OT-LXX, ᾅδης means "grave," "place of the dead," and "death." 2. No conscious souls, except in the parable (Luke 16:19-31). 3. The wicked will be judged and punished in γέεννα at the last day when the Son of Man comes (except in the parable where the wicked and righteous seem to have been rewarded and punished already.
James	1. He does not mention about ᾅδης. 2. It only mentions γέεννα where the wicked will be punished at the last day.
Paul	1. He does not mention ᾅδης nor γέεννα but the concept could be found. 2. He mentions that the dead are asleep in the dust in the intermediate state. 3. Both the wicked and the dead will be resurrected At the *Parousia*. The wicked will be destroyed The righteous will be clothed with immortality, and with the Lord.
John	1. He mentions a[]dhj and it means, "grave," or "death." It is temporary, and it will be destroyed at the last day. 2. The dead sleep in the dust or grave. 3. Souls were figuratively described as conscious. But the meaning of "soul" may carry its OT meaning rather than the Greco- Roman.

Table A5——*Continued*

Peter and Jude	Peter does not mention either ᾅδης or γέεννα. He rather mentions ταρταρώσας, the noun is ταρταρος, the place for the rebellious angels while waiting the judgement. The idea of tartaroj is present also in Jude.
NT Apocrypha and Early Church Fathers	1. ᾿Αδης is the place where the souls of the wicked go. The souls of the wicked would suffer in the fire while waiting for the resurrection. 2. Unlike the OT-LXX, Jewish extra-biblical, and NT, early Christians believed that the souls of the righteous would go to heaven in the intermediate state.

BIBLIOGRAPHY

Aalen, S. "St. Luke's Gospel and the Last Chapter of I Enoch." *New Testament Studies* 13 (1966-67): 1-13.

Achtemeier, Paul J., Joel B. Green, and Marianne Meye Thompson. *Introducing the New Testament: Its Literature and Theology.* Grand Rapids: Eerdmans, 2001.

Agustin, Alfredo G., Jr. "The Locus of the Millennial Reign of Christ and His Saints in Rev 20:1-10." M.A. thesis, Adventist International Institute of Advanced Studies, Silang, Cavite, Philippines, 2002.

Aland, Barbara, Kurt Aland, Johannes Karavidopoulos, Carlo M. Martini, and Bruce M. Metzger, eds. *The Greek New Testament* (GNT-UBS4), 4th ed. (Corrected). Stuttgart: United Bible Societies, 1993.

Allen, Leslie. *Ezekiel 1-39.* Word Biblical Commentary, vol. 28. Dallas, TX: Word, 1994.

Anderson, Arnold A. *2 Samuel.* Word Biblical Commentary, vol. 11. Dallas, TX: Word, 1989.

Andreasen, M. L. *Man: Here and Hereafter.* Mountain View, CA: Pacific Press, 1937.

Arndt, William F. *Luke.* Concordia Classic Commentary Series. St. Louis, MO: Concordia, 1956; reprint, St. Louis, MO: Concordia, 1986.

Arnobius *Against the Heathen.* Translated by Hamilton Bryce. Ante-Nicene Fathers. 6:413-543.

Aune, David E. "The Apocalypse of John and Greco-Roman Magic." *New Testament Studies* 33 (1987): 484-89.

_____. *Revelation 1-5.* Word Biblical Commentary, vol. 52A. Dallas, TX: Word, 1997.
Aune David E. *Revelation 6-16.* Word Biblical Commentary, vol. 52B. Dallas, TX: Word, 1998.

_____. *Revelation 17-22.* Word Biblical Commentary, vol. 52C. Dallas, TX: Word, 1998.
Bailey, Kenneth E. *Poet and Peasant: A Literary-Cultural Approach to the Parables in Luke.* Combined Edition. Grand Rapids: Eerdmans, 1983.

Baldwin, Joyce G. *1 & 2 Samuel.* Tyndale Old Testament Commentaries, vol. 8. Downers Grove, IL: InterVarsity, 1988.

Ball, Michael. "The Parables of the Unjust Steward and the Rich Man and Lazarus." *Expository Times* 106 (1995): 329-30.

Barclay, William. *And Jesus Said: A Handbook on the Parable of Jesus.* Philadelphia: Westminster, 1970.

Barnett, Paul. *The Second Epistle to the Corinthians.* New International Commentary on the New Testament. Grand Rapids: Eerdmans, 1997.

Batzler, Louis Richard. "The Parable of Jesus Concerning the Afterlife: Spiritual and Psychical Insights." *The Journal of Religion and Psychical Research* 23 (2000): 83-90. Journal on-line. Available from Academic Search Premier database. Internet. Accessed 19 January 2007.

Bauckham, Richard. *The Fate of the Dead: Studies on the Jewish and Christian Apocalypses.* Leiden: Brill, 1998.

_____. "Hades." *The Anchor Bible Dictionary.* Edited by David Noel Freedman. New York: Doubleday, 1992. 3:14-15.

_____. *Jude, 2 Peter.* Word Biblical Commentary, vol. 50. Waco, TX: Word, 1983.

_____. "The Rich Man and Lazarus: The Parable and the Parallels." *New Testament Studies* 37 (1991): 225-46.

Bauer, Walter. *A Greek-English Lexicon of the New Testament and Other Early Christian Literature.* Translated and adapted by William F. Arndt and F. Wilbur Gingrich. 3d ed. Revised and augmented by F. Wilbur Gingrich and Trederick W. Danker 3d Edition. Edited by Frederick William Danker. Chicago: University of Chicago Press, 2000. S.v. "ᾅδης," "ἀκούω," "ἀνίστημι," "ἀπολέσαι," "δέ," "διαφθορά," "διήγησις," "ἐκμυκτηρίζω," "ἔνοχος," "γέεννα," "καθεξῆς," "κατισχύω," "κρίσις," "μετανοέω," "ὅμοιοj," "παραβολη," "φιλαργυρία," "ταρταρόω," "τελώνης," "ὑποκριτής."

Bennett, W. H. "*The Prayer of Azariah and the Song of the Three Children.*" In *Apocrypha and Pseudepigrapha of the Old Testament in English.* Edited by R. H. Charles. Oxford: Clarendon, 1978. 1:625-37.

Best, Ernest. *Second Corinthians.* Interpretation. Louisville, KY: John Knox, 1987.

Bible Works. *Version7.* Norfolk, VA: LLC, 2007.

Bietenhard, Hans. "ᾅδης." *New International Dictionary of New Testament Theology.* Edited by Colin Brown. Grand Rapids: Zondervan, 1976. 2:206-08.

_____. "γέεννα." *New International Theological Dictionary of New Testament Theology.* Edited by Colin Brown. Grand Rapids: Zondervan, 1976. 2:208-09.

Blenkinsopp, Joseph. *Isaiah 1-39.* Anchor Bible, vol. 19. New York: Doubleday, 2000.

Block, Daniel I. *The Book of Ezekiel 1-24.* New International Commentary on the Old Testament. Grand Rapids: Eerdmans, 1997.

_____. *Judges, Ruth: An Exegetical and Theological Exposition of Holy Scripture*. New American Commentary, vol. 6. Nashville, TN: Broadman & Holman, 1999.

Blomberg, Craig L. *1 Corinthians*. NIV Application Commentary. Grand Rapids: Zondervan, 1994.

_____. *Interpreting the Parables*. Downers Grove, IL: InterVarsity, 1990.

Blomberg, Craig L. *Matthew*. New American Commentary, vol. 22. Nasville, TN: Broadman, 1992.

Blum, Edwin A. "2 Peter." *The Expositor's Bible Commentary*. Edited by Frank Gaebelein. Grand Rapids: Zondervan, 1981. 257-89.

Bock, Darrell L. *Luke*. NIV Application Commentary. Grand Rapids: Zondervan, 1996.

_____. *Luke 1:1-9:50*. Baker Exegetical Commentary on the New Testament. Grand Rapids: Baker, 1999.

_____. *Luke 9:51-24:53*. Baker Exegetical Commentary of the New Testament. Grand Rapids: Baker, 1996.
Boettner, Loraine. *Immortality*. Philadelphia: Presbyterian & Reformed, 1956; reprint, Cavite, Philippines: Presbyterian Theological Seminary, 1989.

Boucher, Madeleine I. *The Parables*. Wilmington, DE: Michael Glazier, 1981.

Box, G. H. "IV Ezra." In *Apocrypha and Pseudepigrapha of the Old Testament in English*. Edited by R. H. Charles. Oxford: Clarendon, 1979. 2:542-624.

Box, G. H., and W. O. E. Oesterley. "The Book of Sirach." In *Apocrypha and Pseudepigrapha of the Old Testament in English*. Edited by R. H. Charles. Oxford: Clarendon, 1978. 1:268-517.

Brenton, Charles Lee. *The Septuagint Version of the Old Testament and Apocrypha*. London: Samuel Bagster, 1851; reprint, Grand Rapids: Zondervan, 1970.

_____. "Tobit." *The Septuagint Version of the Old Testament and Apocrypha with an English Translations; and with Various Readings and Critical Notes*. London: Samuel Bagster, 1851; reprint, Grand Rapids: Zondervan, 1978.

Brooks, James A. *Mark*. New American Commentary, vol. 23. Nashville, TN: Broadman, 1991.

Brown, Francis, with S. R. Driver and Charles A. Briggs. *A Hebrew and English Lexicon of the Old Testament with an Appendix Containing the Biblical Aramaic*. Based on the lexicon of William Gesenius. Oxford: Clarendon, 1952. S.v. "בּוֹר", "דּוּמָה", "חִידָה", "מָשָׁל", "מָוֶת", "מוּת", "שְׁאִיָּה", "שָׁאַל", "שְׁאֵלָה", "שְׁאוֹל", "שָׁאַל", "שְׁאוֹל", "שָׁאַל", "רְפָאִים", "צַלְמָוֶת", "נָאַם".

Bruce, F. F. *The Book of Acts*. New International Commentary on the New Testament. Grand Rapids: Eerdmans, 1979.

Budd, Philip J. *Numbers.* Word Biblical Commentary, vol. 5. Waco, TX: Word, 1984.

Buis, H. "ᾅδης." *The Zondervan Pictorial Encyclopedia of the Bible.* 1976. 3:7-8.

Bultmann, Rudolf. *History of the Synoptic Tradition.* Translated by John Marsh. Rev. ed. Oxford: Blackwell, 1972.

Buttrick, George A. *The Parables of Jesus.* Grand Rapids: Baker, 1973.

"By Which" (1 Pet 3:19). *Seventh-day Adventist Bible Commentary.* Rev. ed. Edited by Francis D. Nichol. Washington, DC: Review & Herald, 1976-80. 7:574.

Caird, George Bradford. *Saint Luke.* Westminster Pelican Commentaries. Philadelphia: Westminster, 1963.

Cairus, Aecio. "The Rich Man and Lazarus: An Apocryphal Interpolation." *Journal of Asia Adventist Seminary* 9 (2006): 35-45.

Calvin, John. *Calvin's Commentaries: A Harmony of the Gospels of Matthew, Mark, and Luke.* Vol. 2. Translated by A. W. Morrison. Edited by David W. Torrance and Thomas F. Torrance. Edinburgh: St. Andrews, 1972.

Carson, D. A., Douglas J. Moo, and Leon Morris. *An Introduction to the New Testament.* Grand Rapids: Zondervan, 1992.

Carson, D. A. "Matthew." *The Expositor's Bible Commentary.* Edited by Frank E. Gaebelein. Grand Rapids: Zondervan, 1984. 60-599.

"Cast Them down to Hell" (2 Pet 2:4). *Seventh-day Adventist Bible Commentary.* Rev. ed. Hagerstown, MD: Review & Herald, 1980. 7:605.

"A Certain Rich Man" (Luke 16:19). *Seventh-day Adventist Bible Commentary.* Rev. ed. Edited by Francis D. Nichol. Washington, DC: Review & Herald, 1976-80. 5:830.

Clement of Alexandria *Stromata.* Ante-Nicene Fathers. 2:480-522.

Clowney, Edmund. *The Message of 1 Peter.* The Bible Speaks Today. Edited by John R. Stott. Leicester, England: Inter-Varsity, 1988.

Cogan, Mordechai, and Hayim Tadmor. *II Kings.* Anchor Bible, vol. 11. Broadway, NY: Doubleday, 1988.

Cole, R. Dennis. *Numbers.* New American Commentary, vol. 3B. Nashville, TN: Broadman & Holman, 2000.

Collins, Adela Yarbro. "Hades." *The HarperCollins Bible Dictionary.* Edited by Paul J. Achtemeier. New York: HarperCollins, 1985. 395-96.

_____. *Mark.* Hermeneia. Minneapolis, MN: Augsburg Fortress, 2007.

Conzelmann, Hans. *Acts of the Apostles.* Hermeneia. Philadelphia: Fortress, 1987.

Collins, Adela Yarbro. *The Theology of St. Luke*. New York: Harper & Row, 1961.

Craddock, Fred B. *Luke*. Interpretation. Louisville, KY: 1990.

Craigie, Peter. *Ezekiel*. Daily Study Bible. Edited by John C. L. Gidson. Philadelphia: Westminster, 1983.

Creed, J. M. *The Gospel According to St. Luke*. London: Macmillan, 1953.

Crossan, John Dominic. "Parable." *The Anchor Bible Dictionary*. Edited by David Noel Freedman. New York: Doubleday, 1992. 5:146-52.

_____. *In Parables: The Challenge of the Historical Jesus*. San Francisco: Harper & Row, 1973.

Cullman, Oscar. "Immortality of the Soul or Resurrection of the Dead." In *Immortality and Resurrection, Death in the Western World: Two Conflicting Currents of Thoughts*. New York: Macmillan, 1965.

Cundall, Arthur E., and Leon Morris. *Judges and Ruth*. Tyndale Old Testament Commentaries, vol. 7. Downers Grove, IL: InterVarsity, 1968.

Dalton, William Joseph. *Christ's Proclamation to the Spirits: A Study of 1 Pet 3:18-4:6*. Analecta Biblica, 2d rev. ed. Roma: Edtrice Pontificio Istituto Biblico, 1989.

Danker, Frederick W. *Luke*. Proclamation Commentaries. Edited by Gerhard Krodel. Philadelphia: Fortress, 1976.

Davids, Peter H. *The First Epistle of Peter*. New International Commentary New Testament. Grand Rapids: Eerdmans, 1990.

Davidson, Benjamin. *The Analytical Hebrew and Chaldee Lexicon*. Peabody, MA: Hendrickson, 1997. S.v. "שָׁאַל‎," "שְׁאֵל‎," "שָׁאֵל‎."

Davidson, Richard M. "Biblical Interpretation." In *Handbook of Seventh-day Adventist Theology*. Commentary Reference Series, vol. 12. Hagerstown, MD: Review & Herald, 2000.

Davies, W. D., and Dale C. Allison, Jr. *The Gospel According to Saint Matthew VIII-XVIII*. International Critical Commentary. Edinburgh: T. & T. Clark, 1991.

Derrett, J. Duncan M. "Fresh Light on St. Luke XVI: Dives and Lazarus and the Preceding Sayings." *New Testament Studies* 7 (1960-61): 364-80.

Dingfield, Walter. "A Study of the Rich Man and Lazarus." Th.M. thesis, Dallas Theological Seminary, Dallas, Texas, 1954.

Dio Chrysostom *Discourses*. Translated by H. Lamar Crosby. Loeb Classical Library.

Drane, John. *Introducing the New Testament*. Rev. ed. Oxford, England: Lion Publishing, 1999.

Driver, S. R. *Deuteronomy*. International Critical Commentary. Edinburgh: T. & T. Clark, 1978.

Duensing, Hugo, and Aurelio de Santos Otero. "Apocalypse of Paul." In *New Testament Apocrypha*. Edited by Wilhelm Schneemelcher and R. McL. Wilson. Louisville, KY: Westminster John Knox, 2003.

Easton, B. S. *The Gospel According to Luke*. New York: Scribner, 1926.

Elliger, K., and W. Rudolph. *Biblia Hebraica Stuttgartensia*. Stuttgart: Deutche Bibelgesellschaft, 1977.

Elliott, J. K. *The Apocryphal New Testament*. Translated by M. R. James. Oxford: Clarendon, 1993.

Elliott, John H. *1 Peter*. Anchor Bible, vol. 37B. New York: Doubleday, 2000.

Ellis, E. Earle. *The Gospel of Luke*. New Century Bible, vol. 42. Greenwood, SC: Attic, 1977.

Elwell, Walter A., and Robert Yarbrough. *Encountering the New Testament: A Historical and Theological Survey*. 2d ed. Grand Rapids: Baker Academic, 2005.

Eubank, John W. *Secrets of the Bible Unlocked*. Book on-line. N.p.: Trafford, 2005. Reproduced at google book search. Accessed 24 January 2007. Available from http://books.google.com/books. Internet.

Evans, C[hristopher] F. *Saint Luke*. TPI New Testament Commentaries. Philadelphia: Trinity Press International, 1990.

Evans, Christopher F. "Uncomfortable Words–V: Neither Will They Be Convinced." *Expository Times* 81 (1969-70): 228-31.

Evans, Craig A. *Luke*. New International Biblical Commentary, vol. 3. Peabody, MA: Hendrickson, 1990.

Fee, Gordon D. *The First Epistles to the Corinthians*. The New International Commentary on the New Testament. Grand Rapids: Eerdmans, 1987.

"Fire" (Deut 32:22). *Seventh-day Adventist Bible Commentary*. Rev. ed. Edited by Francis D. Nichol. Washington, DC: Review & Herald, 1976-80. 1:1070.

Fitzmyer, Joseph A. *The Gospel According to Luke X-XXIV*. Anchor Bible, vol. 28A. Garden City, NY: Doubleday, 1985.

_____. *Luke I-IX*. Anchor Bible, vol. 28. Garden City, NY: Doubleday, 1981.

_____. *Luke the Theologian: Aspects of His Teaching*. London: Geoffrey Chapman, 1989.

Flender, Helmut. *St. Luke: Theologian of Redemptive History*. Translated by Reginald H. and Ilse Fuller. London, SPCK, 1967.

Fokkelman, J. P. *Narrative Art and Poetry in the Books of Samuel.* Vol. 1, *King David.* Assen, The Netherlands: Van Gorcum, 1981.

France, R. T. *The Gospel of Matthew.* New International Commentary on the New Testament. Grand Rapids: Eerdmans, 2007.

Freedman, H. *Baba Mezia.* London: Socino, 1935.

_____. *Kiddushin.* London: Socino, 1936.

_____. *Pesahim.* London: Socino, 1938.

_____. *Sanhedrin.* London: Socino, 1935.

_____. *Shabbath.* London: Socino, 1938.

Froom, LeRoy Edwin. *The Conditionalist Faith of Our Fathers.* 2 vols. Washington, DC: Review & Herald, 1966.

Fudge, Edward William. "The Case for Conditionalism." In *Two Views of Hell: A Biblical and Theological Dialogue.* Downers Grove, IL: InterVarsity, 2000.

_____. *The Fire That Consumes.* Carlisle, UK: Paternoster, 1994.

Furnish, Victory Paul. *2 Corinthians.* Anchor Bible, vol. 32A. Garden City, NY: Doubleday, 1984.

Garcia-Martinez, Florentino, and Eibert J. C. Tigchelaar. *The Dead Sea Scrolls: Study Edition.* 2 vols. Leiden: Brill, 1997-98.

Geldenhuys, Norval. *Commentary on the Gospel of Luke.* New International Commentary on the New Testament. Grand Rapids: Eerdmans, 1979.

Gerleman, G. "שְׁאוֹל." *Theological Lexicon of the Old Testament.* Edited by Ernst Jenni and Claus Westermann. Translated by Mark Biddle. Peabody, MA: Hendrickson, 1997. 3:1279-82.

Gesenius, Freidrich Heinrich Wilhelm. *Gesenius' Hebrew and Chaldee Lexicon.* Translated by Samuel Prideaux Tregelles. Grand Rapids: Eerdmans, 1978. S.v. "שְׁאֹל."

Gilmour, Michael J. "Hints of Homer in Luke 16:19-31." *Didaskalia* 10 (1999): 23-33. Journal on-line. Available from Academic Search Premier database. Internet. Accessed 24 January 2007.

Goulder, Michael. *Midrash and Lection in Matthew.* London: SPCK, 1974.

Gowler, David B. "'At His Gate Lay a Poor Man': A Dialogic Reading of Luke 16:19-31." *Perspectives in Religious Studies* 32 (2005): 249-65. Journal on-line. Available from Academic Search Premier database. Internet. Accessed 4 December 2007.

Gowler, David B. *What Are They Saying about the Parables?* New York: Paulist, 2000.
    Graf, W. "Dives and Lazarus (Luke 16:19-31)." *Homiletic & Pastoral Review* 38 (1937-38): 1184-85.

Gray, John. *1 & 2 Kings.* Old Testament Library. London: SCM, 1977.

Green, Joel B. *The Theology of the Gospel of Luke.* Cambridge: Cambridge University Press, 1995.

Greenberg, Moshe. *Ezekiel 1-20.* Anchor Bible, vol. 22. Garden City, NY: Doubleday, 1983.

Gregg, J. A. F. "Addition to Esther." In *Apocrypha and Pseudepigrapha of the Old Testament in English.* Edited by R. H. Charles. Oxford: Clarendon, 1978. 1:665-84.

Griffith, F. L. *Stories of the High Priests of Memphis.* Oxford: Clarendon, 1900. Quoted in John Nolland, *Luke 9:21-18:34.* Word Biblical Commentary, vol. 35B, 826. Dallas, TX: Word, 1989.

Griffiths, J. Gwyn. "Cross-Cultural Eschatology with Dives and Lazarus." *Expository Times* 105 (1993): 7-12.

Grobel, Kendrick. ". . . Whose Name Was Neves." *New Testament Studies* 10 (1963-64): 373-82.

Gromacki, Robert G. *New Testament Survey.* Grand Rapids: Baker, 1974.

Guthrie, Donald. *New Testament Introduction.* 4th rev. ed. Downers Grove, IL: InterVarsity, 1990.

Haenchen, Ernst. *The Acts of the Apostles: A Commentary.* Oxford: Basil Blackwell, 1971.

Hafemann, Scott. *2 Corinthians.* NIV Application Commentary. Grand Rapids: Zondervan, 2000.

Hagner, Donald A. *Matthew 1-13.* Word Biblical Commentary, vol. 33A. Dallas, TX: Word, 1993.

Hamlin, E. John. *Judges: At Risk in the Promised Land.* International Theological Commentary. Grand Rapids: Eerdmans, 1990.

Harrington, Daniel J. *1 Peter.* Sacra Pagina, vol. 15. Collegeville, MN: Liturgical Press, 2003.

_____. "Pseudo-Philo." In *Old Testament Pseudepigrapha.* Edited by James H. Charlesworth. Garden City, NY: Doubleday, 1983. 2:299-377.

Harris, Murray J. "2 Corinthians." *The Expositor's Bible Commentary.* Edited by Frank E. Gaebelein. Grand Rapids: Zondervan, 1978. 301-406.

_____. *The Second Epistle to the Corinthians.* New International Greek Testament Commentary. Grand Rapids: Eerdmans, 2005.

Harrison, Everett F. *Introduction to the New Testament.* New rev. ed. Grand Rapids: Eerdmans, 1971.

Hauck, Friedrich. "parabolh,." *Theological Dictionary of the New Testament*. Edited by Gerhard
    Kittel and Gerhard Friedrich. Translated by Geoffrey Bromiley. Grand Rapids: Eerdmans,
    1964-76. 5:744-61.

Hendriksen, William. *The Gospel of Luke*. New Testament Commentary, vol. 3. Grand Rapids:
    Baker, 1978.

Hertig, Paul. "The Jubilee Mission of Jesus in the Gospel of Luke: Reversals of Fortunes."
    Missiology 26 (1998): 167-79.

Hillyer, Norman. *1 and 2 Peter, Jude*. New International Biblical Commentary, vol. 16. Peabody,
    MA: Hendrickson, 1992.

Hippolytus *The Extant Works and Fragments*. Ante-Nicene Fathers. 5:204-41.

_____ *Fragments from Commentaries*. Translated by S. D. F. Salmond. Ante-Nicene Fathers.
    5:174.

Hock, Ronald F. "Lazarus and Dives." *The Anchor Bible Dictionary*. Edited by David Noel
    Freedman. New York: Doubleday, 1992. 4:266-67.

_____. "Lazarus and Micyllus: Greco-Roman Backgrounds to Luke 16:19-31." *Journal of
    Biblical Literature* 106
    (1987): 447-63.

Holmes, Samuel. "The Wisdom of Solomon." In *Apocrypha and Pseudepigrapha of the Old
    Testament in English*. Edited by R. H. Charles. Oxford: Clarendon, 1978. 1:518-68.

Homer *The Odyssey*. Translated by A. T. Murray. Loeb Classical Library.

House, Paul H. *1 & 2 Kings*. New American Commentary, vol. 8. Nashville, TN: Broadman &
    Holman, 1995.

Huie, Wade P., Jr. "Poverty of Abundance: From Text to Sermon." *Interpretation* 22 (1968): 403-
    20.

Hultgren, Arland J. *The Parables of Jesus: A Commentary*. Grand Rapids: Eerdmans, 2000.

Huntingford, Thomas, and Jean Calvin. *Testimonies in Proof of the Separate Existence of the Soul
    in the State of Self-Consciousness between Death and Resurrection*. Book on-line. London:
    C. J. G. & F. Rivington, 1829. Reproduced at google book search. Accessed 25 January
    2007. Available from http://books.google.com/books. Internet.

Hutcheon, Cyprian Robert. "'God with Us': The Temple in Luke-Acts." *St. Vladimir's Theological
    Quarterly* 44 (2000): 3-33.

Irenaeus *Against Heresies*. Ante-Nicene Fathers. 1:315-567.

Isaac, E. "1 Ethiopic Apocalypse of Enoch." In *The Old Testament Pseudepigrapha*. Edited by
    James H. Charlesworth. Garden City, NY: Doubleday, 1983. 1:1-89.

Isaac, Sherly. *Is Jesus God.* Book on-line. N.p.: n.p., 2001. Reproduced at google book search. Accessed 24 January, 2007. Available from http://books.google .com/books. Internet.

Jackman, David. *Judges, Ruth.* Communicator's Commentary, vol. 7. Dallas, TX: Word, 1991.

Jeremias, Joachim. "ᾅδης." *Theological Dictionary of New Testament.* Edited by Gerhard Kittel and Gerhard Friedrich. Translated by Geoffrey W. Bromiley. Grand Rapids: Eerdmans, 1964-76. 1:146-49.

_____. "γέεννα." *Theological Dictionary of the New Testament.* Edited by Gerhard Kittel and Gerhard Friedrich. Translated by Geoffrey W. Bromiley. Grand Rapids: Eerdmans, 1964-76. 1:657-58.

_____. *The Parables of Jesus.* 2d rev. ed. New York: Scribner, 1972.

Johnson, Alan. "Revelation." *The Expositor's Bible Commentary.* Edited by Frank E. Gaebelein. Grand Rapids: Zondervan, 1981. 399-603.

Johnson, Luke Timothy. *The Gospel of Luke.* Sacra Pagina, vol. 3. Edited by Daniel J. Harrington. Collegeville, MN: Liturgical, 1991.

_____. *The Writings of the New Testament: An Interpretation.* Rev. ed. Minneapolis, MN: Fortress, 1999.

Johnston, Robert M. *Peter and Jude.* Abundant Life Bible Amplifier. Boise, ID: Pacific Press, 1995.

Jones, Peter Rhea. *Studying the Parables of Jesus.* Macon, GA: Smyth & Helwys, 1999.

Josephus *Jewish Antiquities.* Translated by St. J. Thackeray. Loeb Classical Library.

_____ *The Jewish War.* Translated by St. J. Thackeray. Loeb Classical Library.

"Justify Yourselves" (Luke 16:15). *Seventh-day Adventist Bible Commentary.* Rev. ed. Edited by Francis D. Nichol. Washington, DC: Review & Herald, 1976-80. 5:828.

Kaiser, Otto. *Isaiah 1-12.* Old Testament Library. London: SCM, 1983.

Keener, Craig S. *1-2 Corinthians.* New York: Cambridge University Press, 2005.

Khoo, Jeffrey. "The Reality and Eternality of Hell: Luke 16:19-31 as Proof." *Stulos* 6 (1998): 67-76.

Kissinger, Warren S. *The Parables of Jesus: A History of Interpretation and Bibliography.* ATLA Series 4. Metuchen, NJ: Scarecrow & The American Theological Library Association, 1979.

Kistemaker, Simon J. "Jesus as Story Teller: Literary Perspectives on the Parables." *The Master's Seminary Journal* 16 (2005): 49-55. Journal-online. Available from Academic Search Premier database. Internet. Accessed 4 Decemebr 2007.

_____. *The Parables of Jesus.* Grand Rapids: Baker, 1980.

Klingbeil, Gerald. "A Semantic Analysis of Aramaic Ostraca of Syria-Palestine during the Persian Period." *Andrews University Studies* 35 (1997): 33-46.

Knight, George R., ed. *Questions on Doctrine.* Adventist Classic Library. Annotated Edition. Berrien Springs, MI: Andrews University Press, 2003.

Knight, George W. "Luke 16:19-31: The Rich Man and Lazarus." *Review & Expositor* 94 (1997): 277-82.

Kofoed, Jens Bruun. "Fact and Fiction in the Near East." SEE-J Hiphil 1 (2004): 1-14. Journal on-line. Available from http://www.see-j.net/hiphil. Internet Accessed 08 February 2008.

_____. *Text and History: Historiography and the Study of the Biblical Text.* Winona Lake, IN: Eisenbrauns, 2005.

Koehler, Ludwig, and Walter Baumgartner. *The Hebrew and Aramaic Lexicon of the Old Testament.* Translated and edited by M. E. J. Richardson. Leiden: Brill, 2000. S.v. "שָׁאַל," "שָׁאוֹל," שָׁאַל."

Kramer, S. N. "Sumerian Myths and Epic Tales." In *Ancient Near Eastern Texts Related to the Old Testament.* 3d ed. Edited by James Benneth Pritchard. Princeton, NJ: Princeton University Press, 1969. 37-59.

Kreitzer, Larry. "Luke 16:19-31 and 1 Enoch 22." *Expository Times* 103 (1992): 139-42.

Krodel, Gerhard. *Acts.* Augsburg Commentary on the New Testament. Minneapolis, MN: Augsburg, 1986.

Kümmel, Werner George. *Introduction to the New Testament.* Rev. ed. Translated by Howard Clark Kee. Nashville, TN: Abingdon, 1975.

Kvalbein, Hans. "Jesus and the Poor: Two Texts and a Tentative Conclusion." *Themelios* 12 (1987): 80-87.

Ladd, George Eldon. *A Commentary on the Revelation of John.* Grand Rapids: Eerdmans, 1972.

Lanchester, H. C. O. "The Sibyline Oracles." In *Apocrypha and Pseudepigrapha of the Old Testament in English.* Edited by R. H. Charles. Oxford: Clarendon, 1979. 2:368-406.

Landry, David. "Honor Restored: New Light on the Parable of the Prudent Steward (Luke 16:1-8a)." *Journal of Biblical Literature* 119 (2000): 287-309.

Lane, William. *The Gospel According to Mark.* New International Commentary on the New Testament. Grand Rapids: Eerdmans, 1974.

Larkin, Clarence. *Rightly Dividing the Word of Truth.* Book on-line. N.p.: Cosimo Classics, 2005. Reproduced at google book search. Accessed 24 January 2007. Available from http://books.google.com/books. Internet.

Lawrence, Richard. *On the Existence of the Soul after Death.* Book on-line. London: C. J. G. & F. Rivington, 1834. Reproduced at the google book search. Accessed 24 January 2007. Available from http://books.google .com/books. Internet.

Lea, Thomas D. *The New Testament: Its Background and Message.* Nashville, TN: Broadman & Holman, 1996.

Leighton, Robert. *Commentary on First Peter.* London: Henry Bohn; reprint, Grand Rapids: Kregel, 1972.

Leitart, Peter. *1 & 2 Kings.* Brazos Theological Commentary on the Bible. Grand Rapids: Brazos, 2006.

Liefeld, Walter. "Luke." *The Expositor's Bible Commentary.* Edited by Frank E. Gaebelein. Grand Rapids: Zondervan, 1984. 797-1059.

Livermore, Daniel Parker. *Proof-Texts of Endless Punishment Examined and Explained.* Book on-line. Chicago, IL: Livermore, 1862. Reproduced at google book search. Accessed 25 January 2007. Available from http://books.google.com/books. Internet.

Lockyer, Herbert. *All the Parables of Jesus.* Grand Rapids: Zondervan, 1963. Quoted in Jeffrey Khoo, "The Reality and Eternality of Hell: Luke 16:19-31 as Proof," 69. *Stulos* 6 (1998): 67-76.

Lohse, Eduard. *The Formation of the New Testament.* Translated by M. Eugene Boring. Nashville, TN: Abingdon, 1981.

Longman, Tremper. *Proverbs.* Grand Rapids: Baker, 2006.

Lorenzen, Thorwald. "A Biblical Meditation on Luke 16:19-31." *Expository Times* 87 (1975-76): 39-43.

Louw, J. P., and E. A. Nida. *Greek-English Lexicon of the New Testament Based on Semantic Domains.* 2 vols. Cape Town: Bible Society of South Africa, 1988.

Lucian *Cataplous—The Downward Journey or the Tyrant.* Translated by A. M. Harmon. Loeb Classical Library.

_____ *The Lover of Lies* 24. Translated by A. M. Harmon. Loeb Classical Library.

_____ *Menippus or the Descent into* "Αιδης. Translated A. H. Harmon, Loeb Classical Library.

Luther, Martin. *Luther's Works.* Vol. 48, *Letters I.* Edited and translated by Gottfried G. Krodel. Philadelphia: Fortress, 1963.

Luz, Ulriz. *Matthew 8-20.* Hermeneia. Minneapolis, MN: Augsburg, Fortress, 2001.

Maier, Gerhard. *Biblical Hermeneutics.* Wheaton, IL: Crossway, 1994.

Mansoor, Menahem. *The Dead Sea Scrolls: A College Textbook and Study Guide.* Grand Rapids: Eerdmans, 1964.

Marincola, John. "Genre, Convention, and Innovation in Greco-Roman Historiography." In *The Limits of Historiography: Genre and Narrative in Ancient Historical Texts*. Edited by Christina Shuttleworth Kraus. Leiden: Brill, 1999.

Marshall, I. Howard. *Acts*. Theological New Testament Commentary, vol. 5. Leicester, England: Inter-Varsity; Grand Rapids: Eerdmans, 1984.

_____. *The Gospel of Luke*. New International Greek Testament Commentary. Grand Rapids: Eerdmans, 1978.

_____. *Luke: Historian Theologian*. Downers Grove, IL: InterVarsity, 1970.

Martin, Ralph P. *New Testament Foundations: A Guide for Christian Students*. Vol. 1. Grand Rapids: Eerdmans, 1975.

_____. *2 Corinthians*. Word Biblical Commentary, vol. 40. Waco, TX: Word, 1986.

Matera, Frank J. *2 Corinthians*. New Testament Library. Louisville, KY: 2003.

Mathews, Edward G., Jr. "The Rich Man and Lazarus: "lms-Giving and Repentance in Early Syriac Tradition." *Diakonia* 22 (1988-89): 89-104.

Mealand, D. L. *Poverty and Expectations in the Gospels*. London: SPCK, 1980.

Merrill, Eugine. "שָׁאוּל." *New International Dictionary of Old Testament Theology and Exegesis*. Edited by Willem A. VanGemeren. Grand Rapids: Zondervan, 1997. 4:6-7.

Metzger, B. M. "The Fourth Book of Ezra." In *Old Testament Pseudepigrapha*. Edited by James H. Charlesworth. Garden City, NY: Doubleday, 1983. 2:525-59.

Michaels, J. Ramsey. *1 Peter*. Word Biblical Commentary, vol. 49. Waco, TX: Word, 1988.

Moore, George F. *A Critical and Exegetical Commentary on Judges*. International Critical Commentary. Edinburgh: T. & T. Clark, 1976.

Moore, Marvin. *Where Is Bobby?* Nashville, TN: Southern Pub. Assn., 1976.

Morris, Leon. *Luke*. Tyndale New Testament Commentaries, vol. 3. Grand Rapids: Eerdmans, 1984.

Mounce, Robert. *The Book of Revelation*. Rev. ed. Grand Rapids: Eerdmans, 1998.

Mussner, Franz. "The Synoptic Account of Jesus' Teaching on the Future Life." In *Immortality and Resurrection*. N.p.: Herder & Herder, 1970.

Nave, Guy, Jr. *The Role and Function of Repentance in Luke-Acts*. Atlanta: SBL, 2002.

Neyrey, Jerome H. *2 Peter, Jude*. Anchor Bible, vol. 37C. New York: Doubleday, 1993.

Nickelsburg, George W. E. *Jewish Literature between the Bible and the Mishnah.* Philadelphia: Fortress, 1981.

_____. "Riches, the Rich, and God's Judgment in Enoch 95-105 and the Gospels According to Luke." *New Testament Studies* 25 (1978-79): 324-44.
Nolland, John. *Luke 1-9:20.* Word Biblical Commentary, vol. 35A. Dallas, TX: Word, 1989.

_____. *Luke 9:21-18:34.* Word Biblical Commentary, vol. 35B. Dallas, TX: Word, 1989.

Odom, Robert Leo. *Is Your Soul Immortal?* Wilwood, GA: Discovery Reading, 1989.

Oswalt, John. *The Book of Isaiah Chapters 1-39.* New International Commentary on the Old Testament. Grand Rapids: Eerdmans, 1986.

Papaioannou, Kim G. "Places of Punishments in the Synoptic Gospels." Ph.D. diss., Durham University, Durham, England, 2005.

Parrot, Douglas M. "The Dishonest Steward (Luke 16:1-8a) and Luke's Special Parable Collection." *New Testament Studies* 37 (1991): 499-515.

Parris, David P. "Imitating the Parables: Allegory, Narrative, and the Role of Mimesis." *Journal for the Study of the New Testament* 25 (2002): 33-53. Journal on-line. Available from Academic Search Premier database. Internet. Accessed 23 January 2007.

Peisker, Carl Heinz. "parabolh,." *New International Dictionary of the New Testament Theology.* Edited by Colin Brown. Grand Rapids: Zondervan, 1975-78. 2:743-49.

Perschbacher, Wesley J. *The New Analytical Greek Lexicon.* Peabody, MA: Hendrickson, 1990. S.v. "ᾅδης," "κατεσθίω," "μέχρι," "τότε."

Peterson, Robert A. "The Case for Traditionalism." In *Two Views of Hell: A Biblical and Theological Dialogue.* Edited by Edward William Fudge and Robert Peterson. Downers Grove, IL: InterVarsity, 2000.

Philo *The Embassy to Gaius.* Translated by F. H. Colson and J. W. Earp. Loeb Classical Library.

_____ *Moses.* Translated by F. H. Colson. Loeb Classical Library.

_____ *On the Posterity of Cain and His Exile.* Translated by F. H. Colson and G. H. Whitaker. Loeb Classical Library.

Pinnock, Charles H. "The Conditional View." In *Four Views on Hell.* Edited by William Crockett. Grand Rapids: Zondervan, 1996.

Plato *Cratylus.* Translated by H. N. Fowler. Loeb Classical Library.

_____ *Georgias.* Translated by W. R. M. Lamb. Loeb Classical Library.

_____ *The Laws* 2. Translated by R. G. Bury. Loeb Classical Library.

_____ *Lesser Hippias.* Translated by H. N. Fowler. Loeb Classical Library.

Plummer, Alfred. *The Gospel According to Luke: A Critical and Exegetical Commentary.* International Critical Commentary. Edinburgh: T. & T. Clark, 1977.

Plutarch *Moralia.* Translated by F. C. Babbit, Herold Cherniss, W. C. Helmbold, E. L. Minar, and F. H. Sandbach. Loeb Classical Library.

Polhill, John B. *Acts.* New American Commentary, vol. 26. Nashville, TN: Broadman, 1992.

Powell, Ivor. *Luke's Thrilling Gospel.* Grand Rapids: Zondervan, 1965; reprint, Grand Rapids: Kregel, 1984.

Powell, W. "The Parable of Dives and Lazarus (Luke 16:19-31)." *Expository Times* 66 (1954-55): 350-51.

"Present with the Lord" (2 Cor 5:8). *The Seventh-day Adventist Bible Commentary.* Rev. ed. Edited by Francis D. Nichol. Washington, DC: Review & Herald, 1976-80. 6:863.

Razafiarivony, David. "The Meaning of the Temple in Stephen's Speech." M.A. thesis, Adventist International Institute of Advanced Studies, Silang, Cavite, Philippines, October 1996.

Regalado, Ferdinand O. "The Jewish Background of the Parable of the Rich Man and Lazarus." *Asia Journal of Theology* 16 (2002): 341-48.

Reichenbach, Bruce. *In Man the Phoenix?: A Study of Immortality.* Washington, DC: Christian University Press, 1978.

Renie, J. "Le Mauvais Riche (Luke 16:19-31)." *L'Année Théologique* (1945): 272-73.

Resseguie, James L. "Point of View in the Central Section of Luke (9:51-19:44)." *Journal of Evangelical & Theological Society* 25 (1982): 41-47.

Rice, John. *The Son of Man: A Verse-by-Verse Commentary on the Gospel According to Luke.* Book on-line. N.p., TN: Sword of the Lord, 1971. Reproduced at google book search. Accessed 24 January 2007. Available from http://books.google.com/books. Internet.

Richards, Larry. *2 Corinthians.* Abundant Life Bible Amplifier. Nampa, ID: Pacific Press, 1998.

Rodriguez, Angel Manuel. "Using a Parable to Make a Point." *Adventist World*, January 2007, 26.

Ryle, John Charles. *Expository Thoughts on the Gospels: St. Luke.* Vol. 2. Book on-line. London: W. Hunt, 1859. Reproduced at google book search. Accessed 23 January 2007. Available from http://books.google.com/ books. Internet.

Sabuin, Richard. "The Growth of Christ: Understanding Luke 2:40,56 in the Light of the Structural Pattern of Luke-Acts." *Journal of Asia Adventist Seminary* 10, no. 1 (2007): 15-25.

Sakenfeld, Katharine Doob. *Numbers.* International Theological Commentary, vol. 4. Grand Rapids: Eerdmans, 1995.

Sandy, D. Brent, and Ronald L. Giese, Jr. *Cracking the Old Testament Codes: A Guide to Interpreting the Literary Genres of the Old Testament.* Nashville, TN: Broadman & Holman, 1995.

Schipper, Jeremy. "Did David Overinterpret Nathan's Parable in 2 Samuel 12:1-6." *Journal of Biblical Literature* 126 (2007): 383-407.

Schnider, Franz, und Werner Stenger. "Die offene Tür und die Unüber-Schreitbare Kluft: Struktur-Analytische Überlegungen zum Gleichnis vom Reichen Mann und Armen Lazarus." *New Testament Studies* 25 (1979): 273-83.

Schweizer, Eduard. *The Good News According to Luke.* Translated by David E. Green. Atlanta: John Knox,   1984.

Scofield, C. I. *The Scofield Reference Bible.* New York: Oxford University Press, 1909. Quoted in Jeffrey Khoo,"The Reality and Eternality of Hell: Luke 16:19-31 as Proof," 69. *Stulos* 6 (1998): 67-76.

Scott, James M. *2 Corinthians.* New International Biblical Commentary, vol. 8. Peabody, MA: Hendrickson, 1998.

Scourfield, J. H. D. "A Note on Jerome's Homily on the Rich Man and Lazarus." *Journal of Theological Studies* 48 (1997): 536-39.

Simon, Maurice. *Gittin.* London: Socino, 1936.

Simon, Uriel. "The Poor Man's Ewe-Lamb: An Example of a Juridical Parable." *Biblica* 48 (1967): 207-42.

Simpson, D. C. "The Book of Tobit." In *Apocrypha and Pseudepigrapha of the Old Testament in English.* Edited by R. H. Charles. Oxford: Clarendon, 1978. 1:174-241.

Skinner, John. *Genesis.* International Critical Commentary. Edinburgh: T. & T. Clark, 1980.

Slotski, Israel W. *Baba Bathra.* London: Soncino, 1935.

_____. *Sukkah.* London: Soncino, 1938.

_____. *Erubin.* London: Soncino, 1938.

_____. *Yebamoth.* London: Soncino, 1936.

Smith, Dennis E. "Table Fellowship as a Literary Motif in the Gospel of Luke." *Journal of Biblical Literature* 106 (1987): 613-28.

Smith, Henry Preserved. *The Book of Samuel: A Critical and Exegetical Commentary.* International Critical Commentary, vol. 9-10. Edinburgh: T. & T. Clark, 1977.

Smith, Matthew Hale. *Universalism, Examined, Renounced, Exposed.* Book on-line. Boston: Tappan & Dennet, 1844. Reproduced at google book search. Accessed 24 January 2007. Available from http://books.google.com/ book. Internet.

Speiser, E. A. "Akkadian Myths and Epics." In *Ancient Near Eastern Texts Related to the Old Testament*. 3d ed. Edited by James Benneth Pritchard. Princeton, NJ: Princeton University Press, 1969. 60-119.

Squires, John T. *The Plan of God in Luke-Acts.* Cambridge, UK: Cambridge, 1993.

Stefanovic, Ranko. *Revelation of Jesus Christ.* Berrien Springs, MI: Andrews University Press, 2002.

Stein, Robert. *Difficult Passages in the New Testament: Interpreting Puzzling Texts in the Gospels and Epistles.* Grand Rapids: Baker, 1990.

_____. *Luke: An Exegetical and Theological Exposition of Holy Scripture.* New American Commentary, vol. 24. Nashville, TN: Broadman, 1992.

Stibbs, A. M., and A. F. Walls. *1 Peter.* Tyndale New Testament Commentary, vol. 17. Grand Rapids: Eerdmans, 1983.

Strack, H. L., and G. Stemberger. *Introduction to the Talmud and Midrash.* Translated by Markus Bockmuehl. Edinburgh: T. & T. Clark, 1991.

Talbert, Charles H. *Reading Luke: A Literary and Theological Commentary on the Third Gospel.* New York: Crossroads, 1982.

Tanghe, Vincent. "Abraham, son Fils et son Envoyé (Luke 16:19-31)." *Revue Biblique* 91 (1984): 557-77.
Tannehill, Robert C. *The Narrative Unity of Luke-Acts: A Literary Interpretation—The Gospel According to Luke.* Vol. 1. Philadelphia: Fortress, 1986.

Taylor, William M. *The Parables of Our Saviour.* Grand Rapids: Kregel, 1975.

Tertullian *A Treatise on the Soul.* Translated by Peter Holmes. Ante-Nicene Fathers. 3:180-235.

Thrall, Margaret E. *2 Corinthians.* International Critical Commentary. Edinburgh: T. & T. Clark, 1994.

Tiede, David L. *Luke.* Augsburg Commentary on the New Testament. Minneapolis: Augsburg, 1988.

Trench, R. C. *Notes on the Parables of Our Lord.* Grand Rapids: Baker, 1945.

Tucker, Jeffrey Thomas. "Four Parables in the Gospel of   Luke: Perspectives on the Example Narratives." Ph.D.   Diss., Vanderbilt University, 1994. Abstract available from http//www.aiias.edu/database/proquest/ dissertation and thesis. Internet. Accessed 22 January 2007.

Vanderkam, James, and Peter Flint. *The Meaning of the Dead Sea Scrolls.* London: T. & T. Clark, 2002.

Vawter, Bruce, and Leslie J. Hoppe. *Ezekiel: A New Heart.* International Theological Commentary. Grand Rapids: Eerdmans, 1991.

Victorinus *Commentary on the Apocalypse of John*. Translated by Robert Ernest Wallis. Ante-Nicene Fathers. 7:344-60.

Vogels, Walter. "Having and Longing: A Semiotic Analysis of Luke 16:19-31." *Église et Théologie* 20 (1989): 27-46.

Wächter, L. "שְׁאוֹל." *Theological Dictionary of the Old Testament*. Edited by G. Johannes Botterweck, Helmer Ringgren, and Heinz-Josef Fabry. Translated by Douglas Stott. Grand Rapids: Eerdmans, 2004. 14:241-42.

Walvoord, John. "The Literal View." In *Four Views on Hell*. Edited by William Crockett. Grand Rapids: Zondervan, 1996.

Watts, John D. W. *Isaiah 1-33*. Word Biblical Commentary, vol. 24. Waco, TX: Word, 1985.

Wehrli, Eugene S. "Luke 16:19-31." *Interpretation* 31 (1977): 276-80.

Wenham, David. *The Parables of Jesus*. Jesus Library. Downers Grove, IL: InterVarsity, 1989.

Wenham, Gordon N. *Genesis 16-50*. Word Biblical Commentary, vol. 2. Dallas, TX: Word, 1994.

Whitehouse, O. C. "The Book of Baruch." In *Apocrypha and Pseudepigrapha of the Old Testament in English*. Edited by R. H. Charles. Oxford: Oxford University Press, 1978. 1:569-95.

Widyapranawa, S. H. *Isaiah 1-39*. International Theological Commentary. Grand Rapids: Eerdmans, 1990.

Williams, Francis E. "Is Almsgiving the Point of the 'Unjust Steward'?" *Journal of Biblical Literature* 83 (1964): 293-97.

Wilson, Gerald. "מָשַׁל." *New International Dictionary of Old Testament Theology and Exegesis*. Edited by Willem A. Vangemeren. Grand Rapids: Zondervan, 1997. 2:1134-36.

Wilson, John A. "Egyptian Myths, Tales, and Mortuary Texts." In *Ancient Near Eastern Texts Related to the Old Testament*. 3d ed. Edited by James Benneth Pritchard. Princeton, NJ: Princeton University Press, 1969. 3-36.

Yarbrough, Robert W. "Jesus on Hell." In *Hell under Fire*. Edited by Christopher W. Morgan and Robert A. Peterson   Grand Rapids: Zondervan, 2004.

Zimmerli, Walther. *Ezekiel 1*. Hermeneia. Translated by Ronald E. Clements. Philadelphia: Fortress, 1979.

Printed in Great Britain
by Amazon

26129273R00129